What Did You *Ask* At School Today?

After completing her PhD in Educational Psychology at
Syracuse University, NY and teaching undergraduates for
a few years, Kamala V. Mukunda returned to India in 1995
and joined Centre For Learning, a non-formal school in
Bangalore exploring the nature of education (www.cfl.in).
She discovered that educators and parents were actively
curious about educational questions that have traditionally
been researched by psychologists. But psychologists rarely
wrote for this audience! Their articles were filled with jargon,
and as Kamala found, not even textbooks in Educational
Psychology could bridge that gap. Thus she began to write
short articles summarizing the research in readable language.
When these articles were well received, she decided to write
a book on psychology for teachers in the Indian context.

What Did You *Ask* At School Today?
A Handbook of Child Learning

Kamala V. Mukunda

Illustrations by Radhika Neelakantan

An Imprint of HarperCollins *Publishers*

First published in India in 2009 by Collins
An imprint of HarperCollins *Publishers* India

ISBN: 978-81-7223-833-9

22nd Impression 2015

HarperCollins *Publishers*
A-75, Sector 57, NOIDA, Uttar Pradesh – 201301, India
1 London Bridge Street, London, SE1 9GF, United Kingdom
Hazelton Lanes, 55 Avenue Road, Suite 2900, Toronto, Ontario M5R 3L2
and 1995 Markham Road, Scarborough, Ontario M1B 5M8, Canada
25 Ryde Road, Pymble, Sydney, NSW 2073, Australia
195 Broadway, New York NY 10007, USA

Typeset in 10.5/15 Janson Text
Jojy Philip New Delhi - 15

Printed and bound in India
by MicroPrints (India), New Delhi

Contents

CHAPTER 1: **Brain, Evolution and Schooling**   7

Gives a brief description of current understandings of the brain structure and function, and an explanation of evolutionary psychology as relevant to education.

Sub-topics: Structure and function; The hippocampus; Evolution of modules in the brain; Innate and non-innate learning; Teaching—a particular human skill.

CHAPTER 2: **Learning**   22

Gives a detailed explanation of conceptual and procedural learning, with examples and suggestions from the research for teachers, and explores the importance of informal reasoning skills in students.

Sub-topics: Constructivism and conceptual change; Discovery learning; Procedural knowledge and skill learning; Context-dependent reasoning.

CHAPTER 3: **Memory**   51

Gives detailed explanations of long-term and short-term memory as relevant to classroom issues, with examples and research.

Sub-topics: The contents of long-term memory; How long-term memories are organized; Working memory, and the teaching-learning process; Automaticity: a special application; 'I'm studying.'

A Few Words About
Kamala V. Mukunda's Book

I have not had the pleasure of reading a book on education as erudite and comprehensive as this one, written by Kamala V. Mukunda. It has many wonderful things that I thought I had discovered. Kamala's scholarly work has deflated my ego – there are few first discoveries in this area.

This is a beautiful work, extremely well written, almost an encyclopaedia for those interested in children's education. I do believe, though, that deep things are learnt more autonomously than most of us in education believe. Perhaps schools often manage to destroy some precious features.

Dr YASH PAL
National Research Professor

Preface

School is the place where children are taught a huge amount of formalized knowledge. A great deal of energy goes into planning and delivering this education, yet surveys both in the West and here in India indicate that the system is deficient. In America, where progressive methods of education have long been in use, reports over the last 25 years show that students are not mastering the fundamentals. And here at home, a national educational survey reported 'alarming gaps in student learning', and this in our 'top schools'. The survey (published in *India Today*, 27 November 2006) concluded that our students do not really understand anything, perhaps because of an over-emphasis on rote learning. Perhaps, they suggested, we need more active and hands-on learning experiences. Both this and the American reports lament the fact that students are not learning 'higher-order thinking skills'.

Where are we going wrong? Obviously, one can address this question at many levels, but in this book I will stick to the psychological principles behind our educational failures.

The typical Indian school curriculum seems to have its own version of the structure of the brain. As far as our curricula are concerned, the brain might well look as in the figure below!

Perhaps this is an exaggeration, but it emphasizes the mismatch between what the brain is good at, and what typical schooling

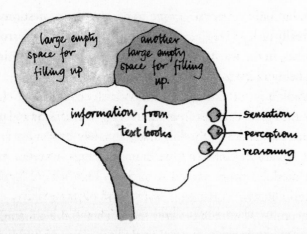

expects from it. To summarize this mismatch in a few brief statements:

- The brain is good at learning from real world contexts. School emphasizes abstract or textbook learning.
- The preschool child is already developing her own 'folk' theories in the areas of biology, physics and psychology. School ignores these and tries to replace them with 'correct' knowledge.
- Memory is constructive and interpretative. School emphasizes reproduction of material learned.
- Emotions are inseparable from learning and memory. School ignores the emotional side of learning.

There are more mismatches, but these seem primary. What now is the solution to this? Maybe we should abandon the idea of formalized instruction! I have heard some progressive educators say things like 'children should be left alone, and they will learn whatever they need to.' Of course this is in reaction to the stifling school environment most children find themselves in, and I can understand the feeling. But it is not clear what is meant by being 'left alone'. Do we provide learning materials and books? Do we teach, but only when they come to us with their questions? Will they really pick up reading and writing just from being surrounded by books, in the way they learn speaking and comprehension just from being in language-rich surroundings?

I think it is certainly true that in a rich environment children will learn a great deal just from interacting with objects and people. But there are limits to this unguided, innately-driven learning. As I will explain in Chapter One, human beings have not evolved brain modules programmed to pick up high school algebra or the periodic table 'naturally'. Some kind of imaginative, explicit instruction *is* required to foster the 'higher-order thinking' that those surveys lamented. Our world has changed to the point where such learning is seen as necessary–core to our successful adaptation. And so, we have to teach. We cannot 'leave our children' to pick up what they will; it would, in my opinion, be irresponsible to do so, given society's demands. How well does schooling accomplish this need? To help us in this discovery, we ought to know more about how the brain works.

Memory, learning, intelligence, child development and other areas of psychology can tell us a great deal that would help us become better teachers. The chapters of this book contain many useful insights under these headings. One thing to keep in mind while reading the book is that the topics are not watertight compartments. One cannot understand learning, memory and intelligence separately; yet by creating chapters with these headings it seems that I am doing just that! In actuality, all are interrelated, which is why there will often be references within a chapter to other chapters, and a fair degree of overlap. I hope you will sometimes return to earlier chapters to re-read sections of interest to you, as this will sharpen your own understanding and questions.

Kamala V. Mukunda
March 2009

Acknowledgements

I am indebted to a number of people for the kind support and encouragement they gave me during the writing of this book. 'Wipro Applying Thought In Schools' gave the financial grant that made it possible, and I am indeed grateful to Anand Swaminathan and Prakash Iyer. Thanks to Sheema Mookherjee at Harper Collins India who has been patient, cheerful and prompt in dealing with my endless queries during editing, and V. K. Karthika who gave me the exciting 'green signal'.

Thanks to Vernon Hall who first taught me how to understand psychology, how to think about education and which questions are useful to ask. The title of the book is inspired by a quote from the physicist Richard Feynman, who credits his mother with asking him this question when he returned from school. Thanks to Radhika Neelakantan, gifted artist, who became right brain to my left brain. Her illustrations breathe life into the text, and this will be her first-of-many books. Sumana Ramanan, childhood playmate who went out of her way to remember me at the opportune moment. Ahalya Chari who has been a dear, wise friend and guide for almost fifteen years. Venu Narayan whose support I have relied on, often taken for granted, for so long. Devika Narayan who interviewed several teachers on my behalf, and got quite carried away in the process. Venkatesh Onkar and

Kirby Huminuik who helped edit parts of the manuscript, and Michael Little who gave the cover idea. Bharathi Pratap, my gifted music teacher, for enriching my life so much. Prof. C. Seshadri who assured me that a book like this would be useful, and started me off with the push I needed.

Usha Aroor, thank you for responding so immediately and generously to the finished work. Your kind appreciation and help has meant the world to me. Arvind Gupta, thank you for being you: energetic, enthusiastic, committed and caring. Just add me to the long list of people who have been inspired by you. Prof. Yash Pal, thank you for your invaluable advice and kind words, coming as they do out of a deep understanding of education in India and a great love of children.

Finally, I would like to thank the following people: my husband Shashidhar for giving me the idea in the first place, making me believe in it, and giving me all the support I needed to complete the project; Shruthi for being the sweetest and most undemanding of children; my parents for appreciating my every little accomplishment in life, and freely supporting my switch from Physics to Psychology twenty-four years ago; my whole big family on both sides, six-month-old to seventy-three-year-old, for their love, encouragement and good company; my CFL family for giving me friendship, and the space and opportunity to work and grow in countless ways; my students who have taught me lessons I could never have learned from a book; and friends and teachers at the Krishnamurti Foundation India whose dedication inspires me.

Introduction

This is a book for teachers primarily, but also for anyone interacting closely with children. As a teacher myself, I often wonder about my students' learning abilities and emotional state. One student finds a topic particularly difficult, another is unmotivated, a third is unable to perform to her potential, and a fourth is distracted. Sometimes we resolve these issues satisfactorily enough to go on with our work, but often they linger unresolved. Actually, the questions that arise from a teacher's daily work are deep and fundamental, with vast implications, and many have no known answers. Still, everyone likes to have their questions answered, and teachers are no different! From our own experience and reading, we draw conclusions and hold beliefs about learning, child development, motivation, intelligence, morality, emotional health and other crucial aspects of teaching. And from these beliefs, we act.

A teacher's beliefs and perceptions are often strongly held. Perhaps this is because beliefs tend to organize our interpretations of events, and we end up seeing only confirmation wherever we look. Many teachers have beliefs that they have never even articulated in words, but which they hold strongly nevertheless. A few examples, expressed in my own words, will give you an idea of what I am talking about:

- Intelligence is not evenly distributed in the population.
- Learning should always be fun.
- School is a means to an end.
- Diversity in a classroom is a problem.
- Children should be taught to be independent thinkers.
- Children should learn to think like adults.
- Anyone can learn anything.
- Children should learn to fit into the real world.
- Children learn best at their own pace.

The significance of our holding these and other beliefs as teachers cannot be overstated. You can see that from each of the statements above, inevitably flow certain decisions and structures. You may say that our actions would be 'right' if our beliefs were 'true'. But when it comes to education and learning, there are not that many absolutely true statements. *Any* strongly held belief has the power to make us rigid and inflexible as teachers, which can make us insensitive to the particulars of a given child in a given situation. On closer examination, practically all the examples given above become very complicated, and their correctness cannot easily be established. This realization is actually quite liberating! It leaves us free to view situations from different perspectives, to question strong positions, to see exceptions and deviations, and to be flexible in our approach. What is needed is time and space for reflection, for questioning our perceptions and ourselves as teachers.

A teacher who can reflect on the teaching-learning process has a naturally investigative, curiosity-driven approach to education. It is an essentially scientific approach, one which fits in beautifully with the scientific methods of psychology. The field of psychology studies all the topics central to our work: learning, memory, intelligence, motivation, child development and emotional health. Psychologists work by formulating theories, testing them, and refining them. For them, no single theory is ever completely and absolutely true—however popular it may become among non-psychologists! Every psychological explanation has its caveats, conditionals and criticisms, and, therefore, understanding the work psychologists do can help us to look critically at our own beliefs as teachers, keeping us on our toes. The truth almost always turns out to be subtle, complex and difficult to pin down into 'tips for a successful teacher'. This, for me, is the beauty of psychology and its strongest contribution to education.

More significantly, a study of psychology can help us take our 'small' questions (about our particular students and classrooms) and fit them into the bigger, eternal questions of intense psychological debate. From 'why doesn't she remember this?' to 'what is memory all about?'; from 'does he have the ability?' to 'what are we born with?'; from 'have they understood?' to 'how is knowledge constructed?', these are short steps. It is exciting to see the connections between our work as teachers and wider social and philosophical issues. It reminds us that teaching is at the heart of what it is to be human.

Some Explanations

In this book, I have attempted to summarize current research in key areas of psychology relevant to education. Of course, 'current' is a relative term! The research reviewed here spans several decades, but most of it is from the last ten or fifteen years. The articles were all published in professional psychological journals, and access to these is limited for readers in India, even using the internet. Nevertheless, I have listed comprehensively, every single paper I read that helped me write the chapters of this book, for readers who would like to track something down. In many cases,

I contacted the authors of papers to request copies via email. Almost without exception, every such request was promptly and kindly responded to, and I am grateful to them all.

A few explanations need to be given about the kind of research I have included. Let me begin with the most obvious thought that strikes anyone reading a psychology book for the Indian context: *if the research has all been done in the West, will it really be relevant to our situation?* Over the two years it has taken me to complete this project, I have been able to sharpen this extremely important question considerably.

I did try to include psychological research conducted in India with Indian participants. Although I found some, it was by no means enough to build an entire psychology of Indian education. The state of Indian psychological research has been studied and commented on by many scholars over the years, and I found a recent survey by Neharika Vohra[1] very informative. She describes three routes to the 'indigenization' of psychological research in India. One route has been via our own cultural explanations of psychological phenomena. For example, there are studies on the effects of yoga on depression and anxiety, or studies on the tridimensional personality theory based on the Sankhya school of Hindu philosophy. However, this is not a popular approach, perhaps because Indians are an extremely culturally diverse people. A second route, much more popular, has been to make our common Indian realities—such as poverty, crowding and gender differences—the subject of psychological study. The third route is to examine Western theories and concepts in Indian contexts.

[1] Neharika Vohra (2004). 'The Indigenization of Psychology in India: Its Unique Form and Progress'. In B. N. Setiadi, A. Supratiknya, W. J. Lonner, & Y. H. Poortinga (Eds.), *Ongoing themes in psychology and culture* (Online Ed.), Melbourne, FL: International Association for Cross-Cultural Psychology. Retrieved from http://www.iaccp.org.

For many years, this amounted to little more than a replication of Western findings, but of late there have been more inventive and original studies of this kind. To give you an idea of the numbers involved, Vohra found that out of 1,895 empirical psychological articles published in Indian journals in the period from 1998–2002, a total of 26 per cent could be called indigenous in one way or another. Of these, 12 followed route one, 394 followed route two, and 85 followed route three. If our aim is a fully autonomous scientific psychology of India, we are only slowly moving toward it. What we need to help this process along, are good quality journals, regional and national psychological associations, and in Vohra's words, '…a critical mass of mature researchers who identify topics of national interest and problems relevant to the Indian context.'

Meanwhile, the field of Western psychology has plenty of insights to offer us. Of course, there are cultural differences. Our specific beliefs and practices are very different from those of people in the West. However, the *mechanisms* of thought and learning (cognition) are the same. Some psychological research findings seem more subject to cultural influences, and others less.[2] More important than the findings themselves are the implications they hold for us as teachers in India, and I found I could usually draw those implications with ease.

A reader may also ask how the topics in this book were chosen. Unlike a traditional textbook of educational psychology, this one has no detailed treatment of history, methods or schools of psychology. None of the traditional favourites (Piaget's or Vygotsky's theories, for example) have been described in detail or depth. There are several excellent books available in the market

[2] An excellent discussion of this can be found in a 2005 paper by Ara Norenzayan and Steven J. Heine titled 'Psychological Universals: What Are They and How Can We Know?' *Psychological Bulletin*, Vol. 131, No. 5, 763-784.

that do this job, but an interested teacher must make the links between theory and practice herself, and these links are not often obvious. In conceptualizing this book, I began from the other end. I first listed several issues that teachers find most interesting or puzzling. These came out of many discussions with fellow teachers, as well as my own questions as a teacher over nearly two decades. Within each chosen topic, I gathered the psychological literature to date, and put it together in a way that I hoped would be relevant, informative and, most of all, enjoyable to read.

In searching through an amazingly rich body of psychological literature relevant to education, I made one decision that I never had cause to regret. Some psychologists work extensively with animals (dogs, cats, monkeys, rats and pigeons) and such research has yielded valuable understanding of animal and human psychology. Even though I admire the ingenuity of their work, the reality remains that research animals are often subjected to painful conditions. I wanted to avoid references to any animal studies, and was pleased to find that all the phenomena I wished to describe have been studied with human beings, and in ways that were ethical enough for my comfort. So you will not read in this book about the familiar rats running through mazes!

While planning and writing this book, I was told by many people (teachers and non-teachers alike), 'But teachers don't read!' While it is true that teachers find very little time to do their own reading after a long day at school, it is definitely an exaggeration to say that they don't read at all. Making time to read about education and wider issues can make the difference between teaching as a job and teaching as a meaningful and exciting vocation. So this book is for you, the busy teacher, because I believe that you want to keep the spirit of learning alive within yourself.

CHAPTER ONE

Brain, Evolution and Schooling

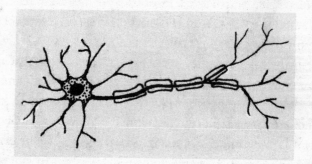

The basics of brain anatomy are learned by most of us in high school. We know that the brain consists of special cells called neurons, that transmit information in the form of electrical impulses. In fact, neurons are distributed throughout the body, to transmit sensations *to* the brain and commands of various kinds *from* the brain. But the work of the one hundred billion neurons *within* the brain represents a fascinating mystery. In ways that we are barely beginning to understand, these neurons give rise to attention, perception, memory, reasoning, intelligence and creativity. Quite a feat!

Structure and Function

Suppose you wanted to understand how some complicated machine works, you might take it apart to closely examine its inner workings. This method works well for clocks, bicycles and cars—but with human brains things are a bit more difficult. When you open the bonnet of a car, you can easily distinguish several different parts inside, even if you are not familiar with their names and functions. When you look at the brain, however, it is harder to see the divisions. At first glance it appears to be a solid mass; closer examination reveals odd shapes and structures that we could call 'parts'.

Just as in the car, we would expect that different parts of the brain have different functions, and to a great extent this is true. Some brain parts are 'older' in an evolutionary sense; that is, we share them with most other animals, including reptiles and fish. They have names such as *corpus callosum*, *basal ganglia*, *medulla* and *cerebellum*. The various functions they serve include reflexes, regulating breathing and heartbeat, coordinating fine and gross movements, regulating sleep cycles and hunger, and much more.

One large section of the brain is its outer covering, called the **neocortex**. It is a wrinkled, grey mass of tissue, three millimetres thick, and doesn't look very exciting. But this is our so-called 'higher' brain, and it is what sets us apart from the other animals. As teachers, most of the things we want our students to do in school—understanding, remembering, associating, communicating, inferring, problem solving and discovering—are accomplished by the neocortex. In proportion to the size of our body, we humans have the largest brains, and almost all of the increase in size is due to an enlarged neocortex. The figures below present an inner and an outer view of the brain.

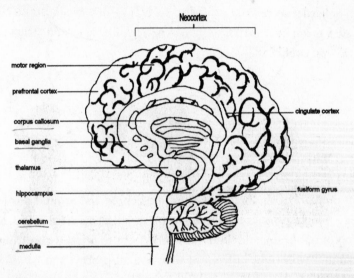

One of the ways in which psychologists have learned to draw labelled pictures, such as these, is through the study of patients with brain damage. Brain damage in a patient can be correlated with specific (sometimes bizarre) symptoms. In other words, we can assume that the particular damaged part was responsible for the particular lost or damaged function. Earlier the location of damage could only be known through an autopsy after the patient's death, but today brain scanning techniques can give us an instant picture of the damage. In fact, as scanning methods improve, psychologists are even able to 'look into' the normal working brain.

Over more than a century, this kind of research has led to a fairly good understanding of the way functions are divided in the brain. For instance, we all process what we see in the lower back portion of the brain, and we all (with few exceptions) process language

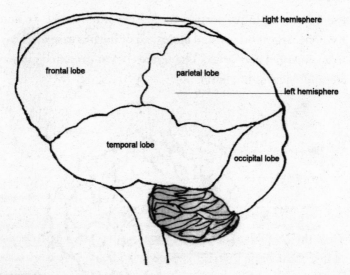

in the part of the brain that lies just behind and around our left ear. We all process bodily sensation in a narrow strip across the top of our brain, and send out instructions to our muscles from a parallel strip right in front of that. We all process and lay down new memories with the help of a small structure in the heart of our brain called the hippocampus.

These 'parts' of the brain can be subdivided quite finely: for example, reading and writing are located separately from speech and comprehension. And there are separate parts for processing *meanings* (semantics) and *grammar* (syntax). We know this because there are patients with damage to one brain area whose speech is rapid, fluent and grammatical, but meaningless nonsense. In contrast, patients with damage to the other area speak in a halting and ungrammatical way, but with the meaning coming across. There are even finer divisions: some patients have difficulty recalling the names of living things and food but not familiar objects, while others can name all objects easily *except* living things and foods! (Box 1 tackles the question of what coordinates the actions of these various parts).

The Hippocampus

Meet the hippocampus, a small and fascinating structure in the centre of the brain that is responsible for 'making new memories'. Recently, it has become the focus of exciting new research into learning and memory-making, but in fact it was many years ago that it first came to the attention of psychologists. Most of our early knowledge about this part of the brain came from patients with damage to the hippocampus and its immediate surroundings, together called the 'hippocampal system'. Such patients forget things from moment to moment: the famous 'short-term memory' deficit. They cannot convert new experiences into lasting memories. Every time you see them, they greet you as if for the first time—even if the last time you met them was only five minutes ago. However, they do retain so-called 'remote memories', which are all the things they had learned and experienced up to a certain point in time. Yet since they are unable to learn and remember new things, they remain in a sense 'stuck' at that point. This makes them far more dysfunctional than amnesia patients who can at least begin life anew.

Here an interesting distinction must be made: hippocampal damage affects **explicit** learning, but not **implicit** learning. Such a patient can learn new skills with repeated practice (implicit learning). For example, if you teach him to ride a scooter every day for a week, by the end of the week he will be able to ride the scooter. But he will have no memory of the learning process, and will even be surprised that he is able to ride so well after a week. He cannot learn new facts, new ideas, or meet and get to know new people (explicit learning). The hippocampus thus appears to be responsible for laying down those memories that can be consciously remembered and verbally expressed. These consist of new connections among events, objects, facts and contexts.

The hippocampus is unique in that it records these connections very quickly, after only a single exposure, unlike other parts of the brain that require several exposures and practice trials. Over time, connections in the hippocampus are 'transferred' to permanent places in the neocortex, and in the process vanish from the hippocampus. Thus when there is damage to the hippocampus but not to the neocortex, recent memories suffer though remote memories are unaffected.

The unique way in which the hippocampus functions, continually making connections in response to stimuli and destroying them as they are transferred to the neocortex, suggests that it may be fundamentally different from other parts of the brain. It is believed that unlike cells in the rest of the body, neurons neither regenerate nor replace themselves. This is mostly true, except for the hippocampus! Recent research is showing that in this region of the brain, neurons are produced even into adulthood (**adult neurogenesis**). Perhaps the special nature of the hippocampus's job makes this necessary; new neurons arise to record new experiences, and probably degenerate as time passes and the memory is transferred to permanent neural networks elsewhere in the brain.

There's more to this interesting story. What do you think are the factors that *reduce* neurogenesis in the hippocampus? Apart from the normal aging process, a prime villain is **chronic stress**, and

Box 1
WHO'S THE BOSS?

Examining the brain under a microscope reveals a world of activity and complexity. The approximately 100 billion neurons, which make up the mass of the brain, work on the basis of electro-chemical reactions. Chemicals called neurotransmitters trigger electric impulses that travel the length of a neuron, and transmit themselves to other neurons across tiny gaps called synapses (again with the help of the neurotransmitters). Messages enter the brain from the outside through our senses, and leave the brain to various limbs and organs so that we can act or respond. The number of messages criss-crossing within the brain snowballs rapidly, since each neuron can be connected to a thousand other neurons.

As we unravel the working of the brain, one question keeps coming up: who is in control, and where is the control centre? Research has found that there is no actual CEO in the brain. The working of the brain is nothing but the ever-changing patterns of connections between neurons. And there is no single neuron or group of neurons that is 'smarter' than the rest.

The boss is nowhere—or everywhere. The brain functions in a special way called Parallel Distributed Processing. First, memories, thoughts and knowledge are widely distributed across the neocortex. Second, processing in the brain takes place in parallel, rather than serial fashion. For example, to activate a particular thought sequence, several thousand connected neurons are firing in different parts of the brain simultaneously. If processing had to be done serially, with a message passing in sequence from one neuron to another and another, the time for even a 'quick thought' would add up. There certainly isn't time for everything to reach some central spot before decisions and actions can be taken. Neuron firing is quite a slow process (between 1 and 100 metres per second!), and the split second speed of our thinking and action shows that brain processes cannot be serial.

However, it is true that we *feel* as though there were someone in charge—and most of us locate that someone in our own heads. The few actions that seem to require the exercise of our 'will'—voluntary attentional processes—are associated with a brain area called the *cingulate cortex*. Every time we make a conscious choice between alternatives, search for a distant memory, purposefully select information for storage, suppress emotional responses or try to suppress thoughts, this particular small part of our brain is active.

the production of glucocorticoids in the body (a chemical released in response to stress). Studies suggest that chronic stress leads to poorer memory ability in human beings. Although this research is a bit new and tentative, perhaps it is not telling us much that we did not already know. Any teacher's first-hand experience will testify that stress inhibits learning! If we want students to learn, school must not be a chronically stressful environment.

The structure and function of different brain parts is closely connected to a relatively new area of thinking, **evolutionary psychology**. For the remainder of this chapter, we will look at some interesting theories in this field as applied to education.

The Evolution of Modules in the Brain

The human brain is very old. Humans as a species have been around for just under three million years. For 99.9 per cent of this time, they have survived as hunter-gatherers who had to cope with a certain range of threats and challenges. The last 10,000 years of agriculture presented a very different set of challenges, and the last 200 years of industrialization, culminating in the computer age, has changed our environment till it barely resembles that of our ancestors any more.

However, human brains and bodies have followed the much slower timetable of evolutionary change over this long period. The process of natural selection required many, many generations to produce the kind of changes that separate us from our ape cousins: standing up, using tools and language, for example. And there have simply not been enough generations for the brain and body to evolve in response to the rapid changes in environment that we ourselves have created in the last few centuries. For this reason, psychologists John Tooby and Leda Cosmides say that 'our modern skulls house a Stone Age brain'!

The 'old' brain was well adapted to a world where there were no electric lights, no refined sugar, and no school! For example, our love of sweet foods was adaptive then, maladaptive today. According to Tooby and Cosmides, the brain evolved separate **modules** that successfully met the challenges of those times. For instance, one to tell us what is edible, one to guide us who will make a good mate, one to help us communicate via facial expressions, one to learn grammar; recognize faces; make spatial maps, and so on. Even processes such as memory, reasoning, decision-making and learning were specialised to fit the contexts faced by our ancestors.

Today we still carry those modules around in our heads, even though our environment presents us with different challenges. Thus even today, logical reasoning is much better for us in social situations that our Stone Age ancestors must have faced. Our recognition memory for faces is much better than for words. Children find learning the rules of spoken language much easier than learning the rules of spelling or written language. Moreover, we do *not* carry around modules suited to our current environment such as one for literacy, one for computer programming, and one for quantum physics. This has, as you can imagine, some implications for education.

Innate and Non-innate Learning

David Geary is another psychologist who writes about modularity, and he describes a very interesting theory. As we have said, any species will evolve modules to help meet its own unique challenges, and for our ancestors these challenges fell into three broad categories: physics, biology and psychology. For successful adaptation, humans needed to

- navigate in a three-dimensional world of physical objects, understand trajectories, judge movement, and mentally represent and manipulate objects (crucial to tool use);
- classify flora and fauna into edible/inedible/medicinal, and prey/predator;
- navigate a social world (especially since they lived in groups): recognize faces, read facial expressions, recognize kin, divide the world into in- and out-group members, use language and infer other people's mental states.

These three areas of human knowledge and skill can be called folk physics, folk biology and folk psychology. (The word folk is used to distinguish it from the formal knowledge we learn in school

and beyond)}̸ A child develops these
three areas of expertise in a natural
way, without any special effort put in
by adults. Geary has attempted to list
the modules that make up these areas
of skill. For some of these modules,
specific brain sites have actually been
found. For example, parts of the
parietal cortex and hippocampus are
involved in mental representation of
physical space. Parts of the posterior

Triple PhD!

neocortex are involved in the ability to name living things but not
nonliving things. Parts of the fusiform gyrus and the prefrontal
cortex are involved with face perception.

Among tribal people who do not have a formal education, we
find knowledge and skill in these three areas very well developed.
Tribal cultures are well known for the depth and sophistication of
their knowledge about plants and animals in their environment.
Similarly, they are highly skilled in the social aspects of living
together and cooperating with each other, and rules of kinship,
hierarchy, status and relationship are well organized. They are
also highly skilled in their use of domestic tools and weaponry.
Psychologists have shown that children too, before they enter
school, have already developed fairly rich folk theories in biology,
physics and psychology. But we ignore this learning completely,
and attempt to supplant it with our school curricula![1]

In a way, we could call these innate skills. Here the word
'innate' does not mean that one is born with the knowledge
already present—of course that is impossible. Rather, it means

---

[1] Chapter Two contains a description of this under the heading
Conceptual Change.

that a part of the brain is 'wired' to make certain connections, to learn certain things.

Language works in this way: it is innate in the sense that babies are **programmed to learn** any language on earth. It is not innate in the sense that they already know a language when they are born.

At this point, you will wonder: is there a 'non-innate' learning? Can we humans learn things we were *not* programmed to learn? We have talked about several innate forms of learning. Now as teachers, we quickly realise that there is little, if any, overlap between a traditional school curriculum and this kind of learning. And yet, many children manage to go through several years of schooling and get certified as having learned several 'non-innate' skills (e.g., reading, writing, calculus, Kepler's laws and classical music). How is this possible? When we look at animals and what they can be trained to do, even the most striking examples of trained animal behaviour pale in comparison to the breadth and novelty of what a human toddler can learn. There is something different about the human brain, and it is this: the human brain is actually *specialised to learn non-innate skills*.

Teaching—A Particular Human Skill

The property of the brain, and cerebral cortex in particular, that makes non-innate learning possible is called **neural plasticity.** The human brain contains plenty of 'spare' circuitry that is available for us to make new associations and connections. For Stone Age man, neural plasticity was a great boon to his innovative use of tools and communication. Today, this same neural plasticity serves us in learning just about anything, right from playing the violin to differentiating exponential functions. Even more important, and what is very different from even our closest relatives the chimpanzees, human learning can be passed on from generation to generation. It is not necessary for each generation to rediscover everything their parents learned, since humans as a species do engage in explicit teaching. The combination of neural plasticity and the ability to communicate and teach, sets us apart as a species.

For another way of looking at the same thing, Geary talks about biologically primary and biologically secondary abilities, which correspond with what we have called innate and non-innate learning. Children acquire the primary abilities, he says, through playful interaction with the environment and a lot of self-driven practice, which develops these skills to a high degree (language is a prime example). But, and this is where education comes in, they can also acquire the secondary abilities—the brain structures can support such learning—but it will require explicit instruction and some (forced!) drill-and-practice. In other words, if we want to learn to play the violin or differentiate exponential functions, we have to be taught how, and we will need deliberate practice in the skill.

Of course, school is the place we have invented for this kind of formal instruction in secondary abilities or non-innate skills. We cannot get away from schools, but this does not mean that we have to teach exactly the way we do now. We can take into account the way the brain works and the way children develop, tailor our teaching to that and avoid the mismatches mentioned earlier. Learning can be meaningful and fun. We already make use of the brain's amazing abilities to stretch learning far beyond what one could have imagined even a hundred years ago, and we could pat ourselves on the back for that, *except* that education is a painful and basically unsuccessful process for many students. Can something better be accomplished, and in a less painful way? That is for us as teachers to discover.

References and Bibliography

1. Barret, H. Clark, and R. Kurzban, 2006. 'Modularity in Cognition: Framing the Debate'. *Psychological Review*, Vol. 113, No. 3, 628–47.

2. Cosmides, L., and J. Tooby, 1997. *Evolutionary Psychology: A primer.*

3. Geary, D.C., 1995. 'Reflections of Evolution and Culture in Children's Cognition Implications for Mathematical Development and Instruction'. *American Psychologist*, Vol. 50, No. 1, 24–37.

4. Geary, D. C., 1996. 'The Evolution of Cognition and the Social Construction of Knowledge'. *American Psychologist*, Vol. 51, No. 3, 265–66.

5. Geary, D.C., and K.J. Huffman, 2002. 'Brain and Cognitive Evolution: Forms of Modularity and Functions of Mind'. *Psychological Bulletin*, Vol. 128, No. 5, 667–98.

6. Gould, E., P. Tanapat, N.B. Hastings, and T.J. Shors, 1999. 'Neurogenesis in Adulthood: a Possible Role in Learning'. *Trends in Cognitive Sciences*, Vol. 3, No. 5.

7. Medin, D.L., and S. Atran, 2004. 'The Native Mind: Biological Categorisation and Reasoning in Development and across Cultures'. *Psychological Review*, Vol. 111, No. 4, 960–83.

8. National Commission on Excellence in Education, 1983. *A Nation at Risk: The Imperative for Educational Reform.* US Department of Education.

9. Nelson, C.A., 2000. 'Neural Plasticity and Human Development: the Role of Early Experience in Sculpting Memory Systems'. *Developmental Science*, 3:2, 115–36.

10. Pinker, S., 2003. 'How to Get Inside a Student's Head'. *The New York Times*, January 31, 2003.

11. Posner, M.I., and G.J. DiGirolamo, 2000. 'Cognitive Neuroscience: Origins and Promise'. *Psychological Bulletin*, Vol. 126, No. 6, 873–89.

12. Sacks, O., 1990. *The Man Who Mistook His Wife for a Hat and Other Clinical Tales.* Harper Perennial, New York.

13. Skoyles, J.R., 1999. 'Neural Plasticity and Exaptation'. *American Psychologist*, Vol. 54, No. 6, 438–39.

14. Squire, L.R., 1992. 'Memory and the Hippocampus'. *Psychological Review*, Vol. 99, No. 2, 195–231.

15. Springer, S.P., and G. Deutsch, 1985. *Left Brain, Right Brain* (revised edn). W.H. Freeman and Co., New York.

16. Thompson, R.F., 1993. *The Brain: a Neuroscience Primer*. W.H. Freeman and Co., New York.

CHAPTER TWO

Learning

In the previous chapter, we looked at some features of the human brain and its evolution that are broadly relevant to education. Now the natural topic for a second chapter is 'learning'. Before getting into how children learn, however, it is important to discuss the kinds of things we want our students to learn, and I will do so first.

Three fields of learning are desirable, and these are what we aim for in schooling: **conceptual** knowledge in various domains (such as biology, chemistry, language), **procedural** knowledge of various skills, and higher-order **reasoning** skills. Conceptual knowledge is the understanding of the basic principles in a domain, and includes an understanding of causal relationships and what is possible in that domain. For example, in the addition of large numbers, children need to have the conceptual understanding of place value in base-ten arithmetic. Procedural knowledge refers to the behavioural skills needed to carry out operations, and in the addition example it would include placing the two numbers correctly one below the other, adding digits and carrying over. Procedural knowledge also has other interesting features which will be explained in this chapter. Reasoning skill is somewhat harder to define in a sentence or two. It may be more useful to define it in terms of its lack—psychologists have used words such as shallow thinking, mindlessness and dysrationalia to describe much of human thinking! As teachers, we must be interested in whether we can improve the *quality* of our students' thinking. This will be explored in the last section of this chapter.

Much of the conceptual and procedural learning we wish to convey in school is 'non-innate'. You remember that in the last chapter we saw the brain as highly capable from an early age in some 'innate' areas of learning, and this would include conceptual as well as procedural learning. A simple example is that when children count objects, they **know that** (conceptually) each item must be counted once and only once, and they also **know how** (procedurally) to touch or point to the objects one by one. In fact, in innate or biologically primary domains, the two kinds of learning are inseparable, and children are not conscious of the difference between them. But as we said, the brain is also capable of a great deal of non-innate learning, and here (in biologically secondary domains) the two kinds of learning can be separated for more effective teaching. In fact, it is interesting that the relative emphases placed on conceptual and procedural learning is one thing that distinguishes progressive from traditional models of education. Perhaps unfairly, we might accuse traditional education of focussing on the latter to the exclusion of the former, while progressive education wants the former to the exclusion of the latter!

If non-innate learning is possible, both conceptual and procedural, how best can we go about teaching? Steven Pinker, a psychologist who has written extensively on the evolution of the human brain, puts the problem very well, 'Educators must figure out how to co-opt the faculties that work effortlessly and to get children to apply them to problems at which they lack natural competence.'

Easier said than done. What are these 'faculties that work effortlessly', and how are they to be 'co-opted'? I have put together a few faculties that I think would qualify—constructivism and conceptual change, practice and procedural learning, and context-dependent reasoning skills. Each of these has an impact on the way students learn best, and thus each should have an impact on the way we teach.

Constructivism and Conceptual Change

Constructivism is a word that has been in use by psychologists since decades, and in India it has recently taken on buzz-word status! In simple terms, it refers to the way that knowledge or information is stored in the brain. Nothing is ever recorded in the brain *exactly* as it was experienced. This is true for the experience we receive from any of our five senses; when two people have seen or heard the same thing, their memories of what they saw or heard will almost certainly differ. Differences in our perceptions and memories arise because we *interpret* everything we experience, and interpretation is always in the light of whatever knowledge we already possess. Thus, our interpretations of experiences become new knowledge, which keeps growing and helping us interpret new experiences. And this is what is meant by knowledge being **constructed** by the learner.

Another important aspect of knowledge in the brain is that it is **organized** in meaningful ways. You know that knowledge is organized differently depending on whether you find it in a textbook, an encyclopaedia or a dictionary. In the human brain, knowledge appears to be organized flexibly in all these and other ways (Chapter Three has a more detailed description of this). Jean Piaget, a psychologist who wrote extensively about child development, called these organized structures of knowledge in the brain 'schemas.' Experiences, he said, are continually being 'fitted into' our schemas (assimilation) and the schemas also need to change to allow new information in (accommodation).

If this is the way the mind works, according to principles of constructivism and organization, are we co-opting these faculties in the way we teach? Unfortunately, the answer is no. Education frequently fails the child on both counts:

- we give our students knowledge in disconnected chunks, and
- we expect our students to reproduce knowledge in more or less the same way it was received.

Presenting disconnected chunks of knowledge makes it difficult for the student to do what she does best—interpret new information in the light of existing knowledge. This makes true conceptual understanding impossible, which, as you will see in Chapter Three, also affects later memory for what one has learned. Also, it is unreasonable to expect that our students' understanding of a given lesson will correspond exactly with the way the textbook is written. In fact, when such correspondence is found, it is usually a sign that the student has parroted the lesson!

To remedy this situation, we need to change the way we approach teaching quite dramatically. We would first have to acknowledge that all children start off with pre-conceptions

of reality. The 'pre' refers to the fact that these conceptions are developed *before* they join a formal school! Each student is far from a blank slate on which we can simply write pages and pages of information. Psychologists have found many examples of the 'naïve' or intuitive theories that children construct, about subjects as varied as force, matter, the earth, and numbers. Sometimes it can happen that a naïve theory coincides with the 'correct' adult theory. For example, children usually figure out that natural numbers are discrete, and that numbers go on forever. But often the student's intuitive knowledge conflicts with textbook or accepted knowledge. These instances are common: for example, senior school students see force as a characteristic of single objects rather than of a system, or explain floating and sinking with reference to weight alone. Our tendency is to say that such statements are *wrong*. Well, from our point of view they are wrong, but the student's explanations are generally based on internally consistent theories (they are not random errors). I am repeatedly struck by the strong drive towards internal consistency in children's explanations of almost any phenomenon.

Nevertheless, we must replace these theories with the correct ones. And here is where we may make a mistake, by assuming that we can simply 'replace' them. That, as we have seen, is not how the brain works. It cannot reject a schema outright in favour of a new one—instead, it must interpret the new in terms of the old, adjusting the old to allow for the new, and so on. Remember, knowledge has to be constructed, it cannot be imported wholesale. This process, according to the research, is usually slow and gradual, not sudden and instantaneous. Along the way, the student's changed schema will contain misconceptions, errors and sometimes inconsistencies, until a complete and thorough understanding is achieved.

This kind of learning is called **conceptual change**, and it has become an extremely promising field of research in education. The fact that students learn best through a process of conceptual change is very important; if such conceptual change does not happen, the old schemas remain as powerful as ever. High school and even college students show surprising misconceptions in their answers to science or mathematics questions—surprising, because they are supposed to have passed through a successful education in all the right theories! The national educational survey mentioned in the last chapter showed how students from 'top Indian schools' can show such gaps in their understanding of concepts in science, mathematics and English. Evidently, they are able to 'perform' satisfactorily in school tests and examinations in spite of these gaps. One psychological explanation of this is that sometimes academics can be very distant from everyday experience. The result is that students build schemas of what is taught in class that are independent from, and unconnected to, their schemas of everyday experience. These schemas are activated in the context of academic work, so that they can perform adequately in tests and homework, but they do not gain a better understanding of real phenomena.

The best way to encourage conceptual change is to confront students with clear examples, which their schemas cannot explain. Then they will have to modify their schemas accordingly, and this is a step-by-step process as they keep encountering new facts that they must explain. For instance, students may assume that multiplication always results in larger numbers, or that more digits imply larger numbers. When they learn to multiply fractions (10x1/2=5), the first concept has to change; and when they encounter decimals (1.234<1.24), the second concept must change. This change, as I said earlier, is usually gradual and not all at once. At the very least, change requires effort on the part of the teacher to make clear and convincing demonstrations. For example, children assume that every part of a moving object moves at the same speed. This is true for objects travelling in straight lines, but for a car on a circular racetrack, its left and right doors are not moving at the same speed! For conceptual change to happen here, a simple physical demonstration, involving two students holding a rod connected to a central pivot and walking around it, will be more effective than an explanation in words.

The student who is further from the pivot will *experience* that she has to walk faster to keep up with the student closer to the pivot.

As the student works to make and remake her schemas, she might reason on the basis of in-between schemas. The psychologist Stella Vosniadou and her colleagues have been studying the way conceptual change happens, and the types of in-between schemas that students construct. A good example comes from the topic of fractions. Vosniadou asked ten- to fifteen-year-old students in Greece to think of the smallest and largest fractions they could, and to explain their answer. The students' responses revealed four distinct schemas for fractions.

1. Smaller numbers in the numerator (or denominator) make smaller fractions. In this schema the size of a fraction is (incorrectly) represented by two independent numbers.

2. *Larger* numbers in the numerator (or denominator) make smaller fractions. Here is an in-between schema based on a partial understanding that fractions behave differently from single numbers—'in fractions, smaller is somehow bigger'.

3. Fractions become larger when the numerator approaches the size of the denominator. Here the fraction is correctly seen as the relationship between two numbers, but understanding is still not complete (the unit is not the largest fraction).

4. Fractions become larger when the numerator becomes larger than the denominator. Some students in this category, therefore, concluded correctly that there is no smallest or largest fraction.

Another example from Vosniadou's work has to do with the density of rational numbers. As you saw earlier, one of the 'naïve' ideas about numbers that children develop is that they are discrete, that is, when counting one goes 1, 2, 3... without anything in between. Of course the list of natural numbers goes on forever—there are infinitely many. The concept of discreteness of natural numbers is very necessary to counting, and children develop it intuitively. But rational numbers behave differently—there are infinitely many rational numbers *between* any two rational numbers. Vosniadou asked fourteen-year-old students several questions about rational numbers, such as how many numbers lay between .005 and .006, between 3/8 and 5/8, and between 5/8 and 8.5. From their responses, four stages of conceptual change could be identified (the fourth one being completely correct).

1. There are no numbers between decimals like .005 and .006, and between 3/8 and 5/8 there is only 4/8.
2. There are a finite number of numbers between decimals like .005 and .006, as between any two fractions.
3. There are a finite number of numbers between .005 and .006, but infinite numbers between any two fractions.
4. There are infinitely many numbers between any two decimals, and between any two fractions.

These two examples should be enough to convince you of the complexity behind a student's 'wrong answer'! We must be aware that our students reason from conceptions, that these 'alternative' conceptions are often in conflict with the 'correct' ones, and further, that it is not always easy for them to change these conceptions. Box 1 describes one theory about alternative conceptions.

It is all very well for a researcher to be investigating the various preconceptions students hold, but how are we as teachers going to find out our own students' schemas? Conversations, classroom discussions, open-ended questions and journal writing can all help. We must frequently ask questions such as, 'What do you mean?', and 'How is that different from what he said?' and 'Can you give an example?'. We may feel that we just do not have the time for this, or that there are too many children in a class for it to work. But if we engage in discussions and conversations with our students at least occasionally, the process might get internalized in their minds. After all, we want them to learn to be good learners, and one thing that will help, is if they can become aware of the process of conceptual change in themselves. As for large classes, even if not everybody can 'get a chance' to speak, everyone can benefit from listening to such exchanges.

Various other good teaching practices encourage conceptual learning. Here are some suggestions from the research to help

Box 1

ALTERNATIVE CONCEPTS, NOT WRONG CONCEPTS

Michelene Chi and others have been working to classify the different types of alternative conceptions that human beings hold, and through that, to understand why some misconceptions are particularly difficult to 'correct'. In any subject, we know that certain concepts are harder to learn than others—could this be related to the kinds of naïve conceptions that humans tend to form? Chi suggests that humans (from infants to adults) have a tendency to explain phenomena in terms of *direct*, sequential cause and effect, rather than as the complex *emergent* properties of systems of independent, simultaneously acting elements. To understand this statement, we need to look at some examples. Consider heat—many naive students think of it as a substance, and explain heat transfer in terms of the transfer of a substance like 'hotness' from one object to another. Similarly, temperature is incorrectly conceived of as an 'amount' of something. There is a human tendency, she says, to explain many concepts in terms of sequential, direct cause and effect. There may also be a tendency to view concepts as *things* rather than *processes* (e.g., heat, electricity, force). Yet, several important phenomena (diffusion, weather patterns, fractals, human behaviour, evaporation, natural selection…) are not like this. Instead, they are properties of a system that *emerge* out of the interactions of individual elements. Because we tend not to see things in this way, we have particular difficulty with understanding emergent processes.

The solution, says Chi, could be for teachers to first make clear that some concepts are processes and not substances, and then create the idea of an emergent process. This can be done using models, or role-playing. Once the schema of an emergent process is in place, new concepts must be understood in relation to that.

your students gain an understanding of the basic principles and relationships in mathematics, for example:

- Ask your students the right questions. Psychologists have classified the questions that mathematics teachers ask into different types. Most questions are of the kind 'What is the answer to so-and-so?', but some teachers also ask 'How would you do so-and-so?', and 'Why is this the right answer?'. Questions of the *how* and *why* kind are less common, but they aid conceptual understanding, and the students of teachers who ask such questions are better at mathematics. This occurs even when the student does not actually answer the question—merely thinking about it encourages higher level conceptualization!

- Ask your students for different ways of solving a problem. Seeing that alternate methods yield the same result and understanding why, will promote conceptual learning. Almost every problem has multiple means of solution, so this is an easy idea to practise.

- Encourage them to classify different problems according to how they must be solved. Problems that appear superficially different have common underlying structures, and recognizing this will strengthen conceptual understanding.

You might have to collect problems or write your own for this—most textbooks cluster the problems according to method, so that this challenge is never given to the students till they face an examination!

- Have your students teach a concept to someone else. Actually, psychological research shows that even reading something with the *intention* of teaching it to another, improves conceptual understanding.
- Ensure that word problems in mathematics are set in contexts familiar or relevant to the student.

In language teaching, you can encourage conceptual understanding by showing students earlier drafts and finished pieces of writing by other writers (yourself, or senior students). They can thus learn for themselves what has been changed or corrected. Students can edit each others' work, as well as their own. In history teaching, the students can be shown different versions of the same event, and encouraged to think about how history is represented, interpreted, and therefore constructed! They can examine evidence (from primary sources such as travellers' accounts or interviews with people) and come up with historical theories themselves, which can then be compared with the theories and explanations in their textbooks.

Whichever subject you teach, let your students learn to ask the 'right questions'—an even more valuable skill than giving the 'right answers'. Use analogies, models or graphic organizers to explain concepts (see examples below). Encourage them to talk about (describe, explain, elaborate) what they are learning. They can keep journals to record, in their own words, what they used to know before a class and how their understanding has changed.

•

Understanding the solar system using analogies:
If the sun is a pumpkin, the earth is roughly as small as a mustard seed, and they are roughly 50m apart. If the sun is a mustard seed, the earth is 50 cm away, and the nearest star is roughly 60 km away!

Solving algebraic equations using the gift wrapping model and the balance scale model:
To model the rearranging of an equation, wrap an object in paper, place it in a box and tie it up with string. To open this 'gift', you have to unwrap it in strictly reverse order. The steps shown below are wrong because it is like trying to open the box without first untying the string.

$$\frac{2x+4}{7} = 10$$

$$\frac{2x}{7} = 10 - 4 = 6$$

Remind the students to always ask themselves 'how the gift was wrapped', so as to know how to unwrap it. In the expression below, they have to be able to say 'first we multiplied x by 2, then we added 4, then we divided the result by 7.'

$$\frac{2x + 4}{7}$$

To solve an equation with one unknown, use fruits (lemons work well) and weights:

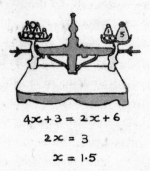

$$4x + 3 = 2x + 6$$
$$2x = 3$$
$$x = 1.5$$

Discovery Learning

A powerful method for conceptual change is the process of self-directed discovery, especially in science and mathematics. Discovery learning has become an extremely attractive idea in Indian educational circles of late! In a typical discovery learning set-up, students are given access to a range of suitable materials, and through self-directed experimentation, it is hoped that they will actively construct the knowledge to accomplish conceptual change. From a constructivist point of view, this is an excellent scenario. It is usually contrasted with the 'expository approach', where the teacher has prepared a lesson and presents it (lecture-style), or the class follows a textbook closely. The table below describes the main advantages and disadvantages of expository lessons.

Advantages	Disadvantages
1. Concepts are made clear and explicit to students. 2. Sequencing of topics aids conceptual change. 3. Relevant ideas are all included so that we are not taking a chance on the student discovering everything.	1. Students may become passive and 'switch off' if they are not called on to speak or think. 2. Teachers need not consider students' backgrounds in order to prepare a coherent lecture, so the lesson may end up being boring or too difficult.

Expository classes do not rule out the possibility of constructive learning—students can 'discover' from listening attentively to a well-delivered lecture, making connections between what is presented and what they know already. But such classes must be well prepared, keep the students' interests and backgrounds in mind, and be peppered with plenty of discussion and questions to keep students on their toes. Unfortunately, too many expository classes end up as monologues. Remember you need to do two things for a student to learn something new: activate relevant existing schemas, and fit new information into existing schemas. In expository teaching, there is the danger that the *first* will not happen, and the dismal failure of this approach has therefore prompted a swing in favour of the discovery approach. Yet in discovery learning, the *second* may not happen if the student never comes across the new information to be learned!

A study conducted by Ilonca Hardy and others in Germany illustrates the problem with the 'pure' discovery approach, and a way to get around it. These researchers conducted a short eight-session course for eight-year-olds in Germany on 'floating and sinking'. The students had never encountered the topic in a formal science class before (it is a rather advanced one). The question posed to the students for investigation was, 'Why does a large iron ship float?'. Young children typically answer questions of floating and sinking with reference to one variable only ('heavy things sink', or, 'big things sink', or, 'things with holes in them can float'). A scientific explanation considers the relationship between the densities of the object and the surrounding fluid, and between gravitational and buoyancy forces. Can we hope that this knowledge, developed in scientific detail by physicists, will be spontaneously discovered by young children?

To this end, several materials were made freely available during the course—chunks of varying size and form, or everyday objects, made from materials such as wood, metal, wax, clay and so on. The materials were designed to provide opportunities to test

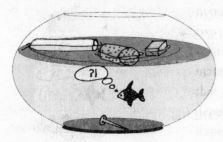

hypotheses. For instance, two pieces of the same volume, but different material, could show that floating does not depend solely on volume. Experimental sites were also set up containing instructions, tips, hints, and guiding questions. And there was also a teacher present in the course.

The study compared two methods of learning: what we might call 'pure discovery' and 'guided discovery'. One group of students was left free to play around with the materials, set up their own experiments and do various worksheets as they liked (called Low Instructional Support). The teacher in this group was available to encourage discussions and make occasional observations, but did not structure the learning in any way. Many spontaneous discussions emerged, and the learning was definitely student-centred. The students were completely free to initiate, do and learn what they wished. A second group received structured guidance from the teacher, who sequenced the course into eight topics, and conducted focussed discussions (called High Instructional Support). These students were led though experiments and completed worksheets in a fixed sequence. The course was designed to systematically change their concepts of floating and sinking by exposing them to counter examples which would encourage them to modify their knowledge schemas. In this group, every student received the benefit of instruction, but there was little freedom in terms of initiating experiments and activities.

What happened? The two groups did equally well on immediate tests of conceptual understanding, and better than a baseline group of children who had not gone through the course. But on a follow-up test given a year later, the children in the Low Instructional Support group, or pure discovery, slipped in their performance. Several misconceptions returned for this group, unlike for the guided discovery group who maintained their understanding even a year later. Like this study, there is a body of research showing that guided discovery is superior to pure discovery for efficient learning, memory and transfer to new problems.

Richard Mayer, an educational psychologist, made an impassioned plea in a 2005 paper to stop equating 'constructivist' with 'hands-on'. We often mistakenly assume that constructivist learning implies *behaviourally* active students. Popular examples of behavioural activity are hands-on work, discussion, group work and a free exploration of materials. However, Mayer stressed that behavioural activity is neither a necessary nor a sufficient condition to say that constructivist learning has occurred. In fact, *cognitive* activity (to look at incoming information, select what is relevant in the given situation, organize and integrate it with existing knowledge) is what we need. As teachers, it may not be enough for us to change the *look* of our classrooms (while that may be beneficial for its own sake).

Lots of activity, movement, and student participation are not ends in themselves. We teachers have to structure our lessons, sequence the teaching of concepts appropriately, and pose challenging questions (if we are following a well-written textbook, much of this is taken care of). With this strong foundation, hands-on activity and time for student-initiated open discussions are much more beneficial.

Ultimately, the way we look at learning will determine the way we teach, and even small or gradual changes in our teaching will be beneficial. We now turn to the second area of learning, procedural knowledge.

Procedural Knowledge and Skill Learning

You would remember that procedural learning refers to *knowing how* to do things, and almost everything we teach in school requires some degree of procedural learning. *How to* skills are needed in mathematics, fine arts, language, science and so on, and these skills are taught through modelling. That is, the teacher demonstrates the skill by doing, whether it is solving equations, parsing sentences or writing neatly, and the student repeats the same to the best of his ability.

But procedural learning is not restricted to the operations students carry out in school! It represents a separate and very important mode of learning in the brain, without which our lives would be dysfunctional. Procedural learning is happening *all the time*, right from day one, as the child learns to turn over, crawl, reach for objects, make meaningful sounds ... handle a spoon, tie her shoelaces, ride a bicycle, light a match ... cross the road, balance an equation, make *chapatis*. As adults, we are gaining new procedures when we learn to drive a scooter, type on a keyboard, or operate a new machine. What is common to all these situations is that they are:

- learned best by doing, not by following verbal instructions, or by watching others performing the actions;
- improved with repeated exposure and practice;
- implicit, or not easily expressible in words (unlike a list of the Mughal kings, for example);
- automatic, effortless, and often out of our conscious control after a point.

In procedural learning, repeated exposure leads to jumps in performance, until the skill becomes so practised that it is automatic. Learning a skill is totally different from learning a concept, and one crucial difference is the need for **practice**. Psychologists tell us that the only effective way to really master a procedural skill is to keep repeating it, which is probably the original aim of all that 'meaningless drill' we did in school. This is a good place to make a general point about psychology and education. Psychologists doing research on procedural learning are investigating the ideal conditions for optimum learning, the underlying mechanisms of it, and so on. They report, for example, that the only way to learn a procedure is to have consistent practice, and plenty of it. Now how is a teacher supposed to respond to this? Should we flood our students with drill-and-practice?

So much has been said about drill and the deadening effect it has on learning that I do not wish to add any more. Many teachers

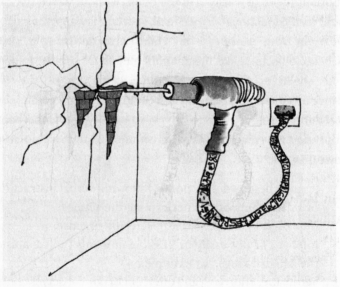

Too much drill...

are aware of these two contradictory facts—drill can be boring, and yet practice is the only way for their students to master certain procedures. The problem with drill comes when we assume that it will **substitute for understanding**. Concepts and procedures are two different things, both of which students need to learn. Practice *alone* cannot lead to conceptual knowledge, and understanding *alone* cannot lead to mastery of a procedure.

Earlier, when we were talking about innate learning, we saw that conceptual and procedural knowledge were both part of it. Very young children spontaneously but diligently practise their procedural skills, repeating sounds or actions again and again till they are mastered. Right from infancy we see this tendency—children seem to enjoy repetition, and we call it 'play'. How wonderful it would be if our students could call a page of multiplication problems 'play'! But practising non-innate procedures just does not seem to be fun beyond a point. Given a choice, students may never engage in the kind of repetition needed to master some procedures.

Dissatisfaction with excessive drill may lead some of us to emphasize conceptual understanding at the cost of procedural learning, says David Geary (we encountered him in Chapter One). Geary is concerned that giving students the idea that learning must always be fun does more harm than good. Social meaning and support must be given to some kinds of learning, he says, so that students will be motivated to practise in spite of a lack of enjoyment. In the context of more 'progressive' educational systems, such as in the U.S., this may be a valid concern. But for us in India, drill is still given undue emphasis, and conceptual teaching takes a back seat in many classrooms. What we need, of course, is a balance of both types of learning.

The idea that people frequently do things that are not necessarily 'fun' is related to motivation, which is covered in Chapter Eight. But a few sentences are relevant here. Children clearly possess the motivation to practise 'innate' skills, and although reduced in some ways, also do show the motivation to practice 'non-innate' skills. This latter motivation is of a different kind—it may lack play, but it gains rewards from small improvements, and perseveres in spite of frustration. The long-term motivation for practice over years can help us to become experts in a wide variety of domains. And please note, we are not talking about the motivation for schoolwork that comes from being afraid of punishment. That kind of motivation is eventually self-defeating.

Can drill actually be an aid to understanding? Many educators believe that the relationship between conceptual and procedural knowledge is unidirectional—understanding a concept well can improve the learning of procedures, but learning a procedure well cannot lead to better understanding of a concept. However, recent research is looking at ways in which each can improve the other, and there can be a continuous back and forth process between procedural and conceptual learning. It appears that the relationship between the two can actually be bidirectional. Reflecting on the use of a procedure reinforces our understanding of the concept. We should ask students *whether* and *why* certain procedures work and other procedures are incorrect. For example, while adding large numbers, why is it important that we place them one under the other in a particular way?

Another advantage of improved procedural knowledge is that when a skill has become automatic, mental resources and attention can be freed up for higher-level reasoning—planning, monitoring, associating, evaluating. We all know that understanding the meaning of text in a new language is extremely effortful and difficult until we have reached automaticity (fluency) in reading the words. Chapter Three contains more on this phenomenon, along with examples.

So practice is not in itself a bad thing, but we must optimize its use. The principles of good practice are that it should:

- involve a *mixture of procedures* in one session;
- include *small doses over longer periods* of time (some psychologists recommend not more than 20 minutes per day for a given skill);
- be supplemented with *reflection on why* certain procedures work.

The phrase 'teaching for understanding' is usually seen as restricting oneself to only conceptual learning. But if, at the close of this section, you see it as embracing both conceptual and procedural learning, I will have achieved my purpose.

Context-dependent Reasoning

In 1985, psychologist David Perkins wrote about schooling, 'One hopes that students will emerge from 12 or more years of study not just better able to read, write, reckon, or recall particular facts, but to *think*.' Perkins referred to this ability to think as **informal reasoning,** or everyday reasoning, and lamented the fact that school pays little or no attention to cultivating it. Informal reasoning differs from formal reasoning in that it does not involve strict deduction or calculation. When we are faced with a claim or situation, we often need to evaluate it after weighing evidence on both (or several) sides. For example, if you are asked 'Does violence on television and in computer games increase violence in society?' your answer cannot be a simple yes or no. You would need to consider several strands of evidence, weighing all aspects carefully. Good informal reasoning would include more lines of argument, more objections to one's own points, and the ability to stick to the issue at hand.

But Perkins's research with high school students, and college graduates alike, showed that people's informal reasoning skills are surprisingly weak. Very few arguments were advanced to the various questions posed, and people gave even fewer objections to their own arguments (this part does not surprise me). This tendency for under-exploration of an issue has been researched earlier. Students often access only a part of all the relevant knowledge they have, and their reasoning falls far short of their intellectual capacity. Many will come up with one argument and rest content with that. This is sometimes called the problem of 'inert knowledge'—a rather apt term, I think. In addition to being generally shallow and narrow, thinking is often hasty or impulsive, fuzzy or imprecise.

As Perkins says, education does not encourage the ability to address open-ended issues. School tasks focus on right answers, quick closure and linear thinking. Yet, thinking about open issues is called for in many situations in the real world. Many of our decisions—concerning everything from money to health to relationships—could be improved by better reasoning. So for this chapter, the question is: can we *learn* to think better? The research shows that there are two possible approaches to this. The first approach is to teach thinking as a separate subject, and several programmes of this kind have been developed and tested for school-age children. The programmes all do two things: make students aware of the process of their thinking (strengths, weaknesses, possible pitfalls) and reorganize their thinking with the help of strategies. The highly successful critical thinking course created by Mathew Lipman is a good example. But one problem is that courses like this take up precious school time—typically two to three periods a week over eight weeks or so. Where is the space in our Indian curriculum for an extra subject?! Another problem is that the courses avoid dealing with subject-matter information, and prefer to stick to abstract problems or puzzles. But this may not give students the skill of 'situated thinking', which is important in developing any domain of knowledge and expertise.

Box 2

RECIPROCAL TEACHING

The Reciprocal Teaching method, developed and tested in the 1980s by psychologist Ann Brown and her colleagues, is a way to make your classroom a **collaborative learning community**, where students take charge of their own learning. It uses dialogue among students (and a teacher) as a means to understanding challenging text material, and in the process improves the students' metacognitive skills. The text can be in any subject, and must be divided into smaller segments, usually paragraphs.

The method has been used with 6–17 students in a group. But if you have a large class, don't despair. You can use the ideas behind reciprocal teaching with small groups of students and minimal teacher support. Just divide your class into several groups of 6–8 students, while you go around giving guidance and help where necessary. Initially, you as the teacher will have to demonstrate all the four skills: summarization, clarification, question generation and prediction (see descriptions below). Gradually, your students will 'get the hang of it' and be able to continue on their own.

Everybody reads a paragraph together, and then one student summarizes it in her own words. The next student clarifies any parts that are difficult to understand, or possible inconsistencies, with the help of the group. A third student asks a question based on the text. This could be a question the answer of which can be found in the paragraph itself, or it could be a question sparked off by the reading. Another student predicts the content of the next paragraph, based on the text so far and his own general knowledge on the topic. The group now moves on to the next segment of text, and the process repeats itself with another set of four students.

On paper, the method almost sounds too simple to be effective, but just try it! It quickly changes the depth at which students are reading text, and the level of understanding they gain. Gradually, this method of reading difficult text becomes internalized in the students so that, more and more, they 'read to learn', and are able to monitor their own understanding of material.

The second approach solves both these problems in one stroke, and that is to teach better thinking through the subjects. Perkins calls this **infusion**, because the hope is that these skills will spread to thinking in general. The best example of the approach is Reciprocal Teaching, developed in the 1980s by psychologist Ann Brown, and described in detail in Box 2. The method can be used for material in any subject area, and it encourages an *awareness of one's own understanding of the material*. This awareness goes by a nice name: **metacognition**. In simple terms, it is the ability to know what one knows, how well one knows it, and what will help to improve one's knowledge. You may be surprised to learn that not many students possess this ability. People in general tend to over- or underestimate their knowledge and understanding, and as a result, do not use appropriate strategies to learn. In Chapter Four on child development, you will read more about the development of the metacognitive ability through childhood. Metacognition is certainly an important part of informal reasoning.

Infusion may also work to the extent that increased knowledge *per se* improves our reasoning ability. Some psychologists would argue the extreme position that good reasoning is nothing but a well-organized knowledge base! Would a person who knows something about sociology, childhood and correlation-and-causation, reason better on the question about TV violence than a person who does not know these things? Quite possibly. The idea is that knowledge, both conceptual and procedural, is developed in various domains (mathematics, science, language, history and so on). The knowledge and skills developed, generalize across domains and eventually can be used in new reasoning situations. In other words, by teaching our subjects in such a way that reasoning skills are developed *in context*, we ensure that our students gain more and better-organized knowledge, which in turn will improve their *general* reasoning abilities. In Chapter Seven on intelligence, you will read more about this idea, because general reasoning ability is one way of defining intelligence.

My own solution would be to teach subjects with conceptual and procedural understanding in mind, use reciprocal teaching methods whenever possible, and have occasional conversations with my students about the nature of learning, understanding and remembering. If you can also slot in a single period a week, for discussions on open-ended questions, this will help them practise informal reasoning skills as well. In these sessions, try to make your students aware of the pitfalls of poor thinking: narrowness, shallowness, imprecision, tangential talking...and let them come up with more themselves.

In Conclusion

It happens that we underestimate our students' capacities to learn—some teachers do this all of the time, and all teachers do this some of the time. Thus, it is good to keep in mind the complex and sophisticated nature of learning, and *go with the grain* of human learning principles. Closely related to learning is the phenomenon of human memory, which is covered in the next chapter. In fact, the two are the same thing: to learn is to remember. In Chapter Three, therefore, you will revisit the idea of concepts and procedures with slightly different terminology, besides encountering other quite different aspects of memory.

References and Bibliography

1. Bransford, J., R. Sherwood, N. Vye, and J. Rieser, 1986. 'Teaching Thinking and Problem Solving'. *American Psychologist*, Vol. 41, No. 10, 1078–89.

2. Chi, M.T.H., 2005. 'Commonsense Perceptions of Emergent Processes: Why Some Misconceptions are Robust'. *The Journal of the Learning Sciences*, 14(2), 164–99.

3. Ericsson, K.A., R.T. Krampe, and C. Tesch-Raimer, 1993. 'The Role of Deliberate Practice in the Acquisition of Expert Performance'. *Psychological Review*, Vol. 100, No. 3, 363–406.

4. Geary, D.C., 1995. 'Reflections of Evolution and Culture in Children's Cognition: Implications for Mathematical Development and Instruction'. *American Psychologist*, Vol. 50, No. 1, 24–37.

5. Geary, D.C., 1996. 'The Evolution of Cognition and the Social Construction of Knowledge'. *American Psychologist*, Vol. 51, No. 3, 265–66.

6. Glaser, R., 1984. 'Education and Thinking: The Role of Knowledge'. *American Psychologist*, Vol. 39, No. 2, 93–104.

7. Glassman, M., 1996. 'The Argument for Constructivism'. *American Psychologist*, Vol. 51, No. 3, 264–65.

8. Gould, E., P. Tanapat, N.B. Hastings, and T.J. Shors, 1999. 'Neurogenesis in Adulthood: a Possible Role in Learning'. *Trends in Cognitive Sciences*, Vol. 3, No. 5.

9. Hardy, I., A. Jonen, K. Moller, and E. Stern, 2006. 'Effects of Instructional Support Within Constructivist Learning Environments for Elementary School Students' Understanding of 'Floating and Sinking'. *Journal of Educational Psychology*, 98(2), 307–26.

10. Keil, F.C., W.C. Smith, D.J. Simons, and D.T. Levin, 1998. 'Two Dogmas of Conceptual Empiricism: Implications for Hybrid Models of the Structure of Knowledge'. *Cognition*, 65, 103–35.

11. Lewis, A.B., 1989. 'Training Students to Represent Arithmetic Word Problems'. *Journal of Educational Psychology*, Vol. 81, No. 4, 521–31.

12. Mayer, R.E., 1992. 'Cognition and Instruction: Their Historic Meeting Within Educational Psychology'. *Journal of Educational Psychology*, Vol. 84, No. 4, 405–12.

13. Mayer, R.E., 2004. 'Should There Be a Three-Strikes Rule Against Pure Discovery Learning? The Case for Guided Methods of Instruction'. *American Psychologist*, Vol. 59, No. 1, 14–19.

14. Nelson, C.A., 1999. 'Change and Continuity in Neurobehavioural Development: Lessons from the Study of Neurobiology and Neural Plasticity'. *Infant Behaviour and Development*, Vol. 22, No. 4.

15. Palinscar, A.S., and A.L. Brown, 1984. 'Reciprocal Teaching of Comprehension-Fostering and Monitoring Activities'. *Cognition and Instruction*, 1(2), 117–75.

16. Perkins, D.N., 1985. 'Postprimary Education Has Little Impact on Informal Reasoning'. *Journal of Educational Psychology*, Vol. 77, No. 5, 562–71.

17. Perkins, D.N., and T.A. Grotzer, 1997. 'Teaching Intelligence'. *American Psychologist*, Vol. 52, No. 10, 1125–33.

18. Perry, M., S.W. VanderStoep, and S.L. Yu, 1993. 'Asking Questions in First-Grade Mathematics Classes: Potential Influences on Mathematical Thought'. *Journal of Educational Psychology*, Vol. 85, No. 1, 31–40.

19. Phillips, D.C., 1997. 'How, Why, What, When and Where: Perspectives on Constructivism in Psychology and Education'. *Issues in Education*, Vol. 3(2), 151.

20. Piaget, J., 1970. *Science of Education and the Psychology of the Child*. Orion Press, New York.

21. Pinker, S., 2003. 'How to Get Inside a Student's Head'. *The New York Times*, January 31, 2003.

22. Posner, M.I., and G.J. DiGirolamo, 2000. 'Cognitive Neuroscience: Origins and Promise'. *Psychological Bulletin*, Vol. 126, No. 6, 873–89.

23. Rittle-Johnson, B., R.S. Siegler, and M.W. Alibali, 2001. 'Developing Conceptual Understanding and Procedural Skill in Mathematics:

An Iterative Process'. *Journal of Educational Psychology*, Vol. 93, No. 2, 346–62.

24. Siegler, R.S., 2005. 'Children's Learning'. *American Psychologist*, 60, 769–78.

25. Skoyles, J.R., 1999. 'Neural Plasticity and Exaptation'. *American Psychologist*, 54, 438–39.

26. Solso, R.L., 2001. *Cognitive Psychology*. Pearson Education (Singapore) Pte. Ltd., Delhi.

27. Stafylidou, S., and S. Vosniadou, 2004. 'The Development of Students' Understanding of the Numerical Value of Fractions'. *Learning and Instruction*, 14, 503–18.

28. Vamvakoussi, X., and S. Vosniadou, 2004. 'Understanding the Structure of the Set of Rational Numbers: a Conceptual Change Approach'. *Learning and Instruction*, 14, 453–67.

CHAPTER THREE

Memory

As I type these words onto an otherwise blank page on the computer, I am struck by the differences between filling a page with text and 'filling' a brain with knowledge. Listing these differences helps to underline some of the most important characteristics of human memory and learning:

- The text I enter will remain in this exact form, potentially forever. Human memory, on the other hand, is extremely gist- and meaning-oriented. Nothing is stored or recalled in verbatim form, unless that were the intention (as when we memorize a poem).

- The page I type on is blank, and new sentences, when typed, do not transform old sentences (thankfully!). Human memory, on the other hand, works by incorporating new information into organized, existing information. And the new information transforms the old: thus, if I read something about birds of South India, it changes my existing knowledge base about those birds. Nothing is literal; nothing remains unchanged.

• The file I type in is stored in a folder, within another folder, within another and so on…to get to a file, you have to open a specific chain of folders, and the chain is fixed. Within the file, the information is stored in a linear fashion, one sentence following the other. Human memory, on the other hand, is organized in exquisitely complicated and subtle ways—in fact, depending on the context, different memories appear to be connected, and therefore, to elicit each other. I can retrieve a particular memory through multiple paths.

Sometimes we teachers, and the school system we are a part of, make demands on our students that are incompatible with these properties of memory. When we use memory inappropriately, we are ignoring its vast powers, its infinite capacities. Psychologists have worked hard on the question of exactly how memory works, and though they still have not arrived at a complete description, they have discovered many interesting things about it. The three points made above refer to three closely related areas of active research: content, encoding/learning and organization. All three are connected with what is called long-term memory, and we begin the chapter with a description of this.

The Contents of Long-term Memory

The long-term memory system is of seemingly limitless capacity. As the name suggests, its contents endure for years, an entire lifetime. But these memories are *never* literal 'copies' of what we have experienced. The difference between a literal recorder and our long-term memory comes from two sources. We don't just experience things; we *interpret* everything we experience (so that no two people experience anything in exactly the same way). On top of that, we don't remember every detail of an experience; there are many gaps in our memory which we subsequently fill in with intelligent guesswork. In short, we never remember external events, only our own mental processing of them. The end result is memories that are meaningful to us, even though they are not accurate copies of our experience. I do not see this property of long-term memory as a defect: it actually helps us to be efficient and effective in daily life. Recording the gist of experiences can lead to deeper understanding, better generalization to other situations and experiences, and is less of a load on the memory system. Of course, it doesn't help students deal with school settings where a lot of rote memorization is demanded!

There are two kinds of long-term memories—those you can talk about, explicit or **declarative**, and those that can only be expressed through actions and behaviours, implicit or **procedural**. The conceptual/procedural distinction made in Chapter Two is the same as the explicit/implicit and the declarative/procedural distinction.

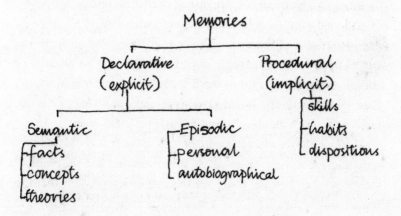

In the figure you see that procedural memory consists of skills, dispositions and habits. An example would be the ability to read, or ride a bicycle. Declarative memories are all the facts, concepts and theories we possess, as well as personal memories of events. An example would be the list of names of the Mughal kings, or the reasons for the Partition, or the name of a best friend in the first standard. It is both useful and right to distinguish between these two types of memories, because in actual fact they are processed separately in the brain. We know this for certain, because of the symptoms of brain-damaged patients. You remember the case of the man with hippocampal damage from Chapter One. He could no longer make new explicit memories, but he could still make new implicit memories. Although he never remembered the doctor who met him every day, and would always greet her as if they were meeting for the first time, he did get progressively better at a particular mirror-drawing task on which he was made to practise daily. Of course, he never remembered having practised the task, but his performance improved nevertheless.

Declarative memories themselves are of two distinct types. There are those to do with ideas and concepts (**semantic** memory) and those to do with events in our own lives (**episodic** memory). Again, we know these two are distinguished in the brain, because of patients with specific brain damage who lose their episodic memories but not their semantic ones. These 'who am I, where am I?' patients do not forget any of their general knowledge or abilities; they simply cannot recall a single personal memory from their lives. For example, one knew the make and year of his car, but could not remember having driven in it even once.

Most of the teaching we do in school adds to our students' semantic memories—ideas, facts and concepts are the stuff of school syllabi. At least, those are the memories we want them to report and retain. If we ask a student to explain the Pythagoras theorem, we don't want her memories of the day she learned it and what she had eaten for lunch just before that class. We just want her to state the theorem.

I said that our teaching 'adds' to semantic memories, but the word 'add' does little justice to the complexity of the process. A student's semantic knowledge base increases along several dimensions. The **size** or the sheer amount of knowledge keeps increasing as he is exposed to new facts and concepts. The **number of interconnections** among the existing pieces of knowledge goes up, as does the **complexity** of these interconnections. The **consistency** among different pieces of knowledge and the **level of abstraction** of his semantic knowledge increases. Do we keep all these in mind when we teach?

I think our education system certainly takes care of the first of these—we have no hesitation adding more and more bits of knowledge to memory! But as teachers, we may have to make special efforts to maximize the more interesting aspects of semantic memory change. We have to help students connect knowledge, confront them with inconsistencies that they have to resolve, and help them build a more complex and abstract knowledge base. Textbooks alone cannot accomplish this—the teacher's role is irreplaceable. When you think about your student's learning in different ways, you will automatically make adjustments to your teaching style.

Speaking of size, how much semantic memory does the average adult have? This may sound impossible to answer, but people have tried anyway. Michelene Chi, whom you encountered in the chapter on learning, makes a conservative estimate that we each possess *at least* one million pieces of knowledge in memory! It goes without saying (especially if you have read the first two chapters of this book) that the over-a-million pieces of knowledge in memory are richly interconnected. The way in which they are

connected is a question of organization, which we look at in the
next section.

How Long-term Memories are Organized

The way information is organized in a storage system will
determine how it is retrieved, and therefore, how useful it is. As
teachers, we want the things we teach our students to be available
to them in a usable form, to 'come to their minds' when they need
it (hopefully beyond the year-end examination!). When a student
has learned how to subtract, the teacher hopes she will subtract
under all the following conditions:

- $456 - 345 = ?$
- $345 + n = 456.$
- Find the difference between 456 and 345.
- Mr. Jai has Rs. 456 and his wife has Rs. 345. How much
  more money does Mr. Jai have than his wife?

And so on.

Each of the above questions is a trigger for the student to
retrieve the knowledge of how to subtract from long-term
memory. When we teach subtraction, along with *how*, we surely
must teach *when* to use it, and to *which* numbers. Because if the
knowledge of *when* or *to which* numbers is missing, or is stored in a
way that cannot be retrieved when needed, the knowledge of *how
to* subtract becomes almost useless!

This analysis applies to any learning—in any field. When a
topic is taught with many connections to things the student already
knows, or is likely to encounter in the world, there are many routes
for retrieval of the information—many triggers for easier recall.

So how are memories organized in the brain? It is not as
simple as, say, one big book where everything we experience from
beginning to end is written. Some have likened memory to a huge

library of thousands of books where everything is stored according to a useful classification system, so that information can be pulled out quickly when needed. But even this is too simple a picture. In a library, books may be classified by theme, and within this, alphabetically by author. So if you want Kipling's *Jungle Book*, you will go to Fiction and look under 'K'. But if you're asked to 'find the book about Mowgli', and you don't have any other information about it, you would literally have to search every book in the library to find it, wouldn't you? That is because library books are not organized by the name of the main character.

Do you have the one about Sherkhan?

Human memories, however, seem to be organized in every possible way. If you have read *Jungle Book*, then you will probably answer all these questions equally rapidly: 'Tell me the name of a popular book by Kipling that's been made into a film'; 'Tell me the name of the story of Mowgli'; 'Tell me the name of the book about Bagheera', and so on. It is as though our memories of books are organized in every possible way, because we can retrieve information (pull books out of shelves) unerringly and rapidly, no matter what kind of question we are asked. The same goes for our personal memories as well: 'What was the book you read when you had chicken pox?' can also get the quick answer, '*Jungle Book*'.

There are currently a few popular explanations of memory organization, two of which I describe here briefly. One is the semantic network theory. Concepts (like chair or rabbit or joy) are linked to each other by relations, and these relations can be of several kinds. Some are subset hierarchies, others are cause-effect, others are before-after (see figure below).

Subset hierarchy

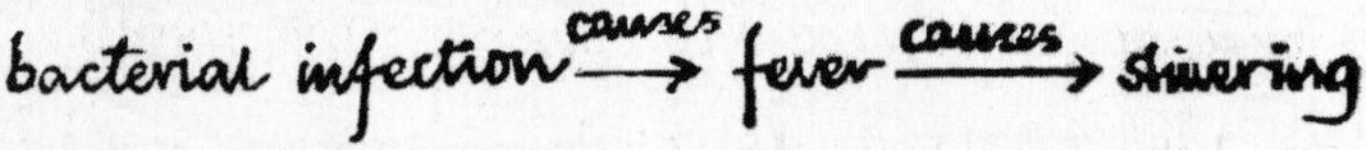

Cause and effect

Concepts that are linked more closely to each other form a domain, and examples of domains are as varied as 'having a bath', 'chemistry' and 'furniture'. To the extent that they overlap, these domains contain many shared concepts, like bathtub, soap and varnish (see figure below). The whole mess has been called 'tangled hierarchies', which I think is a lovely description of memory.

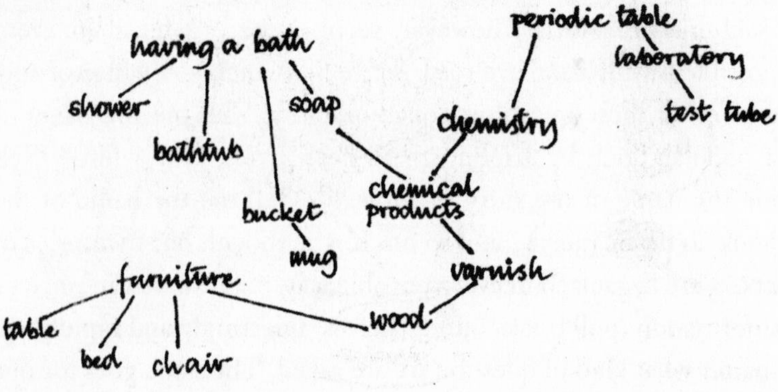

According to another theory, declarative knowledge can be seen as recurring patterns in experience—stored as scripts, plans, maps or explanations that guide our interpretation of new experiences—these are Piaget's schemas. Schemas are abstract because they represent the patterns underlying many different experiences. If a schema is activated by something in the environment (for example, my 'Indian education' schema is activated by the mention of NCERT) the entire schema is retrieved as a package. The new experience is then interpreted in the context of this schema.

Whichever theory we subscribe to, it is clear that our teaching must encourage connections and relationships of different kinds. If memory naturally tends to be organized, let's use that property to the student's advantage. Where appropriate, we should:

- demonstrate hierarchies (like taxonomies);
- highlight correlations (among different phenomena);
- look for cause-effect relations;
- distinguish central principles from examples (in theories or laws, for example);
- use analogies (across and within domains).

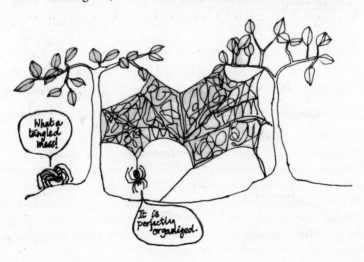

Working Memory

All long-term memories are *potentially* available to us when we need them (or frustratingly not, as happens to all of us at one time or another!). You will agree that all of long-term memory is not in your conscious awareness all the time—that would be like reading every word of every book in a huge library at the same time, which is impossible. So when you are aware of some memory, when you are thinking about it, that bit of knowledge has been retrieved. The 'space' in which this occurs is another memory system, called 'working memory'.[1] You can think of this kind of memory as similar to working at a desktop. On the desk is some information from long-term memory as well as some information from your senses: new, incoming information. You are working on whatever is on the desktop, but since it is rather small, you cannot focus on more than a little bit at a given time. If something new comes along—a new thought from long-term memory or a new sound from the outside— you will get distracted, because the new information will cover your desk and the old material will fall off. And the only way to keep material on this desk is to keep working on it, thinking about it, or rehearsing it. (In this regard, working memory is definitely *not* like a desk. There are things on my desk that have been sitting there for months, and I have done no work on them whatsoever!) Thus, the working memory system is of limited capacity and duration, in the sense that, unlike a long-term memory, it is lost if you stop giving your attention to it. But it is *the* space for new learning to happen.

[1] Working memory is most closely connected with the hippocampus. In Chapter One, you were introduced to this small structure in the brain. You will remember (thanks to the efforts of your own hippocampus!) that this brain part is responsible for the initial recording of all declarative or explicit memories. All through our lives, our experiences and learning are diligently registered by the hippocampus, which transfers memories in due course to various parts of the neocortex. The memories will remain stored here for the long term, and eventually be 'erased' from the hippocampus itself.

It is best to think of working memory as a *dynamic space*, with both storage and processing parts to it. If you are more efficient with processing the work on your desktop, you can store more on it. For example, if you organize your papers into stacks—one for bills, one for lists, one for letters—you can work more easily and efficiently and with more material. In much the same way, when information in working memory is organized efficiently, more can be stored. This organization is dependent on information available in long-term memory, and here is a simple example that will help clarify this. If you hear a list of eight random digits (an unfamiliar phone number, say) and you cannot immediately write it down, you must maintain it in working memory by repeating it to yourself (rehearsal). This eight-digit number will strain the limits of your working memory, and any more digits would become very difficult, if not impossible, as you must have experienced when you try to retain a new mobile phone number in the same way. But if the first five digits of the mobile number are the same as your friend's, you will easily be able to hold ten digits in working memory.

The first five digits become a 'chunk', and therefore a single unit. Any kind of organization helps to increase the capacity of working memory, so that it is as easy to remember a string of six unconnected letters as a string of six unconnected words.

Thus, the capacity of working memory is a function of both process and storage. It has to be measured using a task that requires you to remember items of information while *at the same time* performing some mental task. A good example is the **sentence span task**, where you listen to a series of sentences, judge whether each is true or false, and at the end of the series you have to recall the last word of each sentence. As the number of sentences in the series increases, you will naturally find it harder to recall all the last words. At the point where you begin to make errors, you have reached the limits of your working memory capacity.

Working Memory and the Teaching-learning Process

It is quite obvious that long-term memory is of great importance to us as teachers. We are naturally interested in how long-term information is organized, how it is retrieved, and how forgetting happens. But no less important is the working memory system. Why is it important, especially when it is so small and lasts only a few seconds? There are at least two good reasons: one to do with individual differences in the efficiency of working memory, and the other to do with the benefits of automaticity.

As we saw earlier, everything we learn has to pass through the working memory system. On each learning occasion, the information that is being presented and relevant prior knowledge, have to be present in working memory. The two have to be manipulated, so eventually, new knowledge is added to long-term memory. But *if a child has a lower working memory capacity, the whole process will be impaired.* New knowledge will have fewer associations with existing knowledge, less can be absorbed, and less is therefore available for recall the next time around. Over time, learning suffers. Thus, the working memory system can potentially become a 'bottleneck' for learning. It sounds reasonable, but does this really happen?

There is enough evidence that it does. At any given age, students vary greatly in their working memory capacity, and this variability is related to their performance on academic work in school. Children with lower working memory capacity usually have difficulty with school work. Susan Gathercole and her colleagues in the U.K. have studied this connection between working memory and academic performance among children in great depth. They have found that:

- working memory capacity increases with age till students are about 12–15 years old;
- among students of the same age, it is strongly correlated with reading, writing and mathematical ability.

Gathercole goes so far as to say that when a student is facing academic difficulties which are *not* due to emotional or behavioural problems, one invariably finds his working memory capacity is significantly lower than the average for his age. This suggests a strong causal role for working memory in school performance.

Recently, Gathercole and others did a very detailed study of three five- to six-year-old students who were having trouble with school work, and had low measured working memory capacity. The children were observed very carefully in their natural classroom setting, and every time they had difficulty with some task, the situation was analyzed to see how the working memory system was acting as a bottleneck for learning. Here are examples of specific difficulties the children had:

- Following a series of instructions from the teacher, they would forget what they had to do along the way.
- Copying information from the board, they would lose their 'place' and leave out words.
- Listening to stories, they would miss some parts while trying to understand other parts; thus their comprehension and long term memory for the story would be poor.

Now, of course, these were very young children, but you can see that as time goes on, they are going to find themselves more and more at a disadvantage in the learning process. Based on Gathercole's research, a set of interventions has been compiled for students with working memory deficits. The suggestions can be summarized in a simple way:

- Look out for signs of overloaded working memory systems in children (this section has given you an idea of what the signs may be).
- Evaluate the work you give them for its load on working memory.
- If the load is high, try and break up the work into smaller parts, write all instructions down, use familiar material and encourage them to use rehearsal or paper and pencil as memory aids.

Automaticity: A Special Application

Many adults have had the experience of learning to read and write a new language. If you have, you know that in the beginning, each letter of the word you want to read takes time and effort to 'decode'. While you are decoding each letter, you need to keep the earlier letters in working memory, so that you can string them together to read the whole word. Often, by the time you have reached the third or fourth letter, all your processing capacity is taken up by the decoding, so that previous letters have 'fallen out of' working memory. Now you have to go back and scan the word again, and so on—this makes the reading process slow and painstaking.

But with practice, the decoding becomes more automatic (that is, needing less conscious effort). Your long-term memory for the letters of this new alphabet improves, as well as the recognition of certain letter combinations—even of certain words as a whole. Thus, reading becomes faster and more effortless—at least at the level of the words. Now, working memory can be used to store earlier words of each sentence while you are reading later words, so that you can integrate information as you read and make sense of sentences. Again, if you have a good vocabulary, which means that your long-term memory has the meanings of many words and phrases encoded in it, each word/phrase can be processed relatively quickly. Thus, even a long sentence, containing big words and several phrases and clauses, can be easily understood, because we are now reading whole words or phrases at a time.

Automaticity refers to the ease of processing that comes about with practice, when larger and more 'chunks' of information can be processed in a given time within working memory. One can also see the advantages of automaticity in the mathematics class.

Suppose the student is doing a word problem: Jai has Rs. 45, and his sister has Rs. 35. Together they invest their money in a scheme that gives them a profit of Rs. 320. How should they divide their profit?

It is useful to get students to solve these problems mentally, thinking aloud as they do so, because it gives them and you a real feel of working memory. If they know how to solve this problem, they may first try to reduce the ratio 45:35. They must remember that 5 x 9 = 45, and keep the number 9 in mind while dividing 35 by 5. [By the time they get the answer 7, they may have forgotten the 9]. Then they add the two to get 16, and divide 320 by 16, which requires them to remember that 16 x 2 = 32, meanwhile keeping both 9 and 7 in mind. (By the time they get the answer 20, 9 and/or 7 may be lost.) Now they must multiply 9 by 20 to get 180 (by which time 7 may be lost), and then 7 by 20 to get 140 (by which time 180 may be lost, and also perhaps the name

Jai). During all this they must also keep in mind the method to be followed at each step. In fact, it seems nothing short of a miracle that a student can do such a complex task at all!

Where can automaticity help this process? The answer is, almost at every step. If students can immediately and with minimal conscious processing divide by 5, add small numbers, divide by 16 and multiply by 2, it is not likely they will forget any of the relevant information in between. It is only when such operations are laborious and heavily dependent on conscious processes, that working memory will be overloaded. For example, if to divide 45 by 9 the student has to recite the tables from the beginning, or repeatedly add 9 to itself 5 times, almost certainly there is no space for anything else on the working memory desk, and things will 'fall off'.[2]

Here then is a good reason to encourage our students to memorize certain number facts, or to become so familiar with them that they are automatically retrieved. The same is true for reading fluency, familiarity with vocabulary, and the use of procedures. In India, we probably suffer from a surfeit of drill and memorization. The point is not to limit learning to those memorized facts, but to use them as *a convenience to allow for higher order thinking to occur more smoothly*. The curriculum must be created in such a way that interesting and challenging material is the main focus, while drill remains a necessary support.

So far we have talked about interesting and intelligent uses of our memory system. But it would be incomplete not to address the issue of memorization for examination, as it is such a reality in our schools.

---

[2] This is probably why we teach our students to 'write the steps' in mathematics. Paper and pencil as external supports for working memory can often relieve demands on it. But nothing can really substitute for overfamiliarity with some facts and procedures.

'I'm studying.'

All through my school years, we used the word 'study' to mean the special kind of mental work needed to get by in a typical Indian school. Looking back, I can recall several things that counted as 'studying'. There was revising or re-reading one's notes or the textbook, re-doing problems and checking the answers. And a large part of it  was memorizing—definitions, formulae, statements, procedures, and in some cases, entire paragraphs. To memorize information, we used a number of tricks, or what are technically called mnemonics. There are whole books written about mnemonics, or creative ways to learn lists and names by heart. Of course, as students we came up with our own mnemonics, some of which worked very well! All this definitely helped us survive the tests and examinations, but I have to ask: what is memorized knowledge good for, other than helping us pass examinations?

If we can call the automaticity of procedural knowledge 'memorization', then I have already talked about its benefits. But this is not strictly *memorization* so much as *practice* of a skill. To memorize means to store in long-term memory with minimal connections to existing stored knowledge. The typical Indian student's 'by heart' learning of large amounts of information seems to serve very little purpose—but let us list those purposes, anyway. If one is interested in reciting poetry, knowing the capitals of countries, learning dates of important events in history, or the names of important people—rote memorization is necessary. This kind of knowledge, however, should constitute only a very small portion of a student's learning in school. Facts are somewhat dead-end objects; it is difficult to reason or derive further knowledge from them. Concepts, on the other hand, are sophisticated tools with which to understand and act in the world. If a student tries to 'memorize' a concept, which is to say commit it to memory without understanding it, it will have no relationship to earlier knowledge in the same domain. It will operate only in school situations (such as on homework and in exams). In real-world situations, the old understandings will continue to operate even if they are incorrect, and any misconceptions will never be righted (we talked about this in Chapter Two).

We also have to ask: how much of what we studied in school is still remembered years later? Many people complain of having forgotten things they once knew. They ask, 'What was the use of all I learnt in school, I've forgotten all of it anyway.' Psychologist Harry Bahrick and his colleagues have done some interesting research on the long-term retention (after a fifty-year gap) of knowledge gained in high school—for example, algebra, geometry, a foreign language...and classmates' names and faces! Overall, they found that rates of forgetting were quite surprisingly low, as long as the original exposure was not over too short a period. Their findings indicate that the best way to retain knowledge for many years, without needing rehearsal in between, is to learn and relearn it over a longer period of time. Thus, if exposure to information and rehearsal of that knowledge takes place over several years, Bahrick says that 'performance levels remain stable for half a century without the benefit of further practice. When the same content is acquired over a shorter period, performance tends to decline rapidly.' This means that very short-term courses, however intense, may not be as beneficial for memory as the same spread over six months or a year. Of course, if after a short course you are going to use what you learnt regularly, memory for that material will remain strong.

In another sense, we never really forget certain crucial skills picked up in school, such as reading and writing, calculation and high-order skills such as comprehension, problem solving, analysis and inference. This is provided such skills are taught in the first place. If children are not encouraged to use these and other similar skills, and are simply given a lot of content, surely when they are older and have forgotten it all, it would seem to have been a waste.

In Conclusion

We have in our possession such a wonderfully complex remembering machine; it would be a shame not to use it more imaginatively. People are fond of quoting the popular belief that 'we use only 10% of our brains'. While this statement does not make sense in terms of absolute brain size or power, perhaps we can use it as a pointer to the poor use of our memory's organizing, associating and learning power. Think about it in that sense: am I, as a teacher, making the best use of my students' natural memory abilities?

References and Bibliography

1. Ackerman, P.L., M.E. Beier, and M.O. Boyle, 2005. 'Working Memory and Intelligence: The Same or Different Constructs?' *Psychological Bulletin*, Vol. 131., No. 1., 30–60.

2. Bahrick, H.P., and L.K. Hall, 1991. 'Lifetime Maintenance of High School Mathematics Content'. *Journal of Experimental Psychology: General*, Vol. 120, No. 1, 20–33.

3. Bjork, R.A., 1994. 'Memory and Metamemory Considerations in the Training of Human Beings'. In J. Metcalfe and A. Shimamura (eds), *Metacognition: Knowing About Knowing*. Cambridge, MA: MIT Press.

4. Chi, M.T.H., and S. Ohlsson, 2005. Complex Declarative Learning. In K.J. Holyoak and R.G. Morrison (eds) *Cambridge Handbook of Thinking and Reasoning.* New York: Cambridge University Press.

5. Gathercole, S.E., and T.P. Alloway, *Understanding Working Memory: A Classroom Guide.* Available on request from the authors, s.e.gathercole@durham.ac.uk or t.p.alloway@durham.ac.uk

6. Ibid., 2008. *Working Memory and Classroom Learning.* In K. Thurman and K. Fiorello (eds), *Applied cognitive research in k-3 classrooms.* Routledge/Taylor and Francis, New York.

7. Gathercole, S.E., and S.J. Pickering, 2000. 'Working Memory Deficits in Children with Low Achievements in the National Curriculum at 7 Years of Age'. *British Journal of Educational Psychology,* 70, 177–94.

8. McClelland, J.L., B.L. McNaughton, and R.C. O'Reilly, 1995. 'Why There Are Complementary Learning Systems in the Hippocampus and Neocortex: Insights From the Successes and Failures of Connectionist Models of Learning and Memory'. *Psychological Review,* Vol. 102, No. 3, 419–57.

9. Moors, A., and J. De Houwer, 2006. 'Automaticity: A Theoretical and Conceptual Analysis'. *Psychological Bulletin,* Vol. 132, No. 2, 297–326.

10. Nelson, C.A., 1995. 'The Ontogeny of Human Memory: A Cognitive Neuroscience Perspective'. *Developmental Psychology,* Vol. 31, No. 5, 723–38.

11. Sacks, O., 1990. *The Man Who Mistook His Wife for a Hat and Other Clinical Tales.* Harper Perennial, New York.

12. Siegler, R.S., 2004. 'Turning Memory Development Inside Out'. *Developmental Review,* 24, 469–75.

13. Solso, R.L., 2001. *Cognitive Psychology.* Pearson Education (Singapore) Pte. Ltd., Delhi.

14. Squire, L.R., 1992. 'Memory and the Hippocampus'. *Psychological Review,* Vol. 99, No. 2, 195–231.

15. Towse, J.N., G.J. Hitch, and U. Hutton, 1998. 'A Re-evaluation of Working Memory Capacity in Children'. *Journal of Memory and Language,* 39, 195–217.

CHAPTER FOUR

Child Development

- Do children think completely differently from adults, or are they just less efficient and know less than adults?
- Are early experiences crucial: can they make or break the child's further growth? Or are children resilient—can later experiences make up for earlier ones?
- Would you agree that a child is born a blank slate, and learns from experiences which are 'written' on this slate (in other words, learning makes us what we are)? Or would you rather say that we inherit most of our tendencies and abilities, so that no matter what our environment, what we will be is almost inevitable right from the start?
- And finally, do you believe that children are naturally 'good', and that exposure to society's ills corrupts them? Or do you feel that children are naturally 'uncivilized', and socialization is necessary to make them moral human beings?

These four questions form the basis for most psychological theories of child development. They could go under the headings of qualitative/quantitative change, critical periods, nature/ nurture, and moral development respectively. Many famous names in psychology can be placed according to where they stood

'Not now, dear, we're busy discussing child development!'

on these questions. Piaget believed that children think in qualitatively different ways from adults. Freud believed that experiences in early childhood could determine personality in lasting ways. Skinner believed that all behaviour could be explained in terms of small, incremental changes due to experience. Rousseau believed that children were born 'noble savages', and that if only we would not corrupt them, they would grow up to create the perfect society.

You might wonder how we will ever sort out the 'truth' of such fundamental questions. Many years of investigation are giving us some tentative answers. As you might expect, the answers indicate that the extreme positions are untenable—in each case, we are discovering that the extremes are neither completely false nor completely true. Actually, we are discovering that if you word the questions differently, a much more interesting picture of childhood emerges. This picture is subtle and powerful, not at all black-and-white, and suggests many important questions for us as teachers and educators.

This chapter will begin with a brief description of the changes that occur in the brain itself from birth to adulthood, followed by discussions on qualitative change and critical periods. The other two questions raised here, on nature/nurture and moral development, deserve entire chapters of their own.

The Development of the Brain

The most obvious change in the brain is that it increases in weight rapidly in the first year from 400 to 850 gm, goes up to 1,100 gm by age three, and reaches 1,450 gm by adulthood. Thus, the one-year-old brain weighs more than half the adult brain, compared to its total body weight, which is only a fifth of the adult's. The rapid pace of human postnatal brain growth contrasts sharply with that of chimpanzees and other primates; their brain growth slows down quickly after birth. This is connected to the fact that, compared with other primates, we are born more immature and helpless, and take longer to reach maturity.

However, all areas of the brain do not grow similarly during childhood. At birth, the brain stem and midbrain are already fairly well developed, in size and organization. But the cerebral cortex is far less mature than it will be in adulthood. Most of the cortex is 'uncommitted' at birth, not yet being used to process information and direct behaviour. The frontal and prefrontal cortices, for example, which are involved in planning, consciousness and the inhibition of inappropriate behaviours, do not reach complete maturity till late adolescence. These facts lead us to call the developing brain 'plastic': even after birth, there is still a lot of brain growth and development happening right through adolescence.

What do we mean when we say the brain is growing? Two factors contribute to brain growth: **the number of connections among neurons**, and **the myelination of neurons**.

Connections among Neurons

There are about 150 billion neurons (all present at birth), each of which can connect with up to 1000 others, leading to a grand total of about 150,000,000,000,000 possible neuron-to-neuron synapses! But information does not consist of *all* connections being made—it is the *selectivity* of connections that codes meaningful information. At certain ages, certain parts of the brain produce an excess of synapses with each other (this is called synaptogenesis). Over several years, most of these connections are pruned away or shed, according to experience. Those synapses which are activated by experience are maintained; others wither away.

This kind of brain plasticity is called **experience-expectant**—the unpatterned overproduction of synapses during childhood, followed by massive 'pruning' depending on experiences that confirm or do not confirm those synapses. But there is also **experience-dependent** plasticity, which is the formation of new synapses in response to experience. Ten to fifteen seconds after a new experience, new synapses are formed in the area of the brain that processed that experience. Here too, more synapses are formed than are needed, and the pruning of unused synapses occurs in time.

These two kinds of brain changes in response to the environment can be understood by very rough analogy. Take the example of swimming. As a child you may have splashed around in the water and learnt floating, freestyle or dog paddling (experience expectant). If you are later taught by a swimming coach, she could change your swimming in two ways: by actually teaching you new strokes like the butterfly (experience dependent) *and* by helping you to keep some of your earlier techniques while shedding others.

Myelination of Neurons

Myelin is a fatty tissue that covers and insulates the nerve fibre, thereby increasing the speed of electric impulses passing through it. At birth, most nerve fibres are unmyelinated. Myelination in the various sections of the brain is a gradual, incremental process that takes place over several years. It could account for what we call automatization of cognitive processing—when an action becomes so practised that it can happen unconsciously and effortlessly. As children grow older, more and more cognitive processes become automatized, or effortless, due to myelination. But the fact that myelination is such a gradual process, is actually thought to be helpful for the growing child, as you will see later in this chapter.

We turn now to the first of those four questions: do children think completely differently from adults, or are they just less efficient and know less than adults?

'I am sorry. My myelination is not yet complete!'

Qualitative Change is Accumulated Quantitative Change

Jean Piaget, the famous Swiss psychologist, gave us a tremendous scientific gift—a convincing theory of child development that explains many of our observations on children. But perhaps his greater gift is the opportunity he left behind for psychologists to disagree with his explanations and come up with convincing alternative theories. Piaget described development as occurring in a series of stages, each stage distinctly different from the previous one in a **qualitative** way. What do we mean by stages? If we notice that children's abilities change suddenly, across a variety of settings, and appear to be completely different in nature rather than simply 'more or better' than before, then we would call that stage-like development.

At each developmental stage, Piaget described children's cognitive abilities in terms of a few central concepts. These concepts—for example, egocentrism, object permanence, conservation—summarize the child's reasoning capacities in terms of what she absolutely *cannot do* until she enters a subsequent stage. Or, in other words, in one stage the child would always answer certain questions incorrectly, but in the next she would always answer the same questions correctly. In describing development as a series of 'cannot-then-can' stages, Piaget's theory gives rise to many educational implications, such as the 'teachability' of concepts, the readiness to learn, and the suitability of the environment to stimulate stage transitions.

Now, what is there to question in Piaget's theory? Psychologists have questioned several aspects of his work, but I have selected just two important ideas for you to consider.

- Perhaps we see stage-like changes because we compare behaviour across periods of time that are too long. Are we then missing the continuous changes that are taking place all along?

Suppose changes in children's abilities are always taking place, in a continuous way, from day to day. These could be changes in speed of processing, in the amount of background knowledge they have, in learning new strategies for reasoning, and in the efficiency and ease of using existing strategies. Every day, every week, the child gets a little better at all these things. Over a long enough period of time, say a few years, these gradual incremental changes will lead to behaviour that seems completely different when compared with behaviour from a few years ago. The long series of small changes 'suddenly' enable a child to do something she never could before. Or perhaps, since she is doing it well enough, one fine day the adults suddenly notice the difference!

- When children do not give the 'correct' answers to questions, we assume that it is because they simply don't know it. But perhaps they are having difficulty with other things, such as high-memory demands, misleading cues, or language interpretation problems.

A child's response to your question or task depends as much on the way you asked the question or set the task in the first place, as on his abilities *per se*. Piaget's test for 'egocentrism' is a good example of this. In this test, children view a complex three-dimensional arrangement of mountains on a table by walking around it. They sit at one end and are asked to choose, from different pictures, the view that someone sitting at the other end would see. Most preschool children do not do well on this task—they pick the picture showing their own view. Piaget took this as evidence for their essential egocentric nature during that stage of development, egocentrism being the inability to see things from another person's point of view.

But imagine the task simplified in the following way: the child, sitting across from the adult, has a card with a picture of a house

on one side and a tree on the other, and holds it upright with the tree side facing herself. Does she realize that the adult can see only the house and not the tree? Of course she does! Preschoolers can do this with ease, which means they do understand that other people have different views than their own, and they are not completely egocentric. The Piaget three mountain task places heavy demands on spatial reasoning, mental imagery and, possibly, memory—it is not testing just egocentric thinking. These other abilities may improve with age in a gradual, incremental way, but we may mistake what we see for an 'egocentrism on-egocentrism off' kind of development.

In the attempts to test Piaget's theory against other competing accounts, two kinds of evidence are obtained again and again: younger children often reason very competently, and older children (as well as adults) often reason incompetently. Instead of going from 'just-cannot-do-it' to 'always-can-do-it', we are finding that children go from 'will-rarely-do-it' to 'will-often-do-it'. These findings are not well explained from Piaget's theory, and this has led to totally different ways of understanding development. One such approach has been taken by Robert Siegler, who has an **information processing** theory of development. Siegler and others like him emphasize an essential continuity between child and adult thinking. That means we can understand children's cognition as a downscaled version of adult cognition. Child-like thinking changes into adult-like thinking as a result of improved brain processes, greater knowledge, and the practice afforded by everyday experiences.

But then, what exactly develops? Can the process of cognitive development be described at all, if not in stages? Certainly it can, and in a very convincing way. Here is a brief summary of the kinds of abilities that develop.

A Continuous View of Child Development

Think of the brain as an information processing machine. There are several things this machine is able to do, both with the information it receives through the senses, as well as the information stored within. The figure below contains a long list of these abilities.

These abilities have been studied with infants, toddlers, preschoolers, children, adolescents and adults. The research shows that many of these general abilities are present very early in life, and that with age and experience, children improve steadily and quantitatively in each cognitive area. Let's look separately and in detail at each of them.

Recognition memory is excellent right from infancy, and **recall** memory is good (in one study fourteen-month-old infants recalled a specific action after a four-month gap) and becomes better with age. Preschoolers tend to emphasize verbatim, literal memory. They do not extract the gist of a situation as easily as older children, probably because to do so would require greater knowledge of the world than they as yet possess. Thus, their

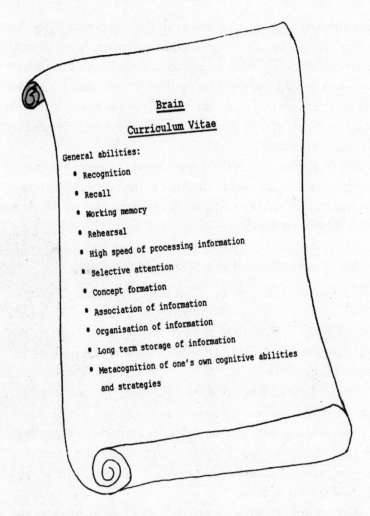

Brain
Curriculum Vitae

General abilities:

* Recognition
* Recall
* Working memory
* Rehearsal
* High speed of processing information
* Selective attention
* Concept formation
* Association of information
* Organisation of information
* Long term storage of information
* Metacognition of one's own cognitive abilities and strategies

memory relies more heavily on the ability to recall an event verbatim, and since such memory is in any case more fleeting than gist memory (plenty of adult research confirms this) it is no surprise that the recall memory of younger children is weaker than older ones.

Working memory (where we place what we are currently aware of; where we combine incoming sensory information with long-term memories to create new knowledge) increases steadily with age. The number of symbols that can be operated upon at a time is said to be about seven, plus or minus two for adults, but for five-year-olds it is about three symbols. What accounts for this increase—'larger' storage or more efficient processing? This is not yet clearly established, but it is likely to be the latter. For example, older children can pronounce words or numbers faster than younger ones, and this allows them to rehearse material in working memory faster. Faster rehearsal means that more material can be maintained, and thus, the 'size' of working memory can appear to be more.

Speed of processing increases exponentially with age (the figure shows a typical exponential curve). Robert Kail, a psychologist who has studied the speed of processing in a variety of tasks—ranging from the simplest reaction time to mental arithmetic—reports that adults respond about thrice as fast as four-year-olds, twice as fast as eight-year-olds, and 1.5 times as fast as eleven-year-olds. These ratios held true no matter what task Kail used, which suggests that a common **structural** mechanism may be responsible for age-related change in speeded performance. Possibly, the growth of myelin sheaths around the nerve fibres could be the reason.

Selective attention, which is the ability to pay attention to only the relevant stimuli from among the barrage around us at every moment, is a strategy whose use increases with age. For example studies show that eight-year-olds are more

systematic and selective than younger children, in what they attend to, while comparing two pictures to 'find the differences'. A large part of the ability to answer a question or perform a task correctly depends on the extent to which a child can 'tune out' irrelevant aspects, and focus only on a few important aspects. If this improves with age, it explains why they might 'suddenly' appear capable of some new kind of reasoning.

Children form **concepts** right from infancy. A concept is a grouping of different ideas that are connected in some way. Even three-month-olds can form abstract concepts of colour and shape and use these to guide their actions (one experiment that demonstrated this with babies and mobiles is described in the next chapter). Early concepts are formed from *probabilistic connections* among features or events. That is, some things usually happen together: you see dogs and tails attached to them much more frequently than you see dogs alone or tails alone. This co-occurrence can become a concept: *dogs have tails*. Later, children are able to distinguish **characteristic** features from **defining**

'But ma'am, that car won't work!'

features, and thus form definition-based concepts as well: dogs *usually* have tails, but *always* have faces. Psychologist Frank Keil, who studies concept formation in young children, believes that children also seek to understand the causes of everything they see. Causal explanations lead to mini 'theories', and these links between causes and effects, form early concepts for children. For example, even a young child realizes there is a fundamental difference between a car with orange wheels and a car with square wheels, even if she has seen neither one before. Keil's work shows that children can answer 'why' questions early on, which shows that this is an important part of their concepts.

Very young children will have fewer concepts and ideas, as well as fewer connections among ideas. But as they develop, so does their sophistication in **associating and organizing knowledge**. Gradually, more and more isolated facts can be connected and 'explained' by new concepts. Thus, over time, children collect an impressive amount of long-term knowledge in a wide variety of areas. The **long-term storage of information** is not just there for retrieval at some later point in life (like annual exams!). Prior knowledge plays an extremely important role in organizing information from new experiences. The more one knows, the more one can know.

There is also in each of us both implicit and explicit knowledge of our own cognitive abilities, and the strategies we can use in a given situation, depending on the demands of the task in front of us. This is called **metacognitive knowledge**. Each one of our cognitive processes can be thought about and evaluated: we can read—and monitor our understanding; learn—and estimate how much of it we will remember; write—and reflect on the quality of our work. Children definitely improve in all these areas with age. By about 10 years of age, children know and can say that it is easier to remember gist than word-for-word, that repetition aids memory, and that recognition is easier than recall. Older children also show better metacognition while reading, as they are better at detecting contradictions in text, know what is important in texts, and are more likely to go back and re-read the parts they have not understood.

In sum, we now believe that children possess many cognitive abilities much earlier than we thought. Perhaps they cannot demonstrate these due to information processing constraints, and, perhaps, at early ages these abilities are more procedural and implicit (young children are less able to reflect on them or describe them verbally). Looking at the brain as an information processor certainly helps us to identify cognitive functions and study their gradual development through childhood. And this provides an impressive alternative to the traditional stage theories of development. A theory such as this is also more useful to teachers because it helps us understand what children find difficult at different ages. Then, perhaps, we can reduce demands of one kind or another, so as to help children process complex situations more effectively.

You will see ways to do this yourself—I suggest just three here as examples.

1. Reduce demands on a young child's working memory by breaking up a task into smaller parts, and writing down instructions. Encourage them to write things down, so that they don't have to keep excess material in working memory—this will free up space for other processes.

2. Give younger children guidelines on what to pay attention to and what to ignore in a given situation. Try to eliminate excessively distracting irrelevant stimuli from the material.

3. Connect all new material with something the child already knows. Also, use familiar contexts to teach new ideas as far as possible.

The above suggestions could *facilitate* learning, but there is a fine line between this and trying to *accelerate* learning. Continuous views of development may tempt us into thinking that we can accelerate learning by getting children to practise more intensely the same things they encounter in everyday experience. Would this be a good idea? Can and should the pace of growing up be tampered with? This question has been debated hotly under the umbrella of 'early childhood education', taken up in the next section.

Take Your Time Growing Up

Give Your Child a Superior Mind and *Don't Push Your Preschooler* are the titles of two books written in the 1980s. Which would you pick up off the shelf? The premises of the books are based on the ideas of quantitative vs. qualitative change during development. If children can do everything (cognitively) that adults can, just less well, then perhaps they can be pushed into improving themselves earlier and earlier. But if, on the other hand, development proceeds in qualitatively different stages, following a maturational clock, so to speak, then it would make no sense to 'push your preschooler'.

It might simply be a waste of time, and it could even have some unintended ill effects.

Indeed, a study conducted by Marion Hyson and others in 1989 indicated this. Two groups of children were put through two different pre-kindergarten programmes, one academic (where they were taught the alphabet and numbers) and one non-academic (where the day was filled with activities initiated by the children). At the end of a year, the two classes were compared on a variety of measures. The academic pre-K children were naturally better at recognizing letters and numbers (they had been taught this). Both groups were equivalent on tests of general intelligence and social competence. By the end of the following year of kindergarten, during which all children went through the same programme, the advantages of the academic pre-K children had disappeared, and they showed more negative attitudes towards school, and greater test anxiety than the other group.[1]

A number of similar studies have been conducted, and the results overall are similar to Hyson's. The lesson we learn is that while we may be increasing cognitive outcomes in the short term by pushing the preschooler, it may be at the cost of 'desirable dispositions' in the long term. The phrase 'desirable dispositions' refers to the love of reading and writing. Understandably, this is lost when the child is subjected to levels of drill and practice that he does not enjoy. Thus, a careful review of the research shows that acceleration may be neither possible nor good for the child, *regardless* of whether we take a qualitative or quantitative view of development.

[1] This study looked only at middle- and upper middle-income children. There is good reason to believe that the findings would not apply to children from disadvantaged homes. Many early intervention programmes have been successful for lower-income children, the reason being that there may not be sufficient intellectual stimulation in their general environment. In such cases, a preschool programme can provide what the home environment lacks. This comes up again in the next section on critical periods.

Within either view, everyone agrees that children are **cognitively immature**. Developmental psychologist David Bjorklund believes that this immaturity serves important functions for normal development. Childhood is a necessary period of growth and maturation. Human beings have developed culture and society to such a degree that children need a long period of dependence on adults, so that they can absorb and learn all the knowledge and skills they need to survive later in life. Compared to our closer relatives among the apes, human children spend many more years in relative immaturity—physical, sexual and cognitive. Bjorklund's focus is on the last of the three.

According to him, we might see cognitive immaturity in children as a kind of *deficiency*, something that needs to be remedied through experience and teaching. But there is another way to see it: cognitive immaturity may serve a necessary function in child development. It may be that some of the *in*abilities of childhood are in fact better seen as qualitatively different *abilities*, useful in structuring experience and, therefore, learning during childhood. A simple example is the fact that babies do not have 20/20 vision, and remain quite myopic for the first few months. This reduces the amount of information they have to deal with while making sense of the world. And further, since they can focus best on objects about a foot away, they are able to make eye contact with the mother during feeding. So it would not make sense to give little babies custom-made spectacles so they can see better.

Could it be that other signs of immaturity in children are similarly 'adaptive' for development? If so, this would have important implications for education. We sometimes see young children's thinking patterns as problematic, to be corrected and fixed. On the other hand, there may be wisdom to 'going with the grain' of the child's development. Bjorklund, for example, identifies several areas of *useful* immaturity, so to speak, and I will summarize two below: metacognition and the speed of processing.

Metacognition refers to our knowledge of our own cognitive processes. Now, young children are famous for overestimating their own cognitive abilities, as confirmed by many studies over the years. Studies of memory show that five-year-olds, for example, will spend very little time memorizing material to be recalled, but will have high predictions of how much they would be able to remember later. Even after, when they can clearly see that their predictions were off the mark, they still continue to make unrealistically high predictions of their recall ability. Children generally tend to overestimate their own skills and future performance (before a certain age, they don't easily confess to not knowing).

This tendency for 'misplaced optimism' may seem to us to be a problem. In fact, among older children and adults, poor metacognition does have negative effects on performance in a variety of activities. But in young children, the misplaced optimism has important and useful consequences for motivation and persistence on difficult tasks. Bjorklund found, for example, that three- to five-year-olds overestimated their own imitative abilities, and so tried to imitate complex actions well beyond their ability, such as juggling with three balls! This led to their trying to learn and practise complex and difficult skills, whereas an adult who 'knew his own limitations' would have given up long before. Bjorklund also points out that younger children have a tendency not to inhibit wrong responses. This tendency is related to the neurological immaturity of the prefrontal cortex, the seat of reasoned, planned actions. We all know that older children and adults are far more hesitant to make mistakes in public than younger ones. But young children's wrong responses prompt important correction and feedback from adults. If they were more 'mature', giving only answers they were very certain would be correct, we would give them less corrective information and they would not learn as much. A two-year-old learning language is a good example of this principle—she freely tries out her new words and sentences, without worrying whether they are right or not ('I goed there...'). And every time she makes a mistake, the adult repeats what she has said after correcting it ('You went there, did you?').

Speed of processing is also known to increase exponentially between the ages of four and twenty or so years, as was described above. At the same time, plasticity, or the ability of the brain to learn new things decreases. Could this, too, play a necessary role in the development of a child? Bjorklund is certain that it does. For a young child, a lot of cognitive activity takes effort and is slow. As she grows older, more and more cognitive activity becomes automatized and quick. This is good—but there is a downside to the efficiency. Responses that are quick and automatic are difficult to suppress or change, which means that those responses are more or less fixed. But an immature nervous system allows greater cognitive flexibility. As we saw earlier, it is myelination that gives greater speed and automaticity to processing, and thus, the young child's incomplete myelination means that she is better prepared to adapt cognitively to later environments.

Here is a beautifully apt quote from Albert Einstein:

> I sometimes ask myself how it came about that I was the one to develop the theory of relativity. The reason, I think, is that a normal adult never stops to think about problems of space and

time. These are things which he has thought of as a child. But my intellectual development was retarded, as a result of which I began to wonder about space and time only when I had already grown up. Naturally, I could go deeper into the problem than a child with normal abilities.

Closely related to these ideas is the next of the four questions. Are early experiences crucial; can they make or break the child's further growth; or are children resilient; can later experiences make up for earlier ones?

Critical Periods in Development

Recently, I came across a flyer announcing a seminar on critical periods for cognitive development and learning. I could imagine that some parents might view the topic with anxiety. There is a kind of irreversibility about the idea of a critical period. What if we don't expose the child to the right thing at the right time? Will it mean that the child will never be able to learn as well later on? Many parents act out of a vague feeling of this sort—filling their child's days with numerous experiences so that there will be no regrets later on.

What is the truth of the situation? One hears both sides: you *can't teach an old dog new tricks*, but it's also *never too late to learn*. The first thing we can say for sure is that the word 'critical' is not always appropriate. It is better to speak of '**sensitive periods**', at least when looking at human development in cognitive and emotional areas. The word critical suggests an all-or-nothing situation. For example, chicks will follow behind any moving object in their first days of life, even if it is not their mother. But if this exposure is absent in the first few days, the behaviour is not learned at all. Zebra finches need to hear a particular song at a particular point in their development in order to learn and remember it, or else they will not learn it at all. Human sensory

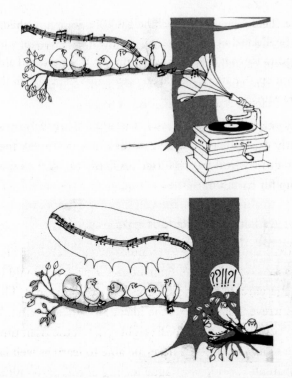

development also contains critical periods. For example, normal visual experience is critical within the first few months of life for the vision processing part of the brain to develop properly.

However, for human emotional and cognitive development, the situation is slightly different. Early childhood is a sensitive, rather than a critical period, for emotional development. Children in orphanages adopted before the age of one are better emotionally adjusted than those adopted later. But being adopted even later into a caring environment can compensate for early deprivation to a great extent. As for cognitive development, it is unclear whether early critical periods exist at all. We can look at language, an ability that one might think is likely to have a critical period of development. The few cases of children reared in extremely impoverished environments early on in life have shown a *decreased* ability to learn language and social skills—but not *zero* ability.[2] Similarly, we know that while learning new languages is much easier during childhood, it is certainly possible even in adulthood. Learning and memory continue through adulthood, and it is possible to learn new skills over one's lifespan.

Psychologist Charles Nelson has written extensively on the role of experience on lifelong learning, and he makes two very important points about critical periods. First, a negative early environment can certainly have long-term consequences. For example, if a child is subject to chronic stress, the volume of the hippocampus will be reduced in adulthood. Since the hippocampus is crucial to learning and memory, these functions can become impaired. But this is not to say that exposure to stress later in life leaves us unscathed. Adults who undergo severe stress can develop anxiety, depression or a host of other problems. Thus, Nelson says that stress and other environmental factors affect a developing brain in a different way than they affect a developed brain.

Nelson's second point is that 'positive' early environments studied in psychology have usually just been 'normal' ones. That is, research has shown that as long as a growing child is exposed to an average amount of stimulation, cognitive development will proceed normally. Not much is known about the effects of exposing children to extraordinary environments, and whether this can lead to extraordinary results that would be difficult, if not impossible, to attain later in life.

This second point is worth reiterating: **the notion of a critical or sensitive period is tied to the notion of normal abilities developing in a normal environment.** If young ones (human

---

[2] There have been a surprising number of cases of babies lost in the wild for years, presumed to have been cared for by wolves because of their 'savage' behaviour when discovered. While attempts were being made to help them adapt to civilized ways, scientists studied various aspects of their development.

or other animal) are deprived of the ingredients of a normal environment, we can expect to see some losses in fundamental abilities. This is not to be confused with the development of special talents given a special environment. In India, in particular, there are two kinds of concerns that people (those who can afford to) have about their children. One is associated with questions such as, 'If we do not introduce our six-year-old to classical music, will it be too late when she is eighteen?' The other is associated with questions such as, 'If we send our six-year-old son through this particular programme, will he become a genius?'

There is very little psychological research directly addressing this kind of question. Early enrichment programmes (such as Head Start for preschoolers in America) do show impressive benefits for children, but we must remember that these were disadvantaged children in the first place. Thus, strictly speaking, the programmes served to improve a deprived environment, not to enrich a normal environment. So any questions about special achievement and environments might have to be answered by popular wisdom, not backed by scientific research!

In Conclusion

It is clear that the outcome of a severely deprived childhood cannot be easily changed in later years. Yet the research reassures us at many levels:

- Within a fairly wide range of acceptable environments, development does proceed normally.
- Even though the first few years of life are significant, from the point of view of brain plasticity, the whole of childhood and adolescence is a sensitive period.
- Humans are able to learn and remember new things in motor and cognitive domains throughout their lifespan.

The brain is designed to do so, as long as it continues to be challenged and stimulated.

Nelson makes a point that we often overlook, which is that brain development during the prenatal months and the first years of life are very sensitive to **biological hazards**. He says, 'There may, in fact, be a stronger scientific basis for arguing that early brain development is assisted by protections from biological hazards (e.g., adequate maternal health care and nutrition, satisfactory postnatal nutrition, avoidance of exposure to environmental toxins and dangerous drugs, protection against viruses, and avoidance of undue chronic maternal prenatal stress) than by the regularity with which caregivers talk to or play with their babies. This means that efforts to enhance brain development should focus at least as much on public health efforts, especially for pregnant women and young children from at-risk populations, as on public information campaigns encouraging greater parental social stimulation of infants and toddlers—although both are important.' Especially for us in India, these words carry a great deal of significance.

The next two chapters will look at two more questions in child development, namely, the nature-nurture debate, and moral development. These are controversial topics, and are hotly debated among psychologists.

References and Bibliography

1. Banks, R., 2001. 'The Early Childhood Education Curriculum Debate: Direct Instruction vs. Child-Initiated Learning'. *Clearinghouse on Early Education and Parenting*, http://ceep.crc.uiuc.edu

2. Bjorklund, D.F., and B.L. Green, 1992. 'The Adaptive Nature of Cognitive Immaturity'. *American Psychologist*, Vol. 47, No. 1, 46–54.

3. Bjorklund, D.F., 1997. 'The Role of Immaturity in Human Development'. *Psychological Bulletin*, Vol. 122, No. 2, 153–69.

4. Bjorklund, D.F., 1997. 'In Search of a Metatheory for Cognitive Development (or, Piaget is Dead and I Don't Feel So Good Myself).' *Child Development*, Vol. 68, No. 1, 144–48.

5. Bornstein, M.H., 1989. 'Sensitive Periods in Development: Structural Characteristics and Causal Interpretations'. *Psychological Bulletin*, Vol. 105, No. 2, 179–97.

6. Bruner, J.S., 1972. 'Nature and Uses of Immaturity'. *American Psychologist*, August 1972, 687–708.

7. Cole, M.C., and S.R. Cole, 1993. *The Development of Children*. Scientific American Books.

8. Hirsh-Pasek, K., M. Hyson and L. Rescorla, 1990. 'Academic Environments in Preschool: Do they Pressure or Challenge Young Children?' *Early Education and Development*, Vol. 1, No. 6, 401–423.

9. Kail, R., 1991. 'Developmental Change in Speed of Processing During Childhood and Adolescence'. *Psychological Bulletin*, Vol. 109, No. 3, 490–501.

10. Kail, R., 1991. 'Processing Time Declines Exponentially During Childhood and Adolescence'. *Developmental Psychology*, Vol. 27, No. 2, 259–66.

11. Keil, F.C., W.C. Smith, D.J. Simons, and D.T. Levin, 1998. 'Two Dogmas of Conceptual Empiricism: Implications for Hybrid Models of the Structure of Knowledge'. *Cognition*, 65, 103–35.

12. Nelson, C.A., 1995. 'The Ontogeny of Human Memory: A Cognitive Neuroscience Perspective'. *Developmental Psychology*, Vol. 31, No. 5, 723–38.

13. Nelson, C.A., 1999. 'Change and Continuity in Neurobehavioural Development: Lessons from the Study of Neurobiology and Neural Plasticity'. *Infant Behaviour and Development*, Vol. 22, No. 4.

14. Nelson, C.A., 2000. 'Neural Plasticity and Human Development: the Role of Early Experience in Sculpting Memory Systems'. *Developmental Science*, 3:2, 115–36.

15. NICHD Early Child Care Research Network, 2005. 'Predicting Individual Differences in Attention, Memory and Planning in

First Graders from Experiences at Home, Child Care and School'. *Developmental Psychology*, Vol. 41, No. 1, 99–114.

16. Piaget, J., 1970. *Science of Education and the Psychology of the Child.* Orion Press, New York.

17. Siegler, R.S., 1998. *Children's Thinking.* Prentice Hall, New Jersey.

18. Siegler, R.S., 2005. *Children's Learning.* American Psychologist, 60, 769–78.

19. Thomas, B., 1992. 'Too Early to Fail? Pressures and benefits of pre-school education'. *Messenger*, Vol. 1, No. 2, p. 6.

20. Thomson, R.A., and C.A. Nelson, 2001. 'Developmental Science and the Media: Early Brain Development'. *American Psychologist*, Vol. 56, No. 1, 5–15.

21. Walker, S.P., T.D. Wachs, J.M. Gardner, B. Lozoff, G. Wasserman, E. Pollitt, J.A. Carter, and the International Child Development Steering Group, 2007. 'Child development: risk factors for adverse outcomes in developing countries'. *Lancet*, 369, 145–57.

CHAPTER FIVE

Nature *and* Nurture

People love explaining human tendencies or abilities in terms of nature or nurture. We like to say: he is brilliant—gets it from his father, of course. Or: she is so helpful—must be the way she has been brought up. The question we posed in the previous chapter presented this dichotomy as two ends of a spectrum of possibilities: Would you agree that a child is born a blank slate, and learns from experiences which are 'written' on this slate (in other words, learning makes us what we are)? Or, would you rather say that we inherit most of our tendencies and abilities, so that no matter what our environment, what we will be is almost inevitable right from the start? But we all recognize that the truth lies somewhere between 'everything is determined by the genes' and 'everything is determined by the environment'.

Recognizing that both nature and nurture obviously play a role in almost all human characteristics, ranging from height to intelligence to mental illness, you might reasonably wonder how much of this is due to nature and how much is due to nurture. Or you might ask, which is more important—nature or nurture?

But questions of nature vs. nurture are fundamentally flawed, when applied to individuals. A simple analogy may help to make this point. Suppose you have a rectangular field, you do not ask how much of its area is due to its width and how much is due to its height. The area is a product of both width and height, and neither is more important than the other. Or, if you buy some material from a store and stitch it into a shirt, you do not ask yourself how much of the shirt comes from the material and how much of it from the stitching. The truth is that the material without the stitching would not be a shirt, and the stitching without any material—well, that would not be a shirt either.

Similarly, the nature vs. nurture question cannot apply to an *individual* person. We cannot say that a child's athletic ability is 75 per cent from her genes and 25 per cent from her environment. After all, we would not say that her athletic ability would be 25 per cent less if she had 'no environment'. The nature vs. nurture question can only be asked of a *group* of genetically and/or environmentally diverse people: **to what extent are differences between people due to differences in nature or nurture?** There is a huge amount of research on this question, and answers have been sought for various human characteristics. For instance, research shows that vocabulary size is fairly 'heritable'.

When something is heritable, it does not mean that we are born with it. We are not born with a ready-made vocabulary! We learn all our words from the environment, but we may *learn more or fewer words depending on our genetic make-up*. Studies of people who are genetically related with each other to differing degrees (identical twins, siblings, parents and children) show that the genetic differences can account for much of the variability seen in vocabulary size. This statement will be easier to understand if we look at some examples. Correlations of vocabulary size between pairs of identical twins are greater than for fraternal twins—the contribution of nature, of course. But correlations of vocabulary size between pairs of fraternal twins are greater than for non-twin siblings!

The significance of this is that although fraternal twins and non-twin siblings share the same amount of their genes (50 per cent), fraternal twins share more similar environments than non-twin siblings who may grow up some years apart. Thus, the second finding alerts us to the influence of the environment. Studies also show that vocabulary size of adopted children is equally highly correlated with both their biological and adoptive mother's vocabulary size. Again, we have evidence for the influence of both nature and nurture.

However, even this is too simple a picture. It turns out that genetic and environmental influences upon human behaviour do not act independently—they are most often correlated. As a simple example, research has found that **identical twins are parented more similarly than fraternal twins**, and **biological siblings are parented more similarly than adopted siblings**. In other words, the genetic similarity brings about an environmental similarity, and when correlations are higher among identical twins than among fraternal twins, or are higher among biological siblings than adopted siblings, the reasons are *both genetic and environmental*. So, we realize that even for a group of individuals, nature and nurture cannot be easily disentangled. And so, even for a group of individuals, the nature vs. nurture question cannot be answered entirely satisfactorily.

Genetic similarity and environmental similarity increase from left to right—and so does vocabulary size correlation.

But do not despair; there are two sets of meaningful questions we can ask about nature and nurture. One is at the level of universals (looking at the human species as a whole), the other is at the level of individual differences (among human beings), and we will look at each in turn below. Since this is a book for teachers, and we are interested in thinking and learning, I will focus on cognitive abilities.

The Universals Question

What are our genetic predispositions, and how are these modulated by the environment? This question takes for granted that we are born into the world with a great deal already 'wired' into the brain—these are our genetic predispositions. So it denies the possibility that we are blank slates at birth. However, the words **predisposition** and **modulate** tell us that the environment does play an important role: it determines the expression of our genes.

How Nature Contributes to Our Cognitive Abilities

From an evolutionary point of view, every creature is born with genetic predispositions that will help it survive and reproduce successfully. Newborn humans are no exception—they instinctively suckle, grasp, and follow moving objects with their eyes, for example. But it is also true that babies of many animals are born rather helpless and immature. You read earlier that brain growth also mirrors this long process of development and growth, right into adolescence. Why? What is the purpose of the period of immaturity, whether short (as in turtles) or long (as in humans)? One answer is that genes equip the newborn only very broadly for a 'normal environment.' Beyond this, there are many specific and unique features of the environment that are not anticipated. To adapt to these, the organism must *learn*. It follows that the organism must be born *able to learn*: learning and memory require sophisticated brain abilities, and these abilities are what the genes give us.

You can look at this as a trade-off between two extreme positions. Either nature can endow us with all that is necessary for survival (in the form of instincts) which means that we would be very quick to reach maturity—but the disadvantage of this is that we would be inflexible in response to changing demands of the environment. On the other hand, if very little was programmed into us by nature, we would be flexible enough to adapt, by learning, to a wide variety of environments, but this would imply a long period of immaturity. Since human cultures and environments are extremely variable and complex, it is clear that we benefit from being at the learning end of the two extremes. Our inborn instincts by themselves would not take us much further than the first few months! For a human being, adapting to the specific and unique aspects of the environment requires a long period of extensive learning. Or another way of putting it is: the long period of human immaturity indicates the importance of learning in our adaptation to the environment.

Two facts from psychological research agree with this line of thinking: (i) babies are extremely active learners right from the beginning, in fact, even within the womb, and (ii) brain growth continues well into adolescence, which allows flexibility and adaptive learning for an extended period during childhood.

Now the nature-nurture question is looking quite different. Obviously, we are born with many abilities already present (vision, hearing, taste, smell, control over movements of the mouth and eyes...). Equally obviously, we are born with a special set of abilities that enable us to learn and make sense of the world through interaction with it. Can we spell out these abilities as well? A large body of research with humans has allowed us to make an impressive list of innate learning mechanisms, and these are listed below with examples:

- One way that our genes make us learning beings is by programming babies to **prefer novel stimuli**—right from birth, they will always pay more attention to something unfamiliar, something new. Babies are also programmed to **prefer complex stimuli**—they will pay more attention to patterned stimuli than plain stimuli for example. Clearly these preferences orient us to learning about our environment.

- Babies are programmed to be classically conditioned, to act according to the laws of association of stimuli. In one study, babies just a few hours old were given drops of sugar water immediately after being stroked on the forehead. They immediately sucked at the sugar water, a natural and instinctive response. But, after a few repetitions, the babies began sucking in response to the stroking alone! In fact, later when they did not receive sugar water following the stroking, they became upset and cried. This suggests that babies can **associate events** very early on, and from such learning can form expectations and predictions about the world.

- Humans are also programmed to **be operantly conditioned**, to act according to the laws of reinforcement and punishment. For example, babies are naturally quite active with their heads, limbs and bodies. We could choose one type of natural movement at random, say head-turning, and reward it by giving the baby a pacifier to suck on every time it turns its head. Very soon, we will find the baby's frequency of head-turning has increased. This ability to be operantly conditioned ensures that babies will practise and learn only those behaviours that lead to favourable outcomes such as food or comfort. In this simple way, they perfect certain early behaviours such as nursing, as well as later more complex behaviours such as language and throwing tantrums.

- Humans are programmed to imitate others—which is a way to learn new behaviours without having to be conditioned. In one study, simply watching an adult push a hinged board down on its base *once* was enough for nine-month-olds to imitate the same action themselves 24 hours later (this is in fact **delayed imitation**: an even more powerful learning tool than immediate imitation).

- Babies are programmed to **generalize** their associations beyond the specific features of the initial situation. In one study, three-month-old babies' feet were tied to a hanging toy with '+'-shaped pieces. They soon began to kick more and more, probably because that shook the toy around in an interesting way. The babies were given three 15-minute sessions with three identical toys, different only in colour, and were eventually kicking at a high rate for all three. The fourth session was the test. This time, half of the babies got a toy with the same '+'-shaped pieces but in a new colour, while the others got a toy with '**B**' shaped pieces in a previous colour. And what happened? The babies who saw the differently coloured '+'-shapes began kicking vigorously immediately; those who saw the '**B**' shapes did

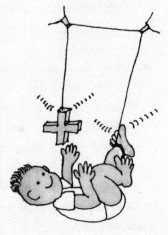

not. They acted as if they had learned the **concepts** of shape and colour.

Experiments of this kind indicate the beginnings of an ability to abstract, to categorize and conceptualize. These are complex and sophisticated abilities, but in a rudimentary form they are present very early in life.

• One of the most written-about and beautiful examples of 'programming to learn' is the way babies learn language. There are a number of innate tendencies in infants that predispose them to respond to a language-rich environment, and learn language as miraculously fast as they do. Here's a sample of these innate predispositions. Babies, just a few months old, prefer voices to instruments; distinguish among a very large number of sound units (phonemes) such as ba/pa and ra/la; produce all consonant and vowel sounds needed for any language on earth (cooing and babbling); parse speech into meaningful units; pay attention to the order of meaningful units; and take turns in communicating! The point of this list is that, according to psychologists, it is impossible for an information-processing system to learn so complex a thing as language, so well and in so short a time, *without* these basic assumptions programmed in from the start.

The capacity to learn that we human beings are endowed with could be seen as a tool-kit of sorts—it helps us to make the most of our environment. And that brings us to the nurture side of the story.

The Contribution of Nurture to Our Cognitive Abilities

The tools we are born with are not worth much by themselves. Each of the innate abilities described above, works in relation to aspects of the environment, thereby increasing the sophistication of our learning. In this sense, the role of the environment is obvious. However, it is an interesting question as to whether learning would proceed in the same way, *regardless of the kind of environment* we find ourselves in. When the environment is rich (in experience and exposure) will learning be superior? And when the environment is poor (when children face deprivation of various kinds) will learning suffer?

A lot of what we think about these questions depends on how we define environments. What do you consider a rich environment, and what then is deprivation? Let me give you one particular definition to begin with. Broadly, we can classify environments as **impoverished, normal** or **enriched**. A **'normal'** environment might imply this rather minimal list:

- sufficient physical support (food and security),
- sufficient exposure to socialisation,
- sufficient exposure to spoken language,
- sufficient availability of, and opportunity for, objects to be manipulated (natural or man-made objects).

Any of a fairly wide range of environments fits this requirement. The reason for coming up with such a minimal list is that babies are predisposed to learn a great deal from the natural environment, from day-to-day experiences. To understand what is meant by 'natural environment', just think about the way children learn to sit up, crawl, stand, walk, talk, and manipulate objects with their hands. No one needs to explicitly *teach* children any of these things; no special materials or aids are required for the normal, healthy child; the only requirement is a **'normal'** environment. According to the psychologist David Geary, in such an environment, the human child is predisposed to develop what are called **biologically primary abilities**. Examples of these abilities are speech and comprehension, implicit understanding of three-dimensional space (e.g., that the shortest distance between two points is a straight line), and the counting of small sets (up to four items). Normal environments all over the world, though vastly different from each other, nurture children who grow up with these abilities.

But what would happen to the child's genetic pre-dispositions if she were in an **enriched** environment, for example, school? From an evolutionary psychology point of view, any ordinary school would be an enriched environment, even if the school were relatively bare and uninspiring in our opinion. Her genetic predispositions do not anticipate a school-like environment, where a conscious effort is made by adults to teach her various things. In other words, will she achieve biologically primary abilities and something beyond them in school? Obviously, she will. With explicit instruction, she can achieve what Geary calls **biologically secondary abilities**.

And examples of these are word decoding (reading and writing) formal understanding of three dimensional geometry, number words, and the counting of large sets (greater than four)...the list is endless, and includes everything in a school

syllabus from classes one to twelve. An enriched environment like school takes the cognitive abilities we are born with and helps us to learn vast quantities of knowledge.

We should spend a little more time on this point, because there is some nice research to look at in this area, based on the question: how does a school environment modulate the 'tool-kit' of cognitive abilities that we are born with? Does schooling improve the way the brain works fundamentally? Studies in different countries have found that schooling appears to increase short-term memory performance, metacognitive skills, and of course, knowledge in certain domains. There are also studies showing that schooling increases IQ.[1]

But the developmental psychologist Michael Cole and his colleagues have studied both schooled and unschooled children and adults in many different parts of the world, and they conclude that schooling does not affect children's ways of thinking 'in any deep and general way.' Instead, **schooling changes the way children perform on school-like tasks**. Here are some interesting examples from Cole's work:

- A group of Vai people in Liberia were asked to judge whether several phrases (spoken in their language) were grammatical or not. Cole found that educated and uneducated Vai could judge this equally well; but only the educated Vai could also explain *why* the phrase was ungrammatical. Explaining *why* is a typical task in school, and quite unnecessary outside school, where it is enough to know that the grammar is wrong and to be able to correct it.

[1] We cannot assume from this that schooling enhances *intelligence per se*—but see Chapter Seven for more on this topic. In any case, as most psychologists will agree, IQ tests are mainly filled with abstract, *school-like* tasks and, therefore, it is no surprise that schooling enhances performance on them.

- In a study of unschooled Mayan children in rural Guatemala, it was found that they performed worse than educated American children of the same age on the task of recalling lists of unrelated words. But when the memory task was changed somewhat, the uneducated Mayan children performed just as well as their American peers. Barbara Rogoff and Kathryn Waddel collected 80 miniature objects (animals, people, furniture etc.) and placed them on a table. They chose 20 of them and placed them here and there in a familiar Mayan village scene. The objects were then returned to the table, and a few minutes later the children were asked to place the 20 objects as before. On this task, the schooled American children showed no advantage. Again, memory ability itself is unaffected by education, but the new skill of learning lists, useful in school, can be trained.

- A third example comes from work in conceptual categorization. Schooled children and adults will usually categorize a list of words into taxonomic groups such as 'animals', 'plants' and 'foods'. But Cole and his colleagues found that unschooled people in Africa categorized the words functionally, into 'edible' and 'inedible' words, for example. Then, when asked to sort '*as stupid people do*', they showed that they were perfectly capable of sorting the words taxonomically too. Schooling influences the *types* of concept and category formation, but not the ability itself.

Cole describes the typical school environment rather aptly:

'...unlike children who are assigned to tend sheep, to care for younger siblings, or to weave rugs to be sold in the market, children who attend school spend vastly more time learning through talking and listening than through doing...not only does the talk in school require the mastery of abstract concepts, it requires that mastery to be used away from the real-world contexts to which they apply. A biology lesson about the way sunlight influences plant growth, for example, may be taught in a windowless room with no plants in it. As a result, children must learn to create meaning from the subtle differences in the ways words are combined.'[2]

Michael and Sheila R. Cole: 'The Development of Children'

Let us step back for a moment and view the picture from a distance. The human being is born with many useful genetic predispositions that make him 'ready to learn' from his environment. This learning is strongly driven by his 'nature'. An enriched environment like school seems to change the child's way of solving certain special kinds of problems—apart from training

---

[2] Cole is speaking of traditional school environments in general. Of course, there are vast differences in the quality of schooling and teaching in the world, and several interesting alternative approaches to education in India. As Chapter Two on learning showed, there are ways of teaching that encourage better learning. The finding that school in general does not fundamentally change brain processes in no way should be taken to mean that a good education teaches the child nothing!

him in abilities like reading, writing and calculation, school gives him plenty of information, and encourages a formal organization of this knowledge. But it does not change the way his mind works fundamentally. Schooled children are not better thinkers in real-world, common sense situations, even if they do perform better on school-world tasks.

So why bother with school then? Because we do *not* usually think of school as an enriched environment. On the contrary, we feel that any child who does not have access to education, is in an **impoverished** environment. Society today, complex and technologically advanced as it is, demands much more from us than biologically primary abilities to succeed (some might argue, to survive, not just to succeed). We have come a long way from our hunter-gatherer ancestors. So, while from an evolutionary point of view, school is an enriched environment, from society's point of view, school is a normal environment. Today, most of us feel strongly that without school, a child is deprived. This point should be kept in mind when we think about nature and nurture—that our brains evolved to solve problems in a very different environment than the one we find ourselves in today. Many, perhaps most, real-world settings today are filled with abstract problems to be solved, and a school education trains us in the necessary skills.

The other side of the coin is, of course, the *truly* impoverished environment. There are several accounts of children in such environments—ranging from children said to have been reared by wolves, to orphans in poorly run institutions. These environments are deprived to the extent that they do not even provide children that minimal list of experiences that you read about a few pages back. Research in this area looks at the question of critical periods in development, which has already been addressed in the previous chapter.

Here is a summary of the 'universals' discussion. Humans have an impressive collection of innate learning mechanisms, and these, in combination with a wide range of 'normal' environments will lead to sophisticated learning. But significant changes in the environment can lead the same genetic predispositions to express themselves differently. For example, if the environment is deprived, children may learn very little, if anything at all, whereas in an enriched environment such as school, they learn vast quantities. Thus, the environment has considerable power to modulate our genetic predispositions.

The Individual Differences Question

Can individual differences at the genetic level be changed by the environment?

This question makes a basic assumption that variety is the norm in most human characteristics. While in the previous section we saw that all babies are born with certain predispositions, it is also true that even babies *differ from each other* on the predispositions. For example, take the preference for novelty. Some babies will get 'used to' a repeated stimulus more quickly than other babies, and thus are more quickly attracted to novel stimuli. Some babies are quicker at being operantly conditioned than other babies. There is a fund of research on early differences in temperamental characteristics[3] such as irritability, distress-proneness, soothability, distractibility and resistance to control. Newborns show clear temperamental differences, and these are thought to be neurologically based.

The next question that springs to a psychologist's mind is whether these innate differences are *enduring*, whether they lead to differences in the future, and how far into the future these effects would go. Would an irritable infant develop into a short-

[3] These are individual differences in behavioural tendencies that can be seen early in life and are relatively stable across various kinds of situations.

tempered student? Would a distress-prone infant develop into an anxious student? To test this, you need to follow groups of children over several years, measuring both early and later differences, and many studies have done so. Psychologist John Bates and his colleagues, for example, followed a large group of infants from six months to ten years of age. During the first two years, they measured something called 'resistance to control' in the babies, which included behaviours such as continuing to play with an object when told not to. These same children were assessed when they were ten years old, when Bates asked their teachers to rate them on *externalizing* behaviour (in other words, disobedient or aggressive behaviour). Bates discovered that many of the students that teachers found 'difficult' at age ten had also shown higher 'resistance to control' as babies.

This kind of continuity sounds rather alarming. If a child is born with certain behaviour tendencies, does this make certain later outcomes inevitable? Believing in the inevitability of something usually makes us 'give up', and if we saw a baby who was highly resistant to control, we might say, 'She is going to turn out difficult in school, and there's nothing you can do about it'. But fortunately, there is evidence that the environment can make a difference in such matters. As part of the same investigation, Bates and his colleagues had also studied the children when they were five years old, and at that time had measured the level of the mother's restrictive control, such as prohibitions and scolding in response to inconvenient or potentially harmful child actions. Their results showed some clear gene-by-environment interactions. For example, those children who had been *resistant* to control as babies but experienced *restrictive* control as five-year-olds had *lower* levels of externalizing behaviour at age ten. But *non-resistant* babies who experienced *restrictive* control as five-year-olds were found *more* difficult at age ten!

What would explain these effects? There are several possible ways in which genetic and environmental effects can co-occur. One possibility is that difficult infant behaviour leads parents to become less playful and more coercive (forceful in their discipline) which in turn influences the child's later behaviour in school. There is plenty of evidence of this phenomenon, and the technical term for it is *reactive covariance*. Another possibility is that children with certain temperaments shape their own environments to lead to certain outcomes. For example, when a fearful or inhibited child avoids social situations, therefore gets less opportunity to learn social skills, and ends up even more inhibited and shy than he would have if his environment had been different. This is termed *active covariance*. Naturally, this leads us to conclude that innate differences could be changed for the better by changing the environment appropriately. Several studies have looked at the effectiveness of training parents to respond better to their child's irritability or distress, and the results do show benefits in terms of the children's exploratory play, social skills, school adjustment, and academic achievement.

In Conclusion

At the end of this detailed exploration of the nature-nurture issue, the question we began with has revealed quite a few complexities. We conclude that the slate is by no means blank, but also that the environment plays a powerful role in developing what we are born with. We also see that nature and nurture interact with each other in cyclical ways, beautifully entangled with each other.

The tone of the discussion in this chapter has remained quite neutral and unemotional, but that is quite unlike the debate in real life between nature and nurture. Top psychologists, brilliant analysts in their respective fields, have battled on opposites sides of the nature-nurture divide. And the reasons for this are not trivial. This is one psychological question that has tremendous and important implications for the way we construct society. If we believe that genes determine outcomes, will we invest in improving environments for those who are deprived? Many fear that when scientists report on innate abilities and tendencies, they are either mistaken or irresponsible, because their results could lead to a belief that **biology is destiny**.

The biology-is-destiny belief implies two things:

- all kinds of outcomes for human beings are fixed or inevitable.
- the force that fixes those outcomes is our biology or inherited characteristics, not our environment.

This appears to be too strong a claim. Most of us believe that outcomes are not fixed and can always be changed by our efforts. Many of us also believe that the environment cannot completely determine outcomes either. So, does anyone really believe that biology is destiny? Sadly, there are enough instances, all over the world and throughout history, where a group of people has been discriminated against because they were considered 'biologically inferior'. Some explanations of social problems such as poverty are made in terms of *abilities* rather than *opportunities*. That is, one political view is that those who have certain abilities will succeed in life, and those who don't are doomed to be poor. But another view is that anyone could succeed if opportunities for good education, health, and jobs were given to all.

These difficult issues will surface again and again. The next chapter prompts us to ask whether, if we conclude aspects of immoral behaviour are innate, we will be forced to condone some crimes? Questions of morality and personal responsibility are strongly tied to the nature-nurture divide. In Chapter Eight, we will have to contend with the question again when it comes to the topic of intelligence.

References and Bibliography

1. Asbury, K., T.D. Wachs, and R. Plomin, 2005. 'Environmental Moderators of Genetic Influence on Verbal and Nonverbal Abilities in Early Childhood'. *Intelligence*, 33, 643–61.

2. Bates, J.E., G.S. Pettit, K.A. Dodge, and B. Ridge, 1998. 'Interaction of Temperamental Resistance to Control and Restrictive Parenting in the Development of Externalizing Behavior'. *Developmental Psychology*, Vol. 34, No. 5, 982–95.

3. Bruner, J.S., and M.C. Cole, 1971. 'Cultural Differences and Inferences about Psychological Processes'. *American Psychologist*, 26, 867–76.

4. Cole, M.C., and S.R. Cole, 1993. *The Development of Children*. Scientific American Books.

5. Collins, W.A., E.E. Maccoby, L. Steinberg, E.M. Hetherington, and M.H. Bornstein, 2000. 'Contemporary Research on Parenting: The Case for Nature and Nurture'. *American Psychologist*, Vol. 55, No. 2, 218–32.

6. Pinker, S., 2002. *The Blank Slate: The Modern Denial of Human Nature*.

7. Rogoff, B., and P. Chavajay, 1995. 'What's Become of Research on the Cultural Basis of Cognitive Development?' *American Psychologist*, Vol. 50, No. 10, 859–77.

8. Wachs, T.D., 2006. 'Contributions of temperament to buffering and sensitization processes in children's development'. In B. Lester, A. Masten, and B. McEwen (eds). *Resilience in Children*. Annals of the New York Academy of Science, Vol. 1094, 28–39.

9. Walker, S.P., T.D. Wachs, J.M. Gardner, B. Lozoff, G.A. Wasserman, E. Pollitt, J.A. Carter, and the International Child Development Steering Group, 2007. 'Child development: risk factors for adverse outcomes in developing countries'. *Lancet*, 369, 145–57.

CHAPTER SIX

Moral Development

Almost forty years ago, newspapers around the world announced the discovery of a gentle and non-violent tribe, unspoiled by civilization, in a remote and beautiful part of the Philippine rainforests. Pictures were published of the Tasaday tribal people going about their daily business in leafy clothing, and news soon spread that they didn't even have words in their vocabulary for 'war' or 'weapon'. The story confirmed many people's deeply-held assumptions about the natural goodness of humankind. Around ten years later, it was 'discovered' that the tribe might have been invented by a trickster who profited from the entire episode. Whether or not the Tasaday were real is undecided even today, but what is interesting is the way the world lapped up the story! It showed how much we believe in the 'noble savage', an idea made popular by the eighteenth-century philosopher, Jean-Jacques Rousseau, who believed that there is 'no original perversity in the human heart'. If savages are noble, then so should be little children who have had very little exposure to tne influence of adult society. And this brings us right to the heart of the role of education in moral development.

Do you believe that children are naturally 'good', and that exposure to society's ills corrupts them? Or do you feel that children are naturally 'uncivilized', and socialization is necessary to make them moral human beings? As teachers, the way we handle situations involving student behaviour will be greatly influenced by which side of the line we fall on; whether we believe that civilisation and society *elevate* or *corrupt* basic human nature. Either way, academic goals are not the only ones that we hold for our students. We want them to tell the truth, to share, to cooperate, to be helpful, kind, respectful and brave...and also

not to tell lies, hurt others, be selfish, lazy, rude or fearful. Now, the seeds of desirable qualities may already be in young children. Some teachers believe that their job is primarily *not to destroy* the child's natural generosity, gentleness and honesty.

But many teachers assume that it is part of their job to *teach* students how to share, cooperate and avoid aggressive behaviour, to 'instil the right ideas', because these things don't come about naturally. Thus, school becomes one of the most powerful socializing influences a child encounters. Actually, the process of socialization begins much earlier than school. Children receive a fair amount of information through discipline encounters beginning even before their first birthday; they are warned, cajoled, threatened, punished, ordered and forbidden. By around four years of age, children are expected to comply with a range of requests or demands, related to safety, respect for possessions, respect for others, family norms and social norms. When they are six years old, they begin formal schooling, and most Indian schools, whether religious or secular, devote time to educating their young in manners and morals. Such moral lessons are imparted regularly, perhaps weekly, right through the school years.

Unfortunately, the end result of the long years of socialization and discipline is not always what we aim for. Perhaps the problem is that moral lessons are abstract and verbal; as the saying goes, values must be caught by example, not taught by instruction. But whatever our approach, we will not be very effective unless we understand more about the true complexities of moral development. There are at least four good reasons why moral development in particular is so complex:

- There is a difference between morals (which might be universal), and conventions (which are limited to one's family or society). How do children understand the difference? That is, how do they know **why certain things are 'right' and other things are 'wrong'?**

- Although socialization starts young, **adult rules are not written on a blank slate.** Research suggests that children probably possess innate tendencies to compete, cooperate, empathize, and be altruistic, aggressive or fearful.
- Children do not simply take in whatever social norms the adults give them. Moral development is not merely a matter of absorbing the rules of behaviour, just as cognitive development is not merely a matter of absorbing knowledge. Here too, **internalization of the rules is a constructive process.**
- Moral behaviour does not always follow from moral knowledge. What makes a person 'act upon her principles'? There is often **a disconnect between what we say and what we do,** and in no area is this more stark than morality.

In this chapter, the above four points are going to be explored in detail with examples from psychological research. We will begin with the moral-conventional distinction, taking a look at some cross-cultural research and psychological history.

Why is it 'Right'?

Do you remember the last time you told one student not to bully another? If you gave her a reason at all, try to remember whether it was 'because in this school we don't tolerate bullying', or 'because the other person will be hurt'. Or, if you told a student to be polite in front of her elders, try to recall whether your reason was 'because it is good manners to be polite', or 'because it makes the other person feel happy'. Whenever a student does something you do not approve of, you can potentially communicate at least these three basic things:

- Stop it!
- Stop it, or else you will be punished in such-and-such way.
- Stop it because of such-and-such reason.

If as teachers, we don't often go beyond the first, psychological research shows that our interventions will not be very effective. The second response is directly from the behavioural school, and is often used to control student behaviour. (Box 1 spells out the specific dangers of using those methods.) The third is what is definitely recommended—when we engage with the student's schemas about the *reasons* for and *consequences* of different kinds of behaviour, there is greater learning. Giving reasons is more effective than not, but the picture is a bit more complex than that. The examples above described two kinds of reasons: the conventional and the moral. That is, we can tell the child that some behaviour is 'right/wrong' because family, school, social or religious **convention** says so. Or, we can tell her that a behaviour is 'right/wrong' because of intrinsic reasons of loss, unfairness or harm—**moral** reasons. Is one type of reason any more effective than the other?

Well, it depends. Not all transgressions are moral. Suppose instead of bullying, the student had failed to remove his cap inside the classroom. Now, as far as I can see, there is no intrinsic moral reason for removing one's cap in the classroom, and there are many similar conventions for which there seem to be no clear moral reasons. Breaking these conventions could not be called moral transgressions. Research shows that children and adolescents can and do distinguish moral from conventional rules at a very young age. Psychologist Larry Nucci, for example, has investigated students' understanding of various rules and their teachers' responses. To summarize one of his findings in very rough terms, teachers are more effective when they give moral or empathic

Box 1

STOP IT OR ELSE...!

The easiest ways to manipulate behaviour come from the **behaviourist school** of psychology, which recommends **punishment and reward** in different forms to get rid of undesired behaviours and boost desired ones. But one should always be suspicious of quick-and-dirty methods! And in this case, there are good reasons to steer clear from punishment and reward in dealing with our students. Suppose, that in order to teach a student to be polite in asking for and giving things in class, you punish him in some way each time he is rude. This could have the following unintended effects:

- He stops the rude behaviour as long as you are around, to avoid punishment, but continues it otherwise.
- He stops the rude behaviour, but has no positive behaviour to replace it.
- If he is required to 'clean the classroom' as a punishment, he learns that cleaning as an activity is a punishment.
- He learns that to get people to do what he wants, punishment is the way.
- He reacts to you with anger and fear.
- He associates you and/or the classroom with the emotions of anger and fear, which now come up automatically whenever either is encountered.

For several years now, many psychologists, including behaviourists themselves, have been saying that punishment *is not* the preferred way to control human behaviour. Some of them recommend instead that we use positive reinforcement such as praise, privileges and other rewards to increase 'good' behaviours. Most of us think of rewards as encouraging students, or at the very least, being harmless, and thus, whenever the student is polite or generous, we might praise him or give him some reward. But here too, there could be subtle unintended effects. The student might increase the desired behaviour, but

'If you share chocolate with your sister, I will buy you a special one tomorrow.'

'If you donate this to charity, I will get you a special tax break.'

only in situations where he will be recognized for his good deeds, or only when the rewarding adults are around. And the behaviour becomes '**overjustified**', that is, comes to be seen as worth doing *only for a reward*. This is potentially the most harmful consequence of rewarding. Rewards are generally given for a behaviour that is otherwise unlikely to occur spontaneously, or when we do not have the patience to wait for something 'good' to happen. As you will see later in this chapter, young children do spontaneously demonstrate generosity or sensitivity to others' feelings. Rewarding acts of generosity or sensitivity sends the message 'you need to be rewarded to do this because otherwise you won't do it'.

However, this does not suggest that we should not appreciate or acknowledge our students' generosity, honesty or sensitivity. The negative effects of rewards come into play when the reward is unrelated to the activity itself. A simple example is when certificates are given for reading more books, instead of a natural consequence such as: reading a book leads to your being able to borrow another. Positive reinforcement works best when it is given in the form of appreciation, encouragement and informative feedback.

reasons rather than conventional ones *for moral transgressions*. For example, children reacted less favourably when a teacher said, 'We have a rule about hitting', than if she said, 'How would you feel if she hit you?' It seems that when it comes to something like hitting (or anything involving harm to another) children are more responsive to an empathic reason than a convention or rule.

'How would you feel if someone hit you?'

Another developmental psychologist, Nancy Eisenberg, found a similar result when she and her colleagues studied generosity in ten-year-olds. The children were given a small amount of money for playing with a game in the laboratory, and were then shown a UNICEF poster asking for donations for poor children. They were told they could share some of their money with the poor children if they wished, but that they didn't have to. Then they watched a short film of an adult playing the same game, and at the end of the film, the adult began thinking aloud about donating money to UNICEF. For some of the children, the adult in the film said that the poor children 'would be so happy and excited if they could buy food and toys. After all, poor children have almost nothing'. For other children, the adult in the film said, 'It's really good to donate to poor boys and girls…Sharing is the right thing to do'. Eisenberg found that the children gave more when they had watched the former film, where the adult gave empathic reasons for sharing money.

Psychological research also consistently shows that children and adolescents view conventions as less important and more negotiable than morals. But most of this work is conducted with children in Western countries, who share more or less the same views on morals and conventions. The question is, do children in all cultures draw the moral-conventional line in the same way? Studies of people in countries such as Kenya and India show that in non-Westernized cultures, morals and conventions may be equally important, and treated similarly by adults and children alike. Richard Shweder is an anthropologist with a strong interest in cross-cultural ideas of moral development. He has questioned the universality of the assumption that 'some events are inherently moral and other events inherently nonmoral'. While there may be universal moral rules, based on ideas such as justice, protection of the weak, keeping promises and unprejudiced judgement, in many societies **conventions have a moral force**. His conclusions stem from in-depth research he has done in the 1980s with a fairly orthodox community in Orissa, where children felt acts such as calling one's father by his first name were *morally* wrong, and a father opening a letter addressed to his fourteen-year-old son was *morally* right. How do we know the children did not think of these as conventions rather than as moral rules? The children were also asked whether it would be better for everyone in the world to adopt those rules; whether America would be a better place if Americans adopted the same rule; and whether it would be alright to change the rule in India if most Indians wanted to.

Their answers (yes, yes and no) indicated that they clearly viewed these as morals, not conventions. In contrast, American children felt it was *not* wrong to call one's father by his first name, and that it *was* wrong for the father to open a letter addressed to his son.

Even in Western cultures, Shweder and others argue, it would be difficult to make the moral-conventional divide clearly. Consider the rule about being on time to class: is it purely a convention, or does it also have an impact on the learning process for the rest of the class? That is, is it 'unfair' for a student to come late because it affects the rest of the class, or is it simply 'against the school rules'? Or, if a student speaks in class without first raising her hand, is she breaking a convention, or being inconsiderate to the needs of others? Looking more closely at the rules in place in our own schools and classrooms, can we make a clear moral-conventional divide? Some psychologists have suggested that moral and conventional transgressions actually lie on the same dimension, the only difference being that the former are more *serious* than the latter.

Today in India, many upper- and middle-class urbanized children are probably much more like their Western counterparts than like fellow Indian children growing up in more traditional or rural settings. Even among more traditionally brought up youngsters, I suspect that difficulties in communication do arise from mismatches between what one generation considers moral but the next generation considers conventional. Discussing your and your students' ideas on morals and conventions would be a fascinating exercise—if you can keep a little time aside for an occasional dialogue on such questions.

With this complex picture of the moral-conventional distinction securely in mind, let us now look at some historical views of moral development. These will help deepen our understanding of the whole question of morals and conventions. Sigmund Freud, Jean

Piaget and Lawrence Kohlberg are familiar names to most people who have done a course or two in psychology. The first two worked in the broad areas of personality and cognitive development, while the third is known specifically for his 'stage theory' of moral development. There is a common thread connecting their theories of childhood morality, but in recent years, the thread has been questioned, pulled and tugged at, till it seems ready to snap! This common thread is the assumption that humanity's highest moral sense emerges only *later* in life, as a result of either socialization by adults or improved cognitive reasoning. Kohlberg's theory in particular states this very clearly, that **morals emerge from conventions**, or at least, *after* conventions. This picture has been challenged, as you will see, by recent data showing that children are moral beings from a very early age. But first, a brief summary of the three approaches to moral development.

In Freud's conception, the young child is born with basic impulses and desires that it seeks to express or satisfy. The *impulses are essentially 'selfish'*, in that there is no consideration of others' needs at this young age. Very soon, however, the child learns that his desires cannot be instantly gratified, his drives cannot be fulfilled, because the world of reality does not allow it. Thus begins a process of socialization, where the adults' repeated warnings, commands and threats prevent the child from doing things that would hurt himself or others, and further teach him to follow family and social conventions. From Freud's point of view, the child's innate impulses are thus continually frustrated, as he struggles to deal with the (sad) realities of a life where he cannot always have what he wants, when he wants it. By around five years of age, Freud said, these external restrictions become internalized, such that the child develops a conscience which guides his actions from within. This allows him to behave properly even when adults are not around to remind or punish, by introducing the complex emotion of guilt.

Piaget described the young child as 'egoistic', not using the word in the sense we use it in everyday language, but as *unable to see things from another's perspective.* According to his theory, it is only by age seven years or so that a child is able to see the consequences of his actions on another, understand cause and effect, as well as understand others' intentions. Presumably, this marks the start of the process of becoming a moral being. Inspired by Piaget's stage theory of cognitive development, Kohlberg proposed a stage theory of moral development. The brief version is as follows: initially children function from personal pleasure and pain, and their own needs (the *pre-conventional* phase). This is followed by *conventional* reasoning—recognizing external consensus, seeking the approval of others, and conforming to social rules. And finally comes the moral or *post-conventional* phase, where the focus is on rational, objective standards for right behaviour. These would include the principles mentioned above: justice, protection of the weak, keeping promises, and unprejudiced judgement.

Pre-conventional→Conventional→Post-conventional

This last stage is, according to Kohlberg, never reached by the majority of human beings. The sequence of stages is invariant from person to person—that is, everybody goes through them in the same order. However, there are no age markers for Kohlberg's stages. Thus, one may find a twelve-year-old girl and a forty-five-year-old woman both at the same stage of moral development, and it follows from this that not everybody will reach the higher stages by adulthood. In fact, research the world over has recorded less than five per cent of the population is at this post-conventional moral stage. (However, see Box 2 for an example of cross-cultural findings on Kohlberg's stages).

While Freud, Piaget and Kohlberg's theories seem to contain truths about human beings, there have been several issues with them. Recent research is showing us that all three psychologists might have seriously underestimated the young child's moral sensibilities. Kohlberg's theory, in particular, has been criticized for being incomplete, if not incorrect. It does not seem to be the case that morals develop only after conventions. One psychologist, Elliot Turiel, has the view that children develop *both* morals and conventions right from the beginning, but that both follow separate developmental trajectories. From the work done by him and his colleagues, very young children seem to distinguish between morals and conventions by correctly interpreting different social interactions. For example, when you pull your friend's hair, she feels pain and cries. But if you don't say 'good morning' to your teacher, the consequence is quite different. Through many such interactions, the child begins to make inferences and judgments about which rules are universal and which are relative. In fact, Turiel asks young children: in another country where parents and schools allow it, would it be alright to (i) wear no clothes to school, or (ii) pull someone's hair? Even three- to five-year-olds are clear that the former can be acceptable whereas the latter cannot.

Box 2

'FORGET HEINZ IN EUROPE'!

Have you heard the story of Heinz, the unfortunate man who could not afford to buy the medicine that would save his dying wife? Thanks to Lawrence Kohlberg and numerous other psychologists, children and adults all over the world have been faced with Heinz's tale of woe. Heinz appeals to the pharmacist who refuses to help him. The question is, should he steal the drug, and why or why not? When the policeman discovers the thief, and learns all the details of the case, should he arrest Heinz, and why or why not?

The research method is to interview people about hypothetical situations with moral conflicts such as the above, and ask them for explanations and justifications of different possible courses of action. According to Kohlberg, whether they feel Heinz should steal the drug or not, the reasons people give indicate their stage of moral reasoning. Yes, he should steal it, because otherwise God will punish him for letting his wife die. No, he should not steal, because stealing is against the law. Yes, he should steal, because he loves his wife and cannot live without her. No, he should not steal, because then he will go to jail. For 30 years people have explained and justified Heinz's actions, and the data show that young children mostly reason pre-conventionally, older children and adults conventionally, and a very few people post-conventionally. But some psychologists believe that the high degree of **self-conscious verbalization** required makes Kohlberg's sequence a theory of the development of 'verbal justifications', not of moral development. Most people around the world *know* and *do* much more than they can *talk* about. This might explain the surprising finding that so few people worldwide reach the higher stages of Kohlberg's developmental sequence.

Further, Kohlberg's theory probably misses other valid but completely different ways of reasoning through conflicting issues. Jyotsna Vasudev and Raymond Hummel interviewed a large number of adults and children in Jaipur, Calcutta and Delhi on the Heinz story, and discovered that many Indians possess different moral principles than Kohlberg had considered. These include the sacredness of all life (not only human), the idea of *ahimsa*, and the feeling that some social issues are greater than individual lives. This last idea led one of Vasudev's participants to say, 'Forget Heinz in Europe, just come to India and you are speaking of the same thing with 60 per cent of the people living below the poverty line...Heinz's story is being repeated all around us all the time with wives dying, with children dying, and there is no money to save them...So...yes, ok, steal the drug, but it is not going to make any difference on a larger scale.'

Turiel and his colleagues have also added a third domain of behaviour, the **personal**. In this category would fall those behaviours that young people feel are really nobody's business but their own (for example, length of hair, what time to sleep, what to wear, how neat their room should be...!). Adults need to allow such issues to remain personal and not spill over into either moral or conventional domains, perhaps for adolescents in particular. We will return to this important idea in Chapter 11 on adolescence. For now, we explore the question of whether there are innate elements of morality, and if so, what are they?

Innate Elements of Morality

Few people would argue against the claim that evolution has bred aggressive and competitive instincts into human beings. We commonly see very young children acting aggressively, grabbing at a precious toy, biting each other, or pulling hair. These behaviours, when they first appear, do not seem imitative or learned from the environment. The urge to compete is also apparent early on. Often two children will fight over an object that neither really wanted in the first place—if one picks it up, the other suddenly feels the need to fight for it, and when the conflict is over, the object is cast aside anyway! Evolutionary arguments say that the instincts of **competition** and **aggression** are important for survival, and therefore inherited.

But these same evolutionary arguments tell us that **cooperative** and **prosocial** behaviours are also important for survival. In many situations, those who help each other in the battle for survival are more likely to live long enough to reproduce than those who help no one, and are in turn not helped. Babies are not, of course, born helpful or cooperative, but the emotional basis of later prosocial behaviour is present right from birth. When they are just a few days old, infants respond to the emotions of those close to them. They can match emotional expressions through imitation (smiles, frowns, fearful expressions). They will cry when they hear another child crying, and become agitated if their mother is distressed. This early form of **empathy** expresses itself as self-distress, but as the child grows older, empathy allows him to respond to others' needs with specific helpful behaviour. This happens as children begin to develop a sense of the difference between the 'self' and the 'other'.

Aspects of morality as sophisticated as **altruism** and **guilt** emerge between one and two years of age. Psychologist Marian Radke-Yarrow, among others, has studied the development of these elements in very young children. One of her studies extended over a year, and involved the mothers of one-year-old children in an unusual and interesting way. The mothers were trained to look for occasions when their child saw someone in distress, and to record the child's responses as faithfully as possible. Once a month, someone from Radke-Yarrow's team would visit the home to interview the mother. On some of those visits, the mother *pretended* to be distressed so that the researcher could videotape the child's response. This provided a useful check of the quality of the mothers' observations.

What did the results reveal? Through the period of study, the children increasingly responded to others' distress with prosocial acts, such as hugging, helping, or verbally comforting. They also showed empathic concern such as sad looks or sympathetic gestures, as well as something called 'hypothesis testing', where they seemed to be seeking the *cause* of the distress. For example, the child might look back and forth from the person's injured foot to the chair that had been stumbled on. The researchers were especially interested in those situations where the distress had been caused by the child himself, since here one might expect to find the roots of guilt and remorse. In adults, guilt seems to create conflict; comforting a friend who has been hurt by someone else is so much easier than when you have hurt him yourself! But would such young children even realize that they were the cause, and if so, how would they respond differently?

Results showed that children were just as likely to help and comfort distressed persons when they had caused the distress, suggesting that empathy is a common root of both compassionate and remorseful behaviour. However, when children caused the distress, they also tended to show more enjoyment, more aggression, less concern for the other, more self-distress (crying or whimpering) and were less likely to explore the reasons for distress than when they had not caused it! Thus, as Radke-Yarrow says, at this early age helping and comforting behaviours arising from remorse, or the early 'conscience', are accompanied by some conflict and ambivalence. Naturally, this is helped along by the adults, who use forceful discipline to stop aggression or make sharing happen. The child feels empathy for another, but when it coincides with knowing that he has *caused* the other's distress, he also feels a conflict that we may later call *guilt*.

Another important element of moral behaviour is the **fear** of consequences. At a very young age, children come to associate

certain acts and situations with fearful consequences, such as punishment or the withdrawal of love. Almost all animal organisms are born with the law of reinforcement wired into their brains: if a behaviour is followed by an unpleasant consequence, it is less likely to occur in the future. Moral development is greatly influenced by this simple law, present even in newborns. As adults, we rely on it to pass on important messages about safety and norms of behaviour: 'If you put your hand there you will get hurt', or 'If you pluck the flowers mummy will be very angry'.

Interestingly, it takes a while for children to figure out that they *can* pluck the flowers, as long as no one catches them at it! And it takes a longer while for children to decide for themselves whether plucking flowers is really wrong or not. This leads us to the next section on socialization and internalization. Whether innate or learned very early on, several moral elements are present well before the child goes to school, and we can say with certainty that young children are far from *amoral*. But what happens when the external world of should and should-not comes into contact with this already fairly complex moral mind?

Internalization as an Active Process

Many psychologists lay great emphasis on the process of socialization and its role in moral development. In Sigmund Freud's conception, for example, the young child's inappropriate impulses and desires can be controlled only through the process of socialization. Here the word 'socialization' refers to the way peers, adults and society in general, condition the child to conform to their rules. But, as you can imagine, things are nowhere near as simple as 'taking in the external rules and acting according to them'. Young people, if and when they attend to the moral values expressed by adults, do not always accept them! Hostility, anger and rejection are common, even when a young person is outwardly obedient. As teachers, we have a large share of the work of socialization falling into our laps. We naturally want our students to **internalize** a number of values, which means that they would think of these values as coming from within themselves, rather than imposed by others. What does the research tell us that could help us in our work?

Although most studies involve parents and their children, the same principles apply to any adult interacting with young people. Psychologists Joan Grusec and Jacqueline Goodnow, for example, have focused on **discipline** encounters, trying to discover what works and what does not. They have discovered several factors that influence internalization, having to do with the situation (type of 'misdeed', for example) the adult's characteristics, and the student's temperament. For example, adult statements may sometimes be tangential or irrelevant, such as when they say,

'This is not the first time you've done this', or 'And another thing you always do is...'. These reduce the possibility of successful internalization. Grusec and Goodnow also note that many adult responses contain irony or humour, such as, 'What is the magic word?' and 'I must be going deaf!' when a child is too soft. These may, they say, serve an interesting purpose. An ironic response requires the child to do a little 'cognitive unpacking' to understand properly, which may aid internalization.

Whatever the situation, ultimately two things *must* happen for a value to be internalized:

- the child's perception of the adult's viewpoint must be accurate, and
- she must accept, not reject it.

To this end, your discipline technique needs to be flexible, in the sense that your response to a child must be contingent on the situation as well as on her temperament. However, note that **flexibility does not imply inconsistency**! The match between the situation and your response is not a random one, and Grusec and Goodnow's work shows that certain types of responses are generally suitable to certain types of situations. What makes an adult response *suitable to the situation*? Remember that anything your student hears has to fit into her existing schemas about social interactions, attitudes, beliefs and behaviours. This means that the way you reason has to aid the process of schema construction and change. Larry Nucci, as you saw earlier, reports that children are most likely to accept the adult's message when it is appropriate to the situation from their point of view. That is, they expect adults to reason differently for moral, conventional and personal transgressions. For example, Nucci found that if a teacher said 'think of the other person' for swearing, or 'it's not allowed' for stealing, students sensed a mismatch and were not likely to accept those reasons. The effects of such a mismatch went beyond simply accepting or rejecting that particular reason: the children even rated such teachers less favourably overall.

We must also keep in mind the student's changing cognitive skill level when we talk of moral reasoning. Important aspects of moral reasoning do rely on cognitive abilities such as being able to take multiple perspectives, and understanding intention, cause and effect. Adults are generally aware of this, which is why we speak in simple, concrete terms with young children, and in more complex, abstract terms with older children and adolescents. But we might mistake 'simple' reasoning for conventional, rule-based (*must* not, *should* not) reasoning, whereas the research we have reviewed here indicates that even primary school children can and do understand empathic, moral reasons. We *can* speak to them about the effects of their actions on others. **'Other-oriented' reasoning**, as it is called, works well for several reasons:

- It develops the child's empathic capacity towards others.
- It is not tied to the adult—that is, the child can be aware of another's feelings even when the adult is absent.
- It encourages the child to think about what she can do to 'repair' hurt inflicted on the other person.
- It leads children to respect the rights of others.

All this should convince us that reasoning with our students, and in ways suitable to the situation, will help the process of internalization of values. The other common discipline technique, badly misused in our schools, is called **'power assertion'**. Some teachers will withdraw privileges or affection, use force, threat, or in the worst cases, physical punishment. Unfortunately, they end up conveying lessons quite different than the ones they intended. There are several reasons why power assertion is a dangerous tool:

- It can lead to insecurity (if we assert power by withdrawing affection).
- It can create anger and hostility, and therefore, internalization will not occur.
- It provides a model for aggressive behaviour.
- It makes the adult's presence the reason for moral behaviour, thus not allowing for internalization.
- It discourages the student from reflecting on moral issues.

One mistake we are liable to make is to underestimate the sophistication in the moral thinking of our young students. For instance, research reveals a complex sense of **justice** in even very young children. Psychologist William Damon studied the way six- and ten-year-olds shared sweets among themselves as a measure of their sense of fairness. Groups of four children were given materials to make as many bracelets as they could, but each group had one child who was younger and therefore produced less than the others. When the time came, Damon gave the groups ten sweets each to be divided as they felt best. Some children tried to divide the sweets in proportion to the work done. Others tried to divide the sweets equally, which of course Damon had made difficult by giving ten sweets to four children! Dividing things equally could happen for two reasons: maybe the children missed the significance of some working more than others, or could not work out the proportions correctly. But equal division also emerged among the older children as a way of being *fair to all regardless of output*. In one group, the ten-year-olds argued at length among themselves until they concluded that the younger one should get the same as them, because 'it's not like he didn't do anything...he did the best he could...so he should get as much as we do'.

Presumably, some of the children's reasoning came about through the process of adult socialization. But here is an interesting thought. Is there a consistency between what adults say is right, and the way adult society actually functions? Social, economic and foreign policies often reflect greed, power seeking, aggression and exploitation of the weak. Growing children are aware not only of their immediate world of interactions, but also the extended world of political and social realities. And many children all over the world live in harsh and difficult conditions, the victims of social injustice. William Arsenio is a psychologist with an interest in what could go wrong with the development of empathy in young people growing up in what he calls **toxic social environments**. Such children might grow up with very few direct experiences of moral reciprocity or fairness, and perhaps, we should not be surprised if they end up feeling: life isn't fair, so why should I be? As Arsenio says, the message they get is that life does not revolve around caring and fairness, but around power and domination. In the worst cases, this could lead the young person into uncaring forms of aggression.

Arsenio's findings are from studies of disadvantaged children in the West. No doubt being poor in a wealthy country, where most of the population live in material comfort, is a different experience from being poor in a country such as India. Do disadvantaged children in India grow up resentful or cynical about their status in society? What are the effects of strong ties within their immediate and extended families as well as within their communities? Perhaps these strong, supportive environments provide children here with the experiences of moral sentiments such as fairness and compassion that they need for their own moral development.[1] There is too little research on this important

[1] One exciting study that may yield answers to these questions is the 'Young Lives' project, a fifteen-year longitudinal study being done in Ethiopia, Vietnam, Peru and India. The work in India began a few years ago in Andhra Pradesh, and involves 3000 young children from economically disadvantaged families. The aim is to understand the impact of social and political policy on young children living in difficult circumstances. You could keep track of their findings at their website, www.younglives.org.uk.

question of the effects of wider social patterns of injustice on children's moral development. One rich source of information is the work of psychologist and writer Robert Coles. Coles spent years getting to know children from various backgrounds, trying to deepen our understanding of moral development. Many of the children he spoke to were victims of poverty and social discrimination. His books are beautiful and moving, because they describe the moral strength of young children living under difficult circumstances. Coles repeatedly encounters children who are neither bitter nor resentful of other children better off than themselves, and tries to identify the reasons why.

One young Brazilian boy he writes about lives in a shack in the *favelas* (slums) with a clear view of wealthy seaside mansions. He begs, does odd jobs, washes the cars and polishes the shoes of wealthy Brazilians for a living. Coles describes how this boy and others like him, being fully aware of the inequities around them, nevertheless have a strong moral sense. They are clear that they will not wrong others, that they will care for each other, sacrifice for those less fortunate or more helpless than they.

These children have 'moral pride, a kind of self respect'. Of course, as Coles cautions, this is not universal: the young boy's neighbour for instance is described as 'mean-spirited, gossipy, altogether unpleasant'! And when Coles talks to children from richer homes, he finds the same variability. Some display 'substantial egoism, insistent self-importance, pushy selfishness', yet '...our well-to-do suburbs also offer rather spirited and ethically sensitive children'. What, Coles wonders, makes for these differences?

Ultimately, it is the way each child processes her social interactions that will determine her own moral sentiments. But holding values is one thing, and acting on them is another. What really matters is moral *behaviour*, and unfortunately, this is not easily predicted from moral knowledge or reasoning.

Moral Behaviour

As adults, we are frequently in situations that require us to make and carry out decisions that affect other people's welfare. Young people, too, frequently encounter such situations, and these can be quite confusing for them. A boy asks his classmate for help with homework during the break, when everyone else is playing cricket. Will he stay back and help? Two girls work jointly on a project, and the teacher gives credit for the best idea to the wrong one. Will this girl tell her teacher that it is her partner who really deserves the credit? A student who happens to be on the school environment task force sees some plastic littering the corridor—and there is no one else around. Will he take the trouble to throw it? A student finds that her teacher has given her five marks too many on a paper. Will she get it reduced?

The actions called for in the examples above fall under the general umbrella of 'responsible behaviour', one definition of which has been given by psychologists Carroll Izard, George Bear and their colleagues: the ability to make decisions concerning others' rights and welfare, and the ability to act according to those decisions. Several factors jointly influence whether a young person behaves responsibly in a given situation. Izard and Bear emphasize the importance of social, cognitive and emotional factors. First, she must be **aware of the need** to act in a certain way, or to inhibit a certain antisocial behaviour. This awareness comes from interpreting social cues, taking another's perspective, and feelings of empathy or sympathy. Second, she must **know what action** to take. This corresponds to the moral reasoning ability we have already examined in detail. Third, she must decide to **act in agreement** with her own moral reasoning, which she may very likely not do, after weighing the personal costs and benefits to herself!

Moral behaviour often conflicts with one's own desires, and this is where the problem lies. In a laboratory study with nine- to twelve-year-olds in America, Nancy Eisenberg found that the call to reasoning within oneself was more likely to happen when there was this sort of a moral conflict. Low-cost helping behaviour (such as picking up someone's fallen pens) came easily to them, and without the need for any kind of moral reasoning. However, high-cost helping (such as anonymously donating a share of one's earnings to a good cause) creates conflict with one's own needs and desires! This conflict is resolved by reasoning, and thus in Eisenberg's study such helping behaviour was more likely among those children who could reason in abstract, internalized terms. It appears that abstract reasoning can help children do what they 'should', even when they don't really feel like.

Eisenberg and her colleagues did another study in a more real-life setting, with ten- to fifteen-year-old middle class students in a Brazilian town. They asked the students to rate each of their peers on how helpful and generous they were, and correlated this data with a test of moral reasoning ability. The test consisted of several stories like the one below.

'One day Mary was going to a friend's party. On the way, she saw a girl who had fallen down and hurt her leg. The girl asked Mary to go to the girl's house and get her parents so the parents could come and take her to a doctor. But if Mary did run and get the girl's parents, Mary would be late to the party and miss the fun and social activities with her friends.'

The students were asked to rate the importance of several reasons why Mary should or should not help the girl, reasons which reflect different patterns of moral thinking. For example,

- It depends how much fun Mary expects the party to be (a **hedonistic** reason).
- It depends whether the girl really needs help or not (a **needs-oriented** reason).
- It depends whether Mary's parents and friends will think she did the right or the wrong thing (an **approval-oriented** reason).
- It depends if Mary thinks it's the decent thing to do (a **stereotypic** reason).
- It depends how Mary would feel about herself if she helped or not (an **internalized** reason).

The researchers found that those students who chose hedonistic or approval-oriented reasons were rated as less helpful and generous by their peers. Age was found to be a factor as well, in that older children more often chose the rather abstract internalized reason, and those who did tended to be the more helpful ones. Thus, the kind of reasoning children used *was* related to their behaviour among peers. But the correlation is not at all perfect; there were exceptions.

The difference between what one 'should' be doing and what one finally does was beautifully captured by Elliot Turiel in a study with primary school children. They were told that a boy had been given a 'dare' by his friends: he had *either* to wear his nightclothes to school, *or* steal an eraser, *or* hit a classmate. Then they were asked: what should he do? And what would he do? The children felt that the boy **should** choose the conventional transgression (wear pajamas to school) because you wouldn't be hurting others by doing so. Yet, when forced to choose which of the three the boy **would** do, most of them said he would make the minor (steal an eraser) or major (hit someone) moral transgression instead of the conventional transgression because of the fear of social disapproval. The distinction between what the boy *should* but *would* do was clear even for children as young as six years old.

As Bear and Izard say, the lack of consistency between what a young person 'knows' to be responsible behaviour and what he finally does is often explained away in excuses: 'I didn't cheat as much as the others', 'I was only playing around', 'She shouldn't have left her money lying outside,' and of course the famous, 'He started it!' On the other hand, certain powerful emotions can close that gap. Many young people report feeling guilt, shame or pride in connection with deciding on some responsible behaviour (eg., 'I couldn't live with myself if I didn't help him').

In Conclusion

While we want our students to internalize the 'right' principles, if we have any humility we also want them to be able to go beyond our values and develop their own moral sense. One way to accomplish this is to make time for frequent and open dialogue among students and teachers, in an environment of trust and affection. This guarantees nothing, of course! Yet it seems only right that young people be given the opportunity to challenge adults and be challenged in return, and most school environments make this difficult, if not impossible.

The other problem with many school environments is that they actively discourage the kind of moral behaviour that they supposedly desire. There are several examples of this: when a student helps another with homework, or (even worse) during a test, it becomes copying or cheating. If a student outranks her friend, the suitable emotion is triumph, not regret. One student's success in school is at the expense of others, but such achievement is praised by all. We are mostly unaware of the powerful effects of these systemic practices on young children's internalization of moral principles. Think of Damon's ten-year-olds. In their own discussions, the younger group member who did not produce as much but 'did his best' clearly deserved as many sweets as the others. We adults often violate that principle when we distribute 'sweets'! In our schools and classrooms, we generally reward *ability* rather than *effort*, and most systems outside school function in a similar way. If we believe that it is worthwhile to question these deeply rooted practices, again it seems that we need to engage our students in open dialogue about these issues. Here, we as teachers are not giving them our rules; rather, we are sharing the complexity of human life with them in the hope that they can truly go beyond us.

References and Bibliography

1. Arsenio, W.F., 2001. 'Moral Education and Domains in the Classroom'. *School Psychology Quarterly*, Vol. 17, No. 1, 100–07.

2. Arsenio, W.F. and J. Gold, 2006. 'The Effects of Social Injustice and Inequality on Children's Moral Judgements and Behaviour'. *Cognitive Development*, 21, 388–400.

3. Bear, G.G., M.A. Manning, and C.E. Izard, 2003. 'Responsible Behaviour: The Importance of Social Cognition and Emotion'. *School Psychology Quarterly*, Vol. 18, No. 2, 140–57.

4. Carlo, G., S.H. Koller, N. Eisenberg, M.S. Da Silva, and C.B. Frohlich, 1996. 'A Cross-National Study on the Relations Among Prosocial Moral Reasoning, Gender Role orientations and Prosocial Behaviors'. *Developmental Psychology*, Vol. 32, No. 2, 231–40.

5. Coles, R., 1986. *The Moral Life of Children*. Houghton Mifflin Company.

6. Damon, W., 1975. 'Early Conceptions of Positive Justice as Related to the Development of Logical Operations'. *Child Development*, 46, 301–12.

7. Eisenberg-Berg, N., and E. Geisheker, 1979. 'Content of Preachings and Power of the Model/Preacher: The Effect on Children's Generosity'. *Developmental Psychology*, Vol. 15, No. 2, 168–75.

8. Eisenberg, N., R. Shell, J. Pasternack, R. Lennon, R. Beller, and R.M. Mathy, 1987. 'Prosocial Development in Middle Childhood: a Longitudinal Study'. *Developmental Psychology*, Vol. 23, No. 5, 712–18.

9. Gibbs, J.C., and S.V. Schnell, 1985. 'Moral Development versus Socialisation: A Critique'. *American Psychologist*, Vol. 40, No. 10, 1071–80.

10. Grusec, J.E., and J.J. Goodnow, 1994. 'Impact of Parental Discipline Methods on the Child's Internalization of Values: A Reconceptualization of Current Points of View'. *Developmental Psychology*, Vol. 30, No. 1, 4–19.

11. Kochanska, G., 1994. 'Beyond Cognition: Expanding the Search for the Early Roots of Internalisation and Conscience'. *Developmental Psychology*, Vol. 30, No. 1, 20–22.

12. Shweder, R.A., M. Mahapatra, and J.G. Miller, 1987. 'Culture and Moral Development'. In Kagan, J., and S. Lamb (eds), *The Emergence of Morality in Young Children*. University of Chicago Press: Chicago.

13. Snarey, J.R., 1985. 'Cross Cultural Universality of Social-Moral Development: a Critical Review of Kohlbergian Research'. *Psychological Bulletin*, Vol. 97, No. 2, 202–32.

14. Tisak, M.S., and E. Turiel, 1988. 'Variation in Seriousness of Transgressions and Children's Moral and Conventional Concepts'. *Developmental Psychology*, Vol. 24, No. 3, 352–57.

15. Vasudev, J., and R.C. Hummel, 1987. 'Moral Stage Sequence and Principled Reasoning in an Indian Sample'. *Human Development*, 30, 105–18.

16. Zahn-Waxler, C., M. Radke-Yarrow, E. Wagner, and M. Chapman, 1992. 'Development of Concern for Others'. *Developmental Psychology*, Vol. 28, No. 1, 126–36.

CHAPTER SEVEN

Intelligence

In many psychology books, the chapter on intelligence begins with the question 'what is intelligence?', and readers are encouraged to come up with their own definitions. When I teach it, I ask my students to do a different exercise, which you may find instructive and interesting. Write down five questions or tasks to measure 'intelligence' (whatever it means to you) in a certain age group. You could choose six-year-olds, or thirteen-year-olds, for example.

Creating this mini intelligence test usually brings up some very important and revealing questions, and you are likely to face these as you go through the exercise.

Can I assume that:

- The children are all Indian?
- They are middle class?
- They are going to school and can read and write?

- How can I make my test reflect ability rather than knowledge?
- Does my test have to be difficult enough so only very few of the children can answer correctly? Or, should it be easy enough so only very few will be *unable* to answer?
- How can a one-time test measure intelligence, which is expressed in the way one lives and adapts to one's environment in the broadest possible sense?

These questions tell us all we need to know about the issues psychologists face in measuring intelligence. To be a reasonably good measure of something as universal as intelligence, the test has to be applicable in any culture, must not discriminate against any class of society, and cannot depend on literacy. It is very difficult to make tests that fulfil these conditions. And if we believe that intelligence is a matter of ability rather than experience, we are soon frustrated, because it is almost impossible to make a test that is completely free of experience. Most questions reduce to tests of knowledge or learned skills. Difficulty levels reflect our own ideology and purpose in testing intelligence—if we want to identify students who have particular problems, we will ask easy questions, but if we believe that intelligence is something that only a few people possess, we will ask hard ones. And finally, we may resist the idea of measuring at all something which is expressed only in the way one adapts to the demands of the environment, not in the way one answers set questions.

For all these reasons, the topic of intelligence testing has remained one of the most controversial and interesting areas of research in psychology. In 1994, a book called *The Bell Curve* was published for the lay public. It made several claims about intelligence, all centred around the shape of the distribution of IQ scores in the general population. This distribution is bell-shaped, with most people scoring around average, and fewer and fewer scoring at the extremes. The bell curve is by itself a common and inoffensive fact of life for many variables (adult height, for instance). But the book offended because it went so far as to claim that IQ is a *stronger explanation for poverty than environmental factors*. You will not be surprised to learn that immediately following its publication, the media and several leading scientists ripped the book apart. For example, writer and scientist Stephen J. Gould wrote, 'For many readers the graphs and charts of *The Bell Curve* confirm a dark suspicion: the ills of welfare, poverty, and an underclass are less matters of justice than biology.' Most criticisms of the book were based on the fact that correlation does not imply causation. That is, simply discovering that social class and IQ scores are correlated does not tell us that intelligence *causes* poverty. Of course, neither does it tell us that poverty causes low IQ. But the critics took pains to explain the following points:

- IQ tests may not measure what most people think of as intelligence;
- what IQ tests measure is only a small part of the array of traits that are important for success in life;
- *both* genes and the environment influence IQ score differences;
- poor children grow up in deprived environments, which can lead to low IQ scores.

Even before the dust could settle, in December 1994, the *Wall Street Journal* published an article about intelligence signed by 52 leading scientists. It was an attempt to 'set the record straight' about what the scientific status of intelligence research really is. And among several other points, it stated clearly that:

- IQ tests *do* measure what most people think of as intelligence;

- what IQ tests measure *is* of 'great practical and social importance';[1]
- genetics plays *an equal or bigger* role compared to the environment in creating IQ differences among people;
- we do not yet know how to manipulate environments to raise low IQs permanently.

The author of the article, psychologist Linda Gottfredson, contacted a total of 100 experts on intelligence research: 52 signed and 48 declined. What reasons might a scientist have for not endorsing a statement like the above? One could be genuine disagreement about the nature and measurement of intelligence. Another could be discomfort with the lack of tentativeness in the article. But, one strong reason has more to do with moral principles than with science. Is it responsible to make claims about intelligence that might lead to large sections of society being further discriminated against, never to get their fair chance of making a success of life?

It is a fact that ideas such as those expressed in *The Bell Curve* provide fuel for social movements such as eugenics. The eugenics movement, which is over a hundred years old, seeks to control human reproduction in such a way as to 'improve' the average intelligence of a population. Their policies would include forced sterilization of anyone believed to be carrying the genes for 'low IQ', or paying such people not to have children, while encouraging others to have more children. It sounds barbaric and straight from the Dark Ages, but sadly, these ideas are alive even today. Naturally, eugenicists welcome any evidence that gives their plans and dreams scientific backing. This includes evidence

---

[1] This statement was made with reference to Western society, and no claim was made in the article regarding countries and cultures outside the U.S.A.

about the genetic nature of IQ and its importance in determining success in life. Even if the scientific basis for eugenics were true, I doubt very much that a world peopled solely by human beings with high IQ would be a just and compassionate one. But in any case, the questions are by no means settled, nor do they show any signs of resolution.

It is interesting that these issues have not raised much dust here in India. Perhaps this is because it is crystal clear to us that poverty implies *severely* reduced opportunities. Any talk of low IQ scores *causing* poverty can be investigated only after we have given everyone equal opportunities to begin with (in the form of prenatal care, infant care, home environment, preschool and school quality, for example), and we are a long way from that. This does not deny, of course, that many people in India have perhaps unconscious yet deeply held images about their fellow human beings from the lower classes. For instance, teachers of poor children may have lower academic expectations for them, and may never have realized or examined their reasons for these low expectations. It is just that statements of the kind made in *The Bell Curve* are rarely to be seen in the mainstream.

But we should become aware of these debates, as they may gain volume here before too long. Already the IQ test is used more and more widely in India as a 'straightforward' measure of intelligence. Of course, there are defensible uses of the IQ test, but many parents and teachers tend to think that 'IQ score equals intelligence'. This assumption, and the consequences that follow from it, can and must be replaced by a more tentative and subtle equation. In the next two sections, we will look separately at the definition and measurement of intelligence, even though these two are closely tied. Along the way, I will describe some serious alternative views of intelligence.

Box 1

THE INTELLIGENCE QUOTIENT TEST

Only a licensed person (a psychiatrist or a school psychologist, for example) is authorized to own and administer an official IQ test. Many amateurs make up their own tests and 'publish' these on the internet, but these should be considered only for their entertainment value. There is quite a fascination for IQ tests in the general public, and I think it is because tests like this tap into our love to be measured and described! But, for a young child and her parents, the stakes are considerably higher than mere entertainment. In India, psychologists use IQ tests on children referred to them for reasons such as suspected learning disabilities, hyperactivity, emotional disturbance, and just about anything preventing a streamlined progression through the school curriculum.

We have been using primarily the same two IQ tests (only slightly modified over the years!) for about a century now—the Stanford-Binet and the Wechsler. These established tests are well-constructed, and when administered by a trained psychologist, will give fairly reliable results. The score is calculated based on the average performance of large groups of children at different ages:

$$IQ = \frac{\text{Mental age (age of children who score the same as the student)}}{\text{Chronological age (age of student in years)}} \times 100$$

A score of 100 denotes 'average' intelligence, because it means that the student has performed as well as others of her age. About two-thirds of the population scores roughly between 85 and 115. The traditional cut off for mental retardation has been 70. All these numbers may seem very reassuring and informative, but as teachers, we must be careful in interpreting the results of an IQ test. Here are some important points to keep in mind about a child's IQ score.

- It is not a number representing a fixed property of the child (unlike her blood group or thumbprint).
- The number may reflect any or all of the following: an ability to solve closed-ended problems requiring verbal/logical/spatial reasoning and memory, the motivation to perform one's best during the two hours of testing, anxiety about the unfamiliar situation and the reasons for being tested, a compliant (obedient) personality.
- There is a certain error of measurement (as in all measuring instruments: see chapter nine), which means that you should not look at the number as precise or exact in any sense.

Defining Intelligence

The *Wall Street Journal* article described in the previous section gave this description of intelligence:

> '...a very general mental capability that, among other things, involves the ability to reason, plan, solve problems, think abstractly, comprehend complex ideas, learn quickly and learn from experience. It is not merely book learning, a narrow academic skill, or test-taking smarts. Rather, it reflects a broader and deeper capability for comprehending our surroundings—"catching on", "making sense" of things, or "figuring out" what to do.'

Although this 'official' definition seems broad enough to please nearly everyone, we need to examine prevailing views of intelligence among teachers, parents and society in general, since these tend to be narrower. There is a widespread preoccupation, in India and elsewhere too, with the concept of intelligence. In our country, advertisements for breakfast cereals and hot drinks routinely promise more 'brain *shakti*'! And the kind of 'brain power' we seek, as a society, is rather narrow—that which allows a child to perform well in academic tasks at school.

It is not as if we value nothing else—we worship sports icons, musicians, dancers, writers and other people with special talents. But the difference is that we readily accept the notion that these talents are not evenly distributed among us all. For example, a non-musical or non-athletic child does not generally pose a problem, to herself or to her family. It doesn't matter if the child can't sing, or can't run fast. But if she can't do well at school, the pressure is immediately on.

Would you *define* intelligence as the ability to do well in school? Probably not; but we do equate the two often enough. In fact, in India we tend to equate intelligence with being good at mathematics and science rather than language and the humanities. That is an inexcusably narrow definition. Each of us will define intelligence in our own way, but some things that most people include in their definition are logical reasoning, analytical thinking and creative problem solving. Some people will also add memory and speed of processing information. In psychological research, definitions range from the more fundamental (neurological efficiency) to higher-order (knowledge of thinking and reflective self-guidance) to context-dependent (the match between a person's talents and the talents valued by their society).

An important aspect of defining intelligence is whether it is 'one thing' or 'many things'. Those who have claimed it is one thing call that g or the general factor, and their position is backed by data showing correlations among different types of tasks on an IQ test. So that means if you are good at one you are good at all, because g is something that influences all abilities, and you just have more of it. One early psychologist (Charles Spearman in 1914) called g a 'general fund of mental energy'. Theories that look at intelligence as neurological efficiency (e.g., speed of processing, sensory discrimination) would endorse the g factor, because according to them, there is something in the wiring of the brain itself that makes people more or less intelligent.

Obviously, such a factor would affect abilities across the board. But the evidence for the presence of g is not very strong— people's scores on the different subtests of an IQ test are only moderately correlated. There are many who look at intelligence as **multidimensional**, having several different aspects to it, and the different dimensions may not even be correlated with each other. The psychologists Howard Gardner and Robert Sternberg fall into this latter group.

Gardner points out that 'school-type intelligence' is valued in society above all other talents. Giving such disproportionate importance to one ability, which surely varies in the population, inevitably causes problems. To understand his position, imagine a world where the only people who 'succeeded' in life were those who could excel at track and field events. It paints a bleak picture indeed for many of us, struggling and failing throughout childhood, higher education and job seeking...and on the other hand, some of us would suddenly be assured of a rosy future! Similar things happen when we make school-type intelligence the most highly

'I've got a 2 GB RAM, you know.'

valued. Gardner's response to this is to redefine intelligence as being of several different types—corresponding loosely, as you can see below, with abilities that we might otherwise call talents. According to his **multiple intelligences** theory, we all have different levels of the different intelligences—thus, each person has a 'profile' of strengths and weaknesses, and education must strive to nurture all these proportionately.

Howard Gardner's seven intelligences
1. Linguistic (e.g., grasping new meaning quickly).
2. Musical (e.g., sensitive to pitch).
3. Logical-mathematical (e.g., abstract reasoning).
4. Spatial (e.g., mental transformation of seen objects).
5. Bodily-kinesthetic (e.g., graceful or athletic actions).
6. Personal (e.g., understanding one's motives).
7. Social (e.g., understanding the feelings of others).

This redefinition can, in principle, be extended to more intelligences if we wish. After all, there is no strong biological basis for coming up with this initial set of seven.[2] Recently, Gardner has added two more to his list—naturalist and spiritual intelligences. This illustrates an important point. *The answer to the question 'what is intelligence?' may be more of a decision than a discovery.* And in that sense, any theory of intelligence must be evaluated

---

[2] There are multidimensional theories of intelligence that do have a biological basis, and these are the **mental module** theories. Evolutionary psychologists Leda Cosmides and John Tooby tell us that humans evolved several separate modules that enable us to learn language, recognize faces, understand others' intentions, and so on. Possibly another module in the brain helps us deal with novel situations through thinking and reasoning—and this could represent the *g* factor. Each of these modules, it is proposed, is a separate kind of intelligence, and humans differ from one another on these abilities. Importantly, neuroscience research has located some of the different modules in specific brain areas, which may give some biological backing to the theory.

in terms of its usefulness in describing behaviour, rather than its 'truth' value. If Gardner's theory of multiple intelligences makes us more sensitive to children's differing strengths in many areas of ability, if it encourages us to widen the scope of education to include

Adaptive Intelligence

these many areas, and if it further provokes a questioning of society's values, it's a good theory in my book. Other theories of intelligence can also be evaluated from this point of view.

Robert Sternberg, an active thinker in the field, offers a different definition. First, he says intelligence is something that applies in any context. We cannot isolate school performance as the only place where intelligence will show—a person surviving on the streets, or in a jungle, also uses his intelligence and displays intelligent behaviour. Second, intelligence is the mental ability required to adapt to or shape the context we are in. So it is not only the ability to perform well on an IQ test, but also the ability to find your way around in the jungle, or to keep one step ahead of trouble on the streets. And third, he says that intelligence represents those mental abilities that are *necessary* for survival, not just useful or desirable. In this respect, some of Gardner's intelligences don't meet Sternberg's criteria for intelligence.

So, in Sternberg's **triarchic** theory there are three kinds of intelligence: analytical, creative and practical. He and his colleagues have conducted a wealth of research, in countries as far flung as India, Russia, Tanzania and the US, showing that these three intelligences are distinct from each other, and yet all correlate with success in real-life situations. The first of the three, analytical intelligence, is the only one that we generally consider the whole of intelligence. This is too narrow a definition, and Sternberg claims that those low in analytical intelligence, but high in creative and/or practical intelligence, do also excel when given the right environment. Too often, he says, such people are lost by the wayside because they did not perform well on measures of analytical intelligence, which is the only kind we seem to value in school.

Here are some examples from Sternberg's tests (I have modified some to suit Indian conditions).

Analytical intelligence:
1. Write the next number in the series: –4, –3, –1, 3, 11, 27
2. Choose the best meaning for the word 'jids' in the following paragraph:

   'Any business that ignores its regular clientele, in order to concentrate on new jids, may discover that sales do not increase. The new interest generated may not be enough to compensate for the loss in sales caused by dissatisfied patrons who begin to shop elsewhere.'

   Jid most likely means:
   a) product
   b) customer
   c) advertisement
   d) investment

Creative intelligence:
1. There is a new mathematical operation called graf. It is defined as follows.

   x graf y = x + y, if x < y

   but otherwise, x graf y = -x -y

   How much is 4 graf 7?

   How much is 7 graf 7?

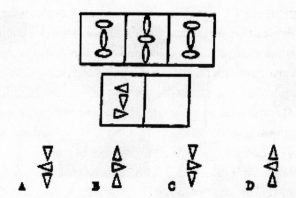

2. Looking at the first sequence, complete the second sequence with one of the given choices.

Practical intelligence:

1. Your friend has not been doing her homework for weeks, even though you keep telling her it is for her own good. Recently, she has started copying your answers at the last minute. If you want to help your friend, yet, if possible, avoid her getting into trouble with the teacher and her extremely strict parents, what is the *best* solution?

    a. Ask your parents for advice, since they are friends with her family.

    b. Suggest that your friend explain everything to the teacher and ask for help.

    c. Tell the teacher what is going on, and request her not to take disciplinary action against your friend.

2. Use the map below to answer the question:

You are walking from the cell phone shop to the shoe store. Your friend is walking from the horoscopes stall to the ice cream shop. Which of these places are you *both* likely to pass?

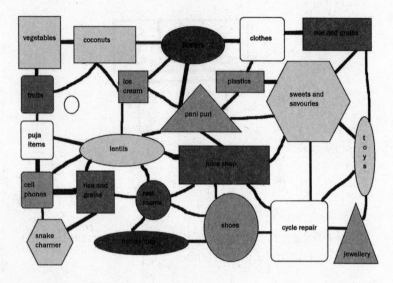

a. rice and grains
b. rest rooms
c. snake charmer
d. lentils

There are numerous examples of interesting studies on the practical intelligence of people in different walks of life, from horse racing bookies to psychology professors to Brazilian street vendors. These studies all demonstrate that practical intelligence is largely unrelated to academic intelligence. Robert Sternberg describes the result of a study of workers at a milk processing plant. 'Workers who assemble orders for cases of various quantities (e.g., gallons, quarts, or pints) and products (e.g., whole milk, two per cent milk, or buttermilk) are called assemblers...experienced assemblers used complex strategies for combining partially filled cases in a manner that minimized the number of moves required to complete an order. Although the assemblers were the least educated workers in the plant, they were able to calculate in their heads quantities expressed in different base number systems, and

Box 2

PRACTICAL INTELLIGENCE, TACIT KNOWLEDGE

Once, a psychologist was hired to administer IQ tests to the children in a school for the mentally challenged. When he arrived, he found the students had managed to outwit school staff and had run away, in spite of elaborate security in the place. When the children were finally rounded up, the psychologist began to administer the Maze Test, a paper and pencil test where you have to find your way out of mazes. None of the students who had escaped the authorities were able to find their way out of the mazes in the test.

This is a true story, and it illustrates a mismatch between what psychologists call practical intelligence and traditional paper-and-pencil tests of intelligence. The table illustrates the differences between such tests and the demands of the real world.

Academic tests of intelligence contain problems which...	*Real-world tests of practical intelligence contain problems which...*
1. have all the required information available from the start;	1. do not have all the required information available at the start;
2. are usually well defined;	2. are not well defined;
3. are not of personal interest;	3. are of personal relevance
4. are detached from everyday experience;	4. are related to everyday experience;
5. have only one correct solution.	5. have many solutions each with its advantages and disadvantages.

they routinely outperformed the more highly educated white collar workers who substituted when assemblers were absent... the order-filling performance of the assemblers was unrelated to measures of school performance, including intelligence test scores, arithmetic test scores, and grades.'

Sternberg also talks of *successful* intelligence, which is the ability to capitalize on one's strengths and compensate for one's weaknesses. In this view, intelligence is what helps us be successful in life. But we cannot disregard the abilities tapped by traditional IQ tests—analytical, logical, verbal abilities. As Sternberg says, by *supplementing* existing traditional tests with measures of practical intelligence, rather than *replacing* them, we will gain a fuller account of intelligence than with either alone.

Gardner's and Sternberg's definitions of intelligence are liberating. Schools that adopt definitions like these would change their curricula to encourage different abilities, as well as practical and creative intelligence. But as long as society as a whole maintains narrow ideas about intelligence, students from such schools will have to 'swim against the current', in a sense. Nowadays, too many interesting, worthwhile and challenging vocations are given little or no respect in our society (teaching is a prime example!).

If psychologists waited to settle issues of definition before turning to measurement, they would wait forever. So, there have been many attempts at measuring this hard-to-define quality over the past 100 years and more, and we turn to these now.

Measurement of Intelligence

Obviously, the way you define intelligence influences the way you measure it. Darwin's cousin, Francis Galton, at the turn of the previous century, believed that intelligence was an inherited property of the brain, a matter of neural efficiency, and as such could be measured using reaction time and sensory discrimination tasks. He set up a stall at a public fair in England offering to test thousands of visitors for a small fee. Unfortunately for him, the data he collected showed that people with quick reaction times or fine discrimination power were not those who were successful in life! So he had to give up on the idea. Over the years, there have been several tests of intelligence based on different definitions. Here are a few examples.

- Those who look at intelligence as the 'ability to learn' suggest the use of *dynamic* tests of it. Dynamic tests measure the process of learning in the test itself, rather than treat the test as a measure of past learning alone. If you answer a question correctly, you move on; if not, you are given guided feedback to help answer. The amount and type of feedback given, as well as progress made, go into the measure of intelligence.

- Gardner and his colleagues have devised tests of the intelligences, based on a system of observational checklists of behaviours, projects and portfolios. For example, athletic movement (power, agility, speed and balance) is assessed as part of kinaesthetic intelligence. These are not yet standardized and widely available.

- There is also the Sternberg Triarchic Abilities Test of analytical, creative and practical intelligence, using multiple choice as well as essay-type items (examples were given earlier). The test has given promising results in different cultures, but is not yet widely used.

- In spite of the variety of theories and tests out there, by far the most commonly used test of intelligence is the IQ test, and it has been so for more than a hundred years. Two IQ tests are used most often: the Stanford-Binet and the Wechsler. They include several subtests, ranging from vocabulary, memory and processing speed, to logical reasoning and spatial puzzles. A good look at the subtests of any IQ test (see table) will tell you how the author of that test defines intelligence.

SUBTESTS ON THE WECHSLER ADULT INTELLIGENCE SCALE

1. Information ('What is steam made of?').
2. Digit span (short-term memory).
3. Vocabulary.
4. Arithmetic.
5. Comprehension ('How do insurance companies make a profit?').
6. Similarities ('In what way are books and television alike?').
7. Picture completion.
8. Picture arrangement (arrange picture cards to tell a story).
9. Block design (assembling coloured blocks to make patterns).
10. Object assembly (jigsaw puzzles).
11. Digit symbol (speeded code substitution).

Individual Differences in Intelligence

There are individual differences in academic abilities among students of the same age. It should not be surprising or disturbing that this is the case; individual differences are found in every single human characteristic and ability. Variety is the norm in nature. But in the case of school-related ability, as we have seen, this variety is not accepted as matter-of-factly as, say, variety in athletic ability. Society and the family place a heavy demand on children to measure up to high standards of school performance, and those who meet these standards are considered more intelligent than those who do not.

Unfortunately, with the lack of consensus on what constitutes intelligence, and therefore how to measure it, any statement about differences becomes questionable as well. Historically, in the US, immigrants from some countries were denied access, because it was believed that their intelligence was inferior to that of immigrants from other countries. The accepted measure of intelligence at that time was a version of today's IQ test, and it contained several questions dependent on a familiarity with American culture and ways of life. If one racial or ethnic group performed worse on the test than another, the reasons were not necessarily, or only, to do with 'intelligence', but with literacy, schooling and familiarity with mainstream culture. Thus, important decisions about people's lives were made on totally wrong bases. Unless you wish to define intelligence as familiarity with mainstream culture, the tests were not measuring true differences among people.

We can never be entirely certain that a given intelligence test is equally fair on any two children. As a simple example, Zambian and English children were asked to reproduce some patterns in three different media—wire models, clay models and paper-and-pencil. The Zambian children did better in wire, the English children did better on paper, and both groups did equally well in clay. If the test had been administered only as a paper-and-pencil measure, we would wrongly conclude that 'Zambian children are less able to reproduce patterns.'

We rarely question the 'invisibles' of the testing process: the language medium of the test, the materials used, the values it embodies, the motivation required to complete it, and the qualities of the examiner. These may contribute substantially to a child's final score, but are usually ignored.

Differences in IQ scores can also be found between groups of people separated in time. Some years ago, a political scientist named James Flynn gathered a great deal of evidence from countries around the world, showing that average IQ scores had increased by 5 to 25 points in a single generation (over roughly thirty years in the mid-1900s). Flynn went on to speculate on what this striking finding really meant. He concluded that IQ tests do not measure intelligence, but something else which correlates only weakly with intelligence. One of his arguments was that such a widespread and significant increase in intelligence levels 'should be highly visible...The result should be a cultural renaissance too great to be overlooked...(but there has been) not a single reference to a dramatic increase in genius or mathematical and scientific discovery during the present generation; no one has remarked on the superiority of contemporary schoolchildren.' In France for instance, where scores went up by 15 to 20 points, Flynn found that the number of patents granted for inventions has actually diminished over the years!

These examples suggest that we are not quite ready to answer questions about the *causes* of differing intelligence levels. Psychologists do, of course, study the relative influence of nature and nurture on IQ test scores, but, as we have seen, this assumes just one answer to the question of what intelligence really is. And then there is the question of teaching intelligence: whether it can be done and to what extent.

At this point, we may feel like someone who started building a house on a flimsy foundation, and is trying to make it to a third floor. If our definitions of intelligence are uncertain, and the cause and nature of individual differences in intelligence is uncertain, what statements can possibly be made with *any* certainty about methods of increasing intelligence?

Educating for Intelligent Behaviour

In the chapter on learning, you encountered the psychologist David Perkins in a section on context-dependent reasoning. Perkins' view of intelligence comes from the understanding that intelligent behaviour is always shown in a context or a domain of knowledge. For him and many other psychologists, intelligence is not an isolated skill. One can look at an economist or a microbiologist and observe any number of signs of intelligence in their behaviour, and we very easily label such people 'intelligent'. But it might be useful for us as educators to distinguish between an expert and an **intelligent novice**. An intelligent novice, as described by psychologist John Bruer, is someone who, when confronted with a new problem or a new field of enquiry, applies her prior learning to the new situation in a flexible way, uses general strategies such as analogy or means-end analysis, and monitors her own approach and progress in learning. She must have three capacities, all of which Bruer believes can be built through education:

- Domain-specific knowledge: a solid foundation of conceptual and procedural knowledge in at least one domain;
- An ability to make these skills more general: understanding of when and how to apply the knowledge and strategies to new situations—in Bruer's words, how to 'stretch it to pose and answer novel problems';
- Metacognitive skills: the ability to think about thinking, and to monitor and control her own mental processing.

Another way to see the difference between an expert and an intelligent novice is by using this hypothetical question, posed by Perkins and a colleague, Gavriel Salomon, in 1989. Suppose a small, peace-loving country is under threat from a large, aggressive neighbour. The small country has no experience in war strategy whatsoever, but it does have the world's reigning champion chess player. So the leader asks the chess champion to use his superior reasoning skills to help them outwit their enemy. Will it work—is a great chess player just generally intelligent, or is his intelligence restricted to the domain of chess?

From one point of view, training the mind in chess could give a person the capacity to handle real-life military strategy, since any mental training exercises the brain and improves its general capacities. This idea was once popular among psychologists, but around the mid-1970s, research in cognition swung the pendulum the other way. The prevailing view became that expertise in a particular domain will result in intelligent behaviour *only* in that domain, or at best, in domains that share almost all elements with the original one. In other words, the chess champion will not be able to do much to save his country, although if he were sent off to compete in an international checkers competition, he would do extremely well.

An example of the research that triggered this view is the famous study done many years ago by William Chase and Herbert Simon on chess experts and novices. The experimenters laid out 25 pieces on a chess board either in random positions, or according to actual possible game scenarios, and then asked people to reproduce those boards from memory. The experts had a far superior memory of actual game board placements, recalling almost all positions correctly (not surprising) but with random placements they were able to recall the positions of only about six pieces. The novices on the other hand recalled about six positions in either condition! Thus, being an expert in a domain had nothing to do with better memorization strategies *in general*.

In a minor way, our students are often like the chess champion. They have learned how to analyze a piece of text in an English class, but they won't automatically do it in a history class. They have mastered the skill of drawing graphs in a mathematics class, but they won't automatically use those skills in a science class. It simply doesn't occur to them to do so. This is called the problem of 'transfer', and for years psychologists have researched the question of whether learning can be transferred from one context to another. Otherwise, of what use is the learning? Although initial results seemed to show that transfer does not happen, in the 1980s, psychologists began to discover that there are conditions under which students *do* transfer skills and strategies to new domains: in other words, become intelligent novices.

First, they established something we have all experienced: that there are students for whom this happens effortlessly, spontaneously. You could say that some students are naturally intelligent novices. They seem able to bring their knowledge to bear in new situations, they ask useful questions, and the interesting thing you notice is that they *learn* quickly in a wide variety of contexts. We need not, however, end on the note that some students can, and some cannot. For example, I have heard that while some people are naturally great golfers, there are also programmes of training that make the skills of golf strokes quite explicit. Such training might not produce a Tiger Woods, but it certainly can develop competent golfers. As Bruer says, we are not *explicit* enough in teaching our students simple strategies, such as how to read for understanding. And psychologists have shown that such explicit training does improve students' use of strategies in new situations. Similarly, they have found that although some students naturally develop good metacognitive skills, these too can be trained explicitly.

Psychologist Scott Paris and his colleagues developed a programme in the 1980s called Informed Strategies for Learning, whose main intent was to make essential reading and metacognitive skills explicit for students. In their words, the programme would 'illustrate strategies concretely and show children the effort required and the benefits derived from their use'. Habits and assumptions of reading were also highlighted explicitly, and students were shown how some strategies are effective and some are not. For example, they were taught that the main goal of reading is to understand the meaning, not to read quickly without mistakes. Skimming is a quick way of finding out what the text is about, and it is not the practice of reading the short words and leaving out the long words. During reading, just as while solving a puzzle, you need to stop in the middle to see if you are understanding what you read. The psychologists also used traffic sign analogies to make the strategies more memorable. For instance, STOP meant to think and say it in your own words. SPEED LIMIT meant to adjust the speed of reading to the difficulty level of the text. DEAD END meant to go back and reread parts not understood well. CURVES meant to skip the hard parts, which was a bad strategy, and one that was to be avoided!

For teaching metacognition, we must make students *become their own critics*. If you correct your students' work in front of them, making explicit the criteria you use by thinking aloud, then the next step can be for them to correct their own work in front of you. Gradually, they internalize the process of self-correction. In a classroom, thinking aloud and commenting on each others' thinking is very useful for making metacognitive strategies explicit.

Although these suggestions may seem narrow in scope (related to academic school tasks only) Bruer says that the mastery of the 'enabling' or 'tool' domains of reading, writing, mathematics and science will bring about high-order cognitive skills in all our students. Armed with these, they can tackle advanced learning in specialized areas more effectively—be intelligent novices! In order for this to work, we must be as aware of *how* we teach as *what* we teach. In the Indian context, we must remember that **a syllabus is only a part of a curriculum** that includes methods, approaches, emphases and attitudes. Our aim must include the teaching of high-order skills to our students, and not be limited to the transmission of knowledge and facts.

On a different note, I must mention here that there have been attempts to **boost IQ scores** specifically. Here the goal is more straightforward, if quite narrow, and the outcomes easily measurable. Most such attempts, such as the Headstart programme in the US, look for increases in IQ test scores (the IQ = intelligence equation again!). They concentrate on the early childhood or preschool age group, and extend over a few years. Their results are typically small gains in IQ scores, which often do not last beyond a few years after the programme. But, by far the most successful programme in raising IQ levels has always been—hold your breath—*regular schooling*.

Research shows clearly that children who spend more time in school have higher IQs, at a modest rate of about two IQ points a year. Now, you might suspect that the relationship is in the other direction—that the higher one's IQ, the longer one is likely to spend in school. But, the research has been able to determine that schooling *causes* the increase in IQ, or to be more precise, prevents its decline. This should not be surprising, since IQ tests are so closely tied to academic skills. Stephen Ceci, a psychologist with a deep interest in intelligence and schooling, has reviewed a large body of literature on the relationship between the two. He finds that starting school late, or dropping out early, lead to declines in IQ. One such study reported that South African Indian children who started school later than their peers in similar villages (because a teacher was unfortunately not available for up to four years) lost an average of five IQ points for every year of delayed schooling. One of his more curious findings is that IQ scores decline slightly during the long summer holidays—something I've often suspected about myself, actually!

Ceci reports that **school quality is not a factor** in this relationship, but his results are primarily from Europe and the U.S. Simply going to school for several years, even if it is of low quality, will help boost IQ. But, the schooling–IQ relationship has not been replicated in India. The quality of education children receive here varies dramatically, and can be extremely poor. Many Indian educational experts say that we need to move from increasing enrolment and retention in our schools to improving quality. It is quite likely that thousands of children in state schools here are gaining next to nothing from the hours they spend in school.

In Conclusion

The research summarized here certainly encourages us to broaden our view of intelligence. But, more important than that, it leads us to question the strong link society has made between a particular definition of intelligence (as measured by the IQ test) and the 'worth' or value of a human being. It is true that whatever the IQ test measures is an interesting aspect of human ability. In today's world, that ability is very important in school and higher education, and fairly important in the real world, depending on one's vocation. Gottfredson suggests that IQ is more important in complex life settings, where there is novelty, unpredictability and ambiguity; and less important in life settings which call for simple problem solving.

Conventional, distorted ideas of intelligence in various social settings can only be changed when we begin to value each and every person for the skills they have worked on. Everyone can make a contribution to society, and every contribution is valuable. We have moved very far away from this basic truth. Recently a student told me, 'My mother, she can't do math and stuff like that, but she knows how to manage anything, she can *really* get things done'. And a highly educated gentleman told me on the phone some months ago, 'My granddaughter has just finished her tenth standard. Unfortunately, she is not so good at mathematics and science, but...' and he proceeded to tell me all the wonderful things she *does* do, which included a passion for the fine arts and learning several languages!

In the next chapter, we look at the all-important question of motivation in school learning. Interestingly, that chapter ends with a story of how a student's understanding of intelligence can affect his or her motivation for challenging work.

References and Bibliography

1. Brody, N., 1997. 'Intelligence, Schooling and Society'. *American Psychologist*, Vol. 52, No. 10, 1046–50.

2. Bruer, J.T., 1995. *Schools for Thought*. MIT Press: Cambridge, Massachusetts.

3. Ceci, S.J., 1990. *On Intelligence—More or Less: a Bio-ecological Treatise on Intellectual Development*. Prentice Hall: New Jersey.

4. Ceci, S.J., and W.M. Williams, 1997. 'Schooling, Intelligence and Income'. *American Psychologist*, Vol. 52, No. 10, 1051–58.

5. Chase, W.G., and H.A. Simon, 1973. 'Perception in Chess'. *Cognitive Psychology*, 4, 55–81.

6. Flynn, J.R., 1987. 'Massive IQ Gains in 14 Nations: What IQ Tests Really Measure'. *Psychological Bulletin*, Vol. 101, No. 2, 171–91.

7. Gardner, H., 1983. *Frames of Mind: The Theory of Multiple Intelligences*. Basic Books: New York.

8. Ibid., 2003. 'Multiple Intelligences After Twenty Years'. Paper presented at the American Educational Research Association, Chicago, Illinois, April 21, 2003.

9. Gottfredson, L.S., 1997. 'Foreword to "Intelligence and Social Policy"'. *Intelligence*, 24(1), 1–12.

10. Ibid., 1997. 'Editorial: Mainstream Science on Intelligence'. *Intelligence*, 24(1), 13–23. Reprinted with permission from the Wall Street Journal, December 13, 1994.

11. Gould, S.J., 1994. 'Curveball'. *The New Yorker*, November 28, 1994.

12. Greenfield, P.M., 1997. 'You Can't Take It With You: Why Ability Assessments Don't Cross Cultures'. *American Psychologist*, Vol. 52, No. 10, 1115–24.

13. Kanazawa, S., 2004. 'General Intelligence as a Domain-Specific Adaptation'. *Psychological Review*, Vol. 111, No. 2, 512–23.

14. Murray, C., and R. Herrnstein, 1994. *The Bell Curve*. New York, NY: The Free Press.

15. Neisser, U., G. Boodoo, T. J. Bouchard, A.W. Boykin, N. Brody, S.J. Ceci, D.F. Halpern, J.C. Loehlin, R. Perloff, R.J. Sternberg, and S. Urbina, 1996. 'Intelligence: Knowns and Unknowns'. *American Psychologist*, Vol. 51, No. 2, 77–101.

16. Paris, S.G., D.R. Cross, and M.Y. Lipson, 1984. 'Informed Strategies for Learning: A Program to Improve Children's Reading Awareness and Comprehension'. *Journal of Educational Psychology*, Vol. 76, No. 6, 1239–52.

17. Perkins, D.N., and G. Salomon, 1989. 'Are Cognitive Skills Context-Bound?' *Educational Researcher*, 18, 16–25.

18. Perkins, D.N., and T.A. Grotzer, 1997. 'Teaching Intelligence'. *American Psychologist*, Vol. 52, No. 10, 1125–33.

19. Sternberg, R.J., R.K. Wagner, W.M. Williams, and J.A. Horvath, 1995. 'Testing Common Sense'. *American Psychologist*, Vol. 50, No. 11, 912–27.

20. Sternberg, R.J., 1997. 'Intelligence and Lifelong Learning: What's New and How Can We Use It?' *American Psychologist*, Vol. 52, No. 10, 1134–39.

21. Ibid., 2003. 'A Broad View of Intelligence: the Theory of Successful Intelligence'. *Consulting Psychology Journal: Practice and Research*, Vol. 55, No. 3, 139–54.

22. Ibid., 2004. 'Why Smart People Can Be So Foolish'. *European Psychologist*, Vol. 9, No. 3, 145–50.

23. Ibid., 2004. 'Culture and Intelligence'. *American Psychologist*, Vol. 59, No. 5, 325–38.

CHAPTER EIGHT

Motivation

What makes us do the things we do? What motivates us to begin an activity, and keep it up until some goal is achieved, sometimes even in the face of great difficulty? The answer to this question can vary from person to person, and from situation to situation. But, there is a universal aspect to motivation as well, since all human beings have the capacity to be motivated. It is important to keep in mind that: when we say someone is 'unmotivated', it is probably because he is not doing the things *we* want him to do. As teachers, we know that if our students are motivated to learn, our work becomes a pleasure. When motivation for school work is lacking, all our teaching efforts seem to disappear into a black hole, leading ultimately to frustration. Thus, an extremely important question is: how do I motivate my students to learn?

Psychologists have traditionally talked about two kinds of motivation: intrinsic and extrinsic. Have you ever watched a small baby trying to turn over onto its stomach for the first time? You must have noticed the determination, the single-minded focus, the persistence till the goal was achieved. Why do babies work so hard to learn and practise all the things they accomplish in their first few years? If you reply 'for the simple joy of it', or something similar, then you have described a situation of internal or **intrinsic motivation**.

Intrinsic motivation is something within us that drives us to accomplish certain goals, to be competent, to feel a sense of freedom and autonomy. We see it in play, in exploration, in challenge seeking—in any unforced, willing activity. In fact, psychologists say that, from an evolutionary standpoint, motivation is an absolute necessity for all humans, because it drives us to action that is good for our survival.

However, and this is very important to us teachers, at some point during childhood, we see that there are increasingly long lists of things that children are *not* intrinsically motivated to do. And on this long list are, more and more, the tasks demanded by school. Even activities such as cleaning, that once were done as 'play', are now resisted and avoided as 'work'.

At this point, to get children to do what we want them to, we begin to introduce external consequences, such as rewards and punishments. We also start saying things like 'if you do this, then...', and 'do it, or else...'. If a child engages in an activity either to avoid a punishment, or to gain a reward, we say the activity is externally or **extrinsically motivated**. Thus we enter an endless loop of promising and threatening to bring about the behaviours we want from children.

Well—so what, you might wonder, if the child is doing what is required of her, what does it matter *why* she does it? Many systems in the world run smoothly on planned (deliberate) systems of extrinsic motivation: threats and promises, rewards and punishments. Examples of such systems are religious traditions, modern corporate houses, schools and institutions of higher learning. I certainly recognize that extrinsic motivators are the quickest and simplest fix in most situations—because most (though not all) people respond to these in predictable ways. Extrinsic motivation is what makes the world go around. But not quite...

Alongside such systems, humans have always also encouraged different ways of motivating people—through understanding, challenge, creating awareness, and self-exploration. We have imposed fines on polluters, but we also run awareness campaigns about the state of the environment. We promise heaven and good karma, but we also appeal to human empathy and compassion. I think nobody is more closely involved with these two motivational systems, the extrinsic and the intrinsic, than a school teacher. Teachers really struggle with these issues. Although the educational system has put in place many extrinsic motivators, teachers are closest to the learning process, and can clearly see the difference when a child is intrinsically motivated. Naturally, teachers want students who are curious and interested in school work, and will leave school with a love of learning for its own sake.[1] In other words, more than motivation to *perform* (which is probably widespread in Indian schools), teachers aim for motivation to *learn*. But this wish is not easily fulfilled.

There are many possible reasons for the lack of intrinsic motivation among school children: emotional or physical

---

[1] Motivation is often seen only as a *means* to achievement, and not as an educational *outcome* in itself. We want our students to be motivated to learn so that they will 'do well'—that is understandable, but we can also look at motivation to learn as a desirable result of education. Students who are motivated to learn will always derive joy from learning, even years after leaving school. That attitude is itself valuable.

insecurity and ill health, evolutionary constraints, the lack of perceived control over the learning process, the misuse of rewards, irrelevance of material and difficult level of work, the classroom environment, and most importantly, teacher behaviours and student beliefs. In this chapter, I describe these factors in turn, and, in the process, suggest various ways to boost sagging motivation levels in our classrooms.

Unmet Physical or Emotional Needs

Abraham Maslow, a familiar name in motivational psychology, proposed that humans have a hierarchy of needs. Only when needs at the base of the pyramid are met, are we motivated to fulfil higher needs. In simple terms, if a child is hungry, anxious or unloved, he will not be motivated to learn at school. But if those needs are met, then he will in fact be intrinsically motivated to achieve competence at school. This point is fairly well borne out by examples in our own experience. When a child goes through an emotionally shaky patch (whether family or peer related) school

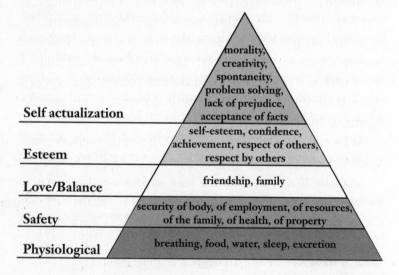

performance suffers immediately. A teacher who wants learning to happen has no alternative but to involve himself with his student's emotional life. As for physical needs, in schools for poor children, teachers spend time, energy, and sometimes their own money, on alleviating their students' hunger—they intuitively recognize the hierarchy of needs.

Unfortunately, a large percentage of children in India are not in a position to have even their physical needs met, let alone their emotional needs. For those children who enjoy physical and emotional security, however, motivation to learn can still be a problem.

Evolutionary Constraints

In Chapter One, I described David Geary's theory of biologically primary and secondary abilities. To remind you, briefly, he proposes that humans evolved to develop certain abilities (biologically primary, such as language) during childhood, through free play and exploration. According to this theory, we are intrinsically motivated to learn/develop a folk psychology, a folk physics and a folk biology. However, we may not be born with the innate drive to master other ideas such as Boyle's Law, Euclidean geometry, grammar, or the periodic table of elements. Thus, Geary says that if we wish our children to learn these things, we must provide the necessary support in the form of deliberate instruction and (perhaps) extrinsic motivators.

As I wrote in that chapter, this theory is a little depressing for a teacher. We are tempted to think that it is 'unnatural' for children to learn the majority of our school curriculum; therefore, we assume, we must use only extrinsic motivators such as ranks and failure, recognition and shame, to get students to work in school. We may feel that we are doomed to work with the carrot and stick, if we want learning to happen at all in school.

But I feel this would be going too far. It has certainly been demonstrated that humans are capable not only of learning large amounts of abstract knowledge, but also of creating more such knowledge for future generations to learn. We *can* do it; and we can *enjoy ourselves* while doing it. Just to repeat the definition of intrinsic motivation at the beginning of this chapter, it is *something within us that drives us to accomplish certain goals, to be competent, to feel a sense of freedom and autonomy.* Such a drive can be applied to any endeavour—I see no reason *per se* that we cannot generate this drive in ourselves or our students for the so-called 'biologically secondary abilities'. In the following pages, you will find suggestions and ideas to guide you in this attempt.

Just remember: evolutionary constraints, if they exist, render the motivation to learn in school neither automatic nor impossible; rather, they indicate that we have to be more imaginative and energetic about our teaching.

Lack of Perceived Control

A new theory, called Self-Determination Theory or SDT, is talking about extrinsic motivation that is **internalized** to a lesser or greater extent. This sounds contradictory: internalized extrinsic motivation—what could it mean? If external reasons for behaviour remain completely external to us, we will act only to comply with them (carrot and stick model) and we will feel controlled by those forces. Suppose we internalize these to a small extent, we will act to maintain or increase our self-esteem (feelings of worth) but we are still controlled by external forces such as others' judgements or images of us. Suppose we internalize them to a greater extent, we will act because we have 'understood' the reasons for the activity, whether it is intrinsically enjoyable or not. I think most of my own motivation to do various things is of this last kind. Take, for example, correcting my students' notebooks. I am rarely intrinsically motivated to do it since it isn't fun. Yet I do it regularly, not to comply with a rule or to feel better about myself, but because I see it as a necessary (even if tiresome) part of my work as a teacher. I know it is an

important way to keep in touch with my students' learning, and that the feedback will help them and myself. The value I have given it allows me to feel a sense of autonomy or control over my actions (*I choose to correct*) rather than feeling controlled by the outside (*I'd better correct or else I'll get into trouble*, or, *I'm a good teacher if I correct*).

The following steps show the progression of increasingly internalized motivations for action.

- I'll do it to get the raise or avoid the blame.
- I'll do it so that others will have a good image of me.
- I'll do it because it's necessary and important.
- I'll do it because I enjoy it.

We as teachers have to encourage learning through two paths, corresponding to the last two entries in the table: conveying a sense of interest and challenge in learning and mastery (intrinsic motivation), and conveying a sense of the relevance of this learning to the student (internally regulated extrinsic motivation). As long as students do not lose the meaning in what they are doing, or their feelings of control over their work, we are doing a good job. In the last section of this chapter, you will read about specific teacher behaviours that discourage or encourage students' intrinsic motivation.

The Misuse of Rewards

One active and fascinating debate taking place in psychology is between those who believe that rewards **diminish** intrinsic motivation, hence reducing the desired behaviour, and those who believe rewards **enhance** both intrinsic motivation and desired behaviour.

How can giving rewards *reduce* a desirable behaviour—isn't it supposed to work in the opposite way, according to the fundamental laws of reinforcement of behaviour? In the behaviourist tradition, rewards always increase frequency of the behaviour, as long as the reward is being given; after you stop rewarding, the behaviour reduces to its original frequency.

When this law was repeatedly demonstrated with rats and other animals, the planned use of rewards was introduced into many areas of human activity as well. Of course, schools were a prime target. But in the 1970s, the psychologist Edward Deci suggested that we might be making a mistake. First, he claimed that some activities are already rewarding in and of themselves (another way of saying we are intrinsically motivated to engage in them). Second, he said that the effect of a reward depends on how the person interprets it (in terms of how it affects the person's sense of autonomy and competence). Thus, a reward is not just the thing in itself, but what meaning it has for the one who receives it. There is a lovely cartoon showing two students cleaning dusters, and one tells the other in dismay, 'You're cleaning dusters as a *punishment*? But I'm cleaning them as a *reward*!'

There was a third problem with the naïve view of rewards, and that was the 'overjustification effect': when you get rewarded for something you already enjoy, you begin to feel that you did the activity for the reward instead of for itself. Several experiments have demonstrated that rewards could lead to *reduced* intrinsic motivation, and therefore *less* time spent in a previously enjoyed activity.[2] One classic study by Mark Lepper gave five-year-olds sketch pens to play with, something most children of that age enjoy. Following this, some of the children were rewarded for 'playing well' (they were given nice-looking

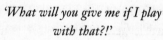

'What will you give me if I play with that?!'

certificates!). And in a later session of free play, these children played less with the pens than a control group of children that had not received certificates. According to Deci, the key variable is the sense of control that one feels while acting. When a reward is seen as controlling your behaviour, you lose a sense of freedom and autonomy, and this reduces intrinsic motivation.

But rewards can be of various kinds, and not all may bring about the same effect. Think about the different rewards you have come across. They can be tangible (a certificate or a prize), or verbal (positive feedback). They may be given for trying a job, or only for completing it. They may be given for attaining a set standard, or for doing better than others. Below is a brief summary of the effects of different types of rewards on intrinsic motivation.

- Tangible rewards (ranging from certificates to sweets) decrease intrinsic motivation, and children are more vulnerable to this effect than college students.

[2] Intrinsic motivation was measured in different ways in these studies: the degree of persistence and amount of time spent on an activity during free choice periods, and self-reported interest in and enjoyment of an activity.

- Rewards for trying, completing, bettering others and meeting standards—*all* decrease intrinsic motivation *when they are seen as controlling our behaviour*.
- Verbal rewards or positive feedback do not decrease intrinsic motivation, and can even increase it. In fact, if any reward is given in the spirit of informational feedback, say to acknowledge good quality performance, and not with the intention to control the student's behaviour, it can increase intrinsic motivation.
- However, many students in our schools who do not perform up to set standards may only rarely, if ever, receive rewards or positive feedback. This amounts to receiving continual negative feedback about one's competence, which will in turn decrease intrinsic motivation for school work.

The above list may suggest to us that we should be praising our students, giving them all positive feedback. But praise, too, has to be carefully administered! In the last section of this chapter, you will read about work that suggests negative effects of praise under certain conditions. Box 1 describes more general issues to keep in mind about praise.

Irrelevant and Unchallenging Work

A lot has been said about school learning being abstract, removed from children's everyday lives and concerns. From an evolutionary point of view, motivation is a necessary drive towards adaptive behaviours (eating, mating, and learning about one's environment so that one can survive better in it). Humans, in fact all animals, possess the motivation to learn things that help them adapt better to their environment. So, when the things we want children to learn seem unconnected with their real-world environment, no wonder their motivation flags.

Box 1

PRAISE

Praise is formally defined as a positive evaluation of another, made by a person who knows the standards of the evaluation. It can be a quick way of making a student feel good about herself, but as it turns out, praise can be tricky. According to psychologists, there can be several negative effects of praising the wrong thing, at the wrong time, or in the wrong way. In 2002, psychologists Jennifer Henderlong and Mark Lepper wrote an extensive review of studies on the effects of praise. Their main conclusions were that:

- Praise can be seen as externally controlling and thus reducing the student's autonomy (which, according to Deci's theory, decreases intrinsic motivation).
- Praise can create a pressure to continue good performance.
- Praise can lead to an obsession with maintaining one's own image while tearing others' images down.
- Praise for extremely easy tasks can lead to a student feeling he has low ability.
- If a student senses praise as insincere, she may reject it outright, or feel that the teacher doesn't really know her that well, or (worse) wonder what is wrong with her that the teacher needs to cover up. One study reported that while children below seven years of age could take praise at face value, most children by the age of twelve viewed praise with suspicion, believing that it was a sign that you lack ability and therefore need extra encouragement!

Of course, all this does not mean that we must never appreciate our students' work. There are right ways to praise, and these can be summarized in brief:

- Praise the *process* of an activity (strategies, ideas, effort), not the *ability* of the student.

- Make your praise descriptive, related to the student's work, such that it works as useful feedback.
- Praise without referring to comparisons with other students.

Another interesting connection is that between praise and high self-esteem, which for years was thought to relate to many positive outcomes, ranging from higher performance to longer life! The self-esteem movement has an interesting history, and has come under fire in recent years. You will find a description of this in Chapter Ten.

However, human society has become so complex that we have no choice but to extend school curricula to include many things that are unconnected to the child's immediate needs and surroundings. This is particularly true for high school curricula. It is difficult, if not impossible, to convince children that they are learning about vectors because 'they need it'. The truth is, if they leave school to study tailoring or European history, they will never need vectors. To demand that most, let alone all, of the high school curriculum be grounded in children's lives and surroundings is unrealistic. Yet, this does not mean that we are doomed to drag

why?

unwilling children through their lessons. Nor does it mean that we have to resort to ranks and failures to motivate them to learn. Very early on, certainly by middle school, children can be made to understand the special nature of their society and its demands— that at a young age, they must learn a great many things in order that, when they are older, they can better decide what they would like to go on with. This understanding can give them what we earlier called *internally regulated extrinsic motivation* to learn— similar to what motivates me to correct students' notebooks. Free of performance anxiety and fear, and taught with imagination and energy, learning anything can be enjoyable. And enjoyment is one of the prime factors that motivate human endeavour!

The second important aspect of school work is its difficulty level. Work that is either too easy or too difficult quickly loses interest for the student. Finding the right level of challenge is something teachers are constantly struggling with, especially in typical classrooms where a large heterogeneous group of students is working through the same material. It almost seems as if, in any class, there are bound to be some students who are unmotivated because the challenge level is either too high or too low for them. There are solutions to this quandary, which require a flexible approach and some hard work.

- For some topics, divide the students into small groups according to their level. Give them tasks appropriate to their level.
- For some topics, divide the students into small mixed level groups. Devise mini-projects where different group members have different responsibilities and can work at their own level without jeopardizing the overall task.
- For some topics, find or create material that the students can work through independently. Allow for some students

to do more and more challenging work than others, by including extension topics. Make sure that everyone has learnt the 'core' concepts and procedures.

- For some topics, hold small group discussions about the material, or use the Reciprocal Teaching method described in Chapter Two. This emphasizes the fact that regardless of 'level', a group of students can be a community of learners, and you do not always need a homogeneous group for meaningful learning to occur.

- For some topics, by all means deliver lectures to the whole class! Keep an eye on the students for signs of boredom or hopeless confusion, interrupt your own flow to ask questions at the right level to particular students, ask one student to summarize for the others...there are many imaginative ways to engage them all together with the same lesson.

Each of the above solutions will have disadvantages if practised alone, so it would not be advisable to latch onto just one as your permanent educational model. If you are flexible enough to try different things at different times, depending on the topic and the class dynamics, they will make up for each others' disadvantages, and you will reap the benefits.

Classroom Environments

One important factor influencing a student's motivation to learn is the **motivational system** in place, or the classroom environment. Psychologists broadly classify these environments as competitive, cooperative or individualistic. All three systems can create the motivation to work, but for different reasons. And these different sources of motivation can have consequences for the way students approach learning. Here is a brief summary of the three distinct classroom environments.

In a **competitive classroom**, the students' attention is focussed towards their peers' performance, and self-vs-other comparisons provide the motivation to work. This leads students to think in terms of ability. 'Am I smart enough to do this? How did I do? How did *he* or *she* do? I don't want to make a mistake…'. Avoiding failure becomes all-important, which means avoiding challenging situations. Paradoxically, some students may avoid trying hard in competitive situations, because if after all that effort they do not succeed, everyone will assume that they do not have the ability. Not trying, therefore, is one way of 'failing with honour'.

In a **cooperative classroom**, the students' attention is focussed towards the performance of the group as a whole. Students think in terms of 'oughts', and a sense of moral responsibility provides the motivation to work. 'Are we working hard enough? I (or he or she) ought to be contributing enough to the work. My friends want me to work hard.' Intentions become all-important, and

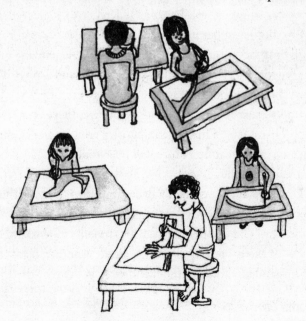

students evaluate each other more in terms of willingness to work rather than ability. Equally, peers *encourage* each others' efforts. Trying is because you 'owe' it to your group mates.

In an **individualistic classroom**, students work completely independently, and each one's work and progress are unrelated to those of others in the class. They are led to think in terms of mastering goals for themselves. 'I know I am improving. I am given a chance to correct my mistakes and my teacher wants me to try new things.' Self-vs-earlier-self comparisons may be heightened, and these provide the motivation for work. Trying is for improving and bettering one's own earlier achievements.

A few interesting contrasts need to be highlighted here. When a student is in an individualistic environment, she can focus on the question, 'How shall I do this? I need to make a plan.'[3] But in a competitive environment, *even if she tries hard*, she may not 'succeed', since success is defined as doing better than other students. So she must ask herself, 'If I try, will I succeed?' The answer to this lies in her judgement of *her own ability relative to the other students*. So, motivation to learn will be dependent on that crucial judgement, which seems such a waste and a pity! This is what psychologists call the 'double-edged sword of effort'. Effort could lead to success, but if it leads to failure, there is shame and a loss of self-esteem. Thus, in competitive environments, difficult tasks which could lead to failure will be avoided.

One caution: the descriptions above, of the three types of classrooms, are almost certainly over-simplified. Even within one classroom, not all students will interpret the goals of the class in the same way. The teacher may ask his students to work together, yet a few of them opt out and work alone. Another teacher may expect his students to work independently, yet two or three of his

---

[3] Presumably, in a cooperative classroom, she will think, '*We* need to make a plan.'

students begin to collaborate with each other. And we all know of students who, in spite of being in competitive classrooms, ignore those compulsions and work simply to master the material.

The choice of which system a class follows is influenced by the school's educational philosophy and, ultimately, by societal values. But, it is the teacher who sends powerful motivational messages to her students in the kinds of expectations she communicates. In the next section, we'll look more closely at the **specific teacher behaviours** that influence student motivation.

Teacher Behaviours and Student Motivation

As a teacher, are you a Controller or an Autonomy Supporter? Read on to find out.

> Sara is an average student. During the past two weeks, she has been looking dull and has not been participating in class. She has not been completing her homework, but whatever work she does is accurate. A phone conversation with her mother did not give any useful information. If you were Sara's teacher, what would you do?
>
> *Option 1*: Tell her the importance of finishing homework, since she needs to learn this material for her own good.
>
> *Option 2*: Tell her that she doesn't have to finish all of the work now, and see if you can help her work out the cause of the problem.
>
> *Option 3*: Make her stay after school until the homework is done.
>
> *Option 4*: Show her how she compares with the other children in terms of homework, and encourage her to catch up with the others.

Deci and his colleagues constructed a test of teacher behaviours in the 1980s with eight short stories like the above. For each story, they gave four options to correspond to four styles of teacher behaviour. In the story above, option 3 is a highly controlling behaviour, the teacher decides what is good for the student and 'makes' her do it. Option 1 is moderately controlling: the teacher decides what is best, and tries to get the student to see it his way. Option 4 is moderately supportive of the student's autonomy: the teacher encourages the child to compare herself with her peers so that she will be motivated to solve the problem. Option 2 is highly supportive of the student's autonomy: the teacher encourages the student to arrive at her own solution to the problem.

Deci and other psychologists who have used this questionnaire over the years find that autonomy-supportive teachers (who follow options like 2 above) have students who *are* more intrinsically motivated in school. But what kinds of behaviours does support for autonomy translate to in the classroom? In a study conducted by a psychologist named Johnmarshall Reeve, one adult was given ten minutes to solve puzzles with the help of another adult who was already familiar with the puzzles. Several such 'student-teacher' pairs were studied, and their behaviour videotaped for later analysis. Everyone had completed the Deci questionnaire a month earlier. Reeve found that those 'teachers' who scored high on autonomy support and those who scored as more controlling in the questionnaire showed *distinctly different behaviours* during the ten minutes of puzzle solving. Specifically, the autonomy-supportive teachers

- listened to the 'students' more,
- held the puzzle materials in their hands for a shorter time,
- avoided giving the puzzle's solutions,
- gave hints in a limited and sparing way,
- expressed fewer commands,
- asked more questions about what the student wanted to do,
- responded more to student-generated questions.

For instance, the more controlling teachers made statements like 'flip it over', 'can you make it like I showed you?', and, 'you've got to get the base first'. On the other hand, the more autonomy-supportive teachers said things like 'which pattern do you want to start with?', 'now you're getting the hang of it', and, 'I can see you're starting to get frustrated!'

'Here, let me show you how!'

There is an interesting finding that crops up here. Deci had intended option 4 in the story above to be a *moderately autonomy-supporting* option. Each of his eight stories contained an option like this, where the teacher appeals to comparison with others to encourage students to 'keep up with the other kids'. But, in all the research using his questionnaire, this option repeatedly correlates more with *controlling* than autonomous behaviours. So Deci says that we should actually look at it as a 'slightly controlling' behaviour. To me, this suggests the interesting possibility that the pressure of comparison is a subtle (or sometimes not so subtle) control on our behaviour—something that diminishes our sense of autonomy. It feeds directly into the ideas presented in Box 2.

How can we make teachers more supportive of their students' autonomy? Deci has looked at the kinds of external pressures that make teachers behave in particular ways. For example, when teachers are told that it is their responsibility to make sure that students 'perform up to standards', if they view this as a controlling demand on themselves, they will pass the pressure they feel on to their students. What applies to students also applies to teachers. If we want teachers who are intrinsically motivated to do their job well, and who support their students' autonomy, we have to support *their* autonomy to be that way! In Deci's words, 'Just as children need autonomy-oriented classrooms to be intrinsically motivated and to perceive themselves as competent, teachers need an autonomy-oriented context within which to benefit from feedback about their own orientations.' I couldn't agree more. A good teacher can only be self-motivated; quality is not something that can be enforced from the outside or from above. One contributing factor is the information teachers receive about teaching and learning, and if anything can improve teaching in a lasting, genuine way, it is this informational feedback. It is the main reason that I felt a book like this one was needed for teachers.

Another valuable emphasis that a teacher can bring into her classroom is the **mastery** orientation. This approach aims for every student to learn everything, without worrying about the time taken to learn. It is based on the important assumption, 'I can if I try', and students focus their attention and thoughts on **effort**. The typical alternative to a mastery orientation is something called a **performance** orientation, where students work in order to keep up with or outdo their peers. Success is measured in terms of performance relative to others, and even the teacher focuses on performance rather than learning. As a result, students focus their attention and thoughts on **ability**.

The mastery-performance distinction runs somewhat parallel to the individualistic-competitive distinction I made earlier in describing classroom environments. The mastery approach can keep motivation levels high—since students will attribute their failures to effort rather than ability, they will be motivated to persevere in the future. Mastery approaches also yield students who use more learning strategies, who move from 'can I do this?' to 'how can I do this?'

Box 2

BORN TO COMPARE

Anyone who spends even a little time around a group of children soon realizes that they are very aware of their *relative* levels of *anything* at a given time. A mastery learning environment, where the teacher deliberately does not encourage comparison and allows each child to work independently, is no exception. I have overheard many revealing conversations among younger students in a mastery classroom:

'I'm on page 72 already. Which page are you on—only 55?!'
'She's seven years old but she's doing level 1, and I'm six but I'm doing level 2!'

Adults and older children are probably no different, even if they do not express things in the same open and frank way! I believe it is neither necessary nor possible to 'do away' with the need to compare. Social comparison, however, brings its own stress for adults and children alike. For this reason at least, it is important to investigate alternative approaches.

As long as we use the same text material for everyone, comparison is inevitable. If all the students are moving through the work together, some will understand better and know more than others. Yet, if we allow each student to move through the work at a pace determined by himself or herself, some will move faster than others. Either way, comparisons arise in students' as well as in teachers' minds. If this makes us uncomfortable, there are two alternatives open to us. One is to have material that is not hierarchically or linearly arranged, such that students can pick their activities in the order they wish. Another is to have completely different materials and tasks for each student. These two solutions may prove to be impractical (except, perhaps, in language classes)—even contrived. Instead of trying to create and maintain situations that make comparison difficult, there are other ways for teachers to reduce the stress of constant comparison.

To begin with, we can avoid using comparison ourselves as a motivating factor. For instance, we need not say to a child, 'Finish it before he does', or 'Why can't you be more like her?' There must be good enough reasons for a child to finish something or behave in a certain way, other than to be as good as or better than someone else! Next, we can help students acknowledge comparisons in a matter-of-fact way, instead of letting them feed into their sense of self-worth. That is, a student who is good at mathematics is not in some fundamental way 'better' or 'smarter' than a student who struggles with mathematics. Different students find different things easy, and the school environment must allow for many activities in its curriculum so that different students' strengths can be discovered. But the school must do more than that. It must also give the strong message that, for example, artistic ability is *as valuable as* mathematical ability. Merely including a long list of 'extra-' or 'co-' curricular activities in a school day will not accomplish this. We in India have a long way to go in this arena; we have not even been able to communicate to young people that *language* ability is as valuable as mathematical ability.

Finally, we can avoid making competition institutional. The obvious benefits of this are in de-stressing the child, but that is not all. Most institutions in our modern society are built upon competition as a fundamental motivating force. But the often heard argument that there are competitive, aggressive instincts in us all is only half the story. There are also instincts of cooperation and altruism in us all. Perhaps, we must make thoughtful choices and decisions about *which* instincts we will encourage and emphasize in society, because the same competitive mentality, globally amplified, results in the social dysfunction we see around us (poverty and inequality, for example).

Teachers can make mastery goals important in class by laying emphasis and value on understanding and effort instead of performance and ability. But practically speaking, many children are themselves highly performance oriented. By this I mean that they spontaneously compare themselves with their friends, without adult prompting. This is the first thing many people say in protest when it is suggested that we 'do away' with competition in school: *but isn't it only natural for children to compare and compete with each other?* Box 2 discusses this interesting question in the context of education.

Closely related to teacher behaviours are the beliefs held by students about ability and effort, so we end this chapter with a section on this important area.

Student Beliefs and Motivation

Carol Dweck is a psychologist who investigates the way students think about intelligence. She has found this a much richer area of research than actually measuring students' intelligence. According to Dweck, if a student believes intelligence is an **incremental** quantity, something that can increase with more learning, he will be motivated to learn. The alternative belief is that intelligence is a more or less fixed **entity**, and a student who believes this will have low motivation to learn challenging material.

In the 1970s, Dweck was studying children who showed a kind of 'helplessness' in the face of challenging school work. Other children would willingly approach and even seek out challenging work. The secret seemed to lie in their beliefs about intelligence, and Dweck found that while younger children possess the incremental intelligence belief, as they grow older some may switch to the entity belief. What triggers the switch? One factor is when adults praise for ability rather than effort. Telling a child, 'That's very good, you're so clever!' immediately does two things. One, it makes him feel very good about himself. But this 'feel-good' state is contingent upon maintaining the impression that he is clever, so it can come crashing down at the first sign of failure. And two, it implies that if one *doesn't* do well, it's because one is *not* clever; this makes the child avoid situations where he may fail in future. This translates to low motivation in the face of challenging tasks.

Dweck and her colleague Claudia Mueller conducted several studies with ten-to-twelve-year-olds, and the results confirmed this. The students were given a set of moderately easy problems to solve, and later told they had done very well. In addition, some were told: '*You must be smart at these problems*,' and others were told, '*You must have worked hard at these problems*'. In the next stage of the experiment, all children were given a choice of what kind of problems they wanted next—problems that are easy, that I'm good at, or harder ones that I'll learn from. The results showed that those students who had received praise for intelligence chose easier problems for the second stage, while those who had received praise for effort chose harder ones. Dweck also asked the students a crucial question: how much they enjoyed the problems and whether they would like to take some home to work on. Here the findings were very curious. Some of the children were asked this question soon after the first set of problems and the praise, and they showed no differences according to type of praise given. But some of the children completed a second set of problems, were told they had not done as well as before, and only then asked the question. Those earlier praised for intelligence then rated their enjoyment of the problems lower than those praised for effort, and were less keen to take any problems home. It seems that the differences in enjoyment and motivation set in only following a failure experience.

Doesn't the student's actual ability level have anything to do with this phenomenon? In Dweck's own words: 'There is *no* relation between students' abilities or intelligence and the development of mastery-oriented qualities. Some of the very brightest students avoid challenges, dislike effort, and wilt in the face of difficulty. And some of the less bright students are real go-getters, thriving on challenge, persisting intensely when things get difficult, and accomplishing more than you expected...(but) having the mastery-oriented mind-set will help students become more able over time.'

In Conclusion

Motivation is a natural human quality, present in abundance in all of us. Unfortunately, we are not highly motivated in every activity we need to do from morning till night. Faced with a sink full of dirty dishes, I am no different from my student faced with a bag full of homework. The overwhelming feeling at that moment is one of **resistance** to what needs to be done. Sometimes, motivation is simply the absence of resistance to the work at hand. Instead of teachers looking for ways to boost students' motivation levels, we can shift the focus of our attention to the force of resistance. Together, teachers and students can learn about what it takes to meet resistance in themselves. After all, this is a force that students will face throughout their lives, and here in school is the perfect opportunity to learn about it.

When we opt for a stick, a carrot or a competition to motivate our students, we have completely sidestepped the issue of resistance. There are thousands upon thousands of highly motivated youngsters in our country, but too many of them have never been encouraged to understand themselves or reflect on their own drives and desires. What would happen to their motivation and drive if we removed the props of external competition? If you believe that it is an important purpose of education for students to be self-reflective and to better understand their emotional and motivational states, you might decide to completely put aside competition as a motivating force in your school or classroom. But do not be disappointed if, as soon as you do so, all your students do not magically fall into place, striving to do their best, producing excellent work, filled with joy at their accomplishments! The move from an emphasis on performance and ability to learning and effort must not be seen as simply a 'better way to motivate our students'. Rather, it opens the door to new questions, new challenges and certainly new frustrations—all of which have immeasurable educational value.

References and Bibliography

1. Ames, C., and R. Ames, 1984. 'Systems of Student and Teacher Motivation: Toward a Qualitative Definition'. *Journal of Educational Psychology*, Vol. 76, No. 4, 535–56.

2. Ames, C., and J. Archer, 1988. 'Achievement Goals in the Classroom: Students' Learning Strategies and Motivation Processes'. *Journal of Educational Psychology*, Vol. 80, No. 3, 260–67.

3. Ames, C., 1992. 'Classrooms: Goals, Structures and Student Motivation'. *Journal of Educational Psychology*, Vol. 84, No. 3, 261–71.

4. Covington, M.V., and C.L. Omelich, 1979. 'Effort: The Double-Edged Sword in Achievement'. *Journal of Educational Psychology*, Vol. 71, No. 2, 169–82.

5. Deci, E.L., A.J. Schwartz, L. Sheinman, and R.M. Ryan, 1981. 'An Instrument to Assess Adults' Orientations Toward Control Versus Autonomy With Children: Reflections on Intrinsic Motivation and Perceived Competence'. *Journal of Educational Psychology*, Vol. 73, No. 5, 642–50.

6. Deci, E.L., R. Koestner, and R.M. Ryan, 1999. 'A Meta-analytic Review of Experiments Examining the Effects of Extrinsic Rewards on Intrinsic Motivation'. *Psychological Bulletin*, Vol. 125, No. 6, 627–68.

7. Eisenberger, R., and J. Cameron, 1996. 'Detrimental Effects of

Reward: Reality or Myth?' *American Psychologist*, Vol. 51, No. 11, 1153–66.

8. Geary, D.C., 1996. 'The Evolution of Cognition and the Social Construction of Knowledge'. *American Psychologist*, Vol. 51, No. 3, 265–66.

9. Grouzet, F.M.E., T. Kasser, A. Ahuvia, J.M.F. Dols, Y. Kim, S. Lau, R.M. Ryan, S. Saunders, P. Schmuck, and K.M. Sheldon, 2005. 'The Structure of Goal Contents Across 15 Cultures'. *Journal of Personality and Social Psychology*, Vol. 89, No. 5, 800–16.

10. Henderlong, J., and M.R. Lepper, 2002. 'The Effects of Praise on Children's Intrinsic Motivation: A Review and Synthesis'. *Psychological Bulletin*, Vol. 128, No. 5, 774–95.

11. Hopkins, G., 2005. 'How can Teachers Develop Students' Motivation—and Success? An Interview with Carol S. Dweck'. *Education World*, School Issues, 2005.

12. Mueller, C.M., and C.S. Dweck, 1998. 'Praise for Intelligence Can Undermine Children's Motivation and Performance'. *Journal of Personality and Social Psychology*, Vol. 75, No. 1, 33–52.

13. Reeve, J., E. Bolt, and Y. Cai, 1999. 'Autonomy-Supportive Teachers: How They Teach and Motivate Students'. *Journal of Educational Psychology*, Vol. 91, No. 3, 537–48.

14. Reeve, J., and H. Jang, 2006. 'What Teachers Say and Do to Support Students' Autonomy During a Learning Activity'. *Journal of Educational Psychology*, Vol. 98, No. 1, 209–18.

15. Ryan, R.M., and E.L. Deci, 2000. 'Self-Determination Theory and the Facilitation of Intrinsic Motivation, Social Development and Well-Being'. *American Psychologist*, Vol. 55, No. 1, 68–78.

CHAPTER NINE

Measuring Learning

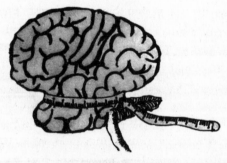

There are so many negative associations with the words 'assessment', 'testing' and 'examinations' that writing a balanced chapter on the topic might seem like an impossible task! Yet, there is no denying that assessment is an inseparable part of teaching, whether done formally or informally, one-on-one, or with masses of students at once. We often think of a test or an examination as the *end-point* of a process of learning. But, assessment can also be woven into the learning process, and classroom tests are good examples of this—made by the teacher, frequently spaced, connected to class work, and used as ongoing feedback for both student and teacher. This is called **formative assessment**; it helps students see their strengths and gaps, and helps teachers fine-tune instruction accordingly. The other kind of assessment is **summative**; it is externally imposed, has high stakes, and makes comparative evaluations of students (as well as teachers and schools). This chapter discusses issues that are applicable to both formative as well as summative assessment.

Testing has a fascinating history, from the ancient Chinese system of mass testing for the civil service (applicants had to write poetry and philosophical essays); through the Greek (Socratic) method of testing interwoven with teaching; to the many present-day examinations that all our students face. It was not always the bane of education; in fact, advances in testing such as the infamous 'multiple-choice' questions were welcomed and praised in their time. Assessment has not been a completely thoughtless or absent-minded invention—but there is no doubt that many things are wrong with it today. We must acknowledge and examine the problems with assessment in India, before we can see ways to set things right. I will simply list some of these issues below—they are too well-known to need much explanation:

- A significantly large percentage of **teaching time** is devoted to preparing for, administering, and recovering from tests.
- **Motivation** has shifted from processes of learning to outcomes, both for teachers and students.
- Curricula are shaped by tests (this is called the '**curriculum backwash**' effect) and when the tests are heavily knowledge-based, the curriculum pays less attention to understanding or application.
- Students experience almost constant **anxiety** about tests.
- Tests make **teachers anxious** too, when they feel responsible for their students' performance.
- Tests encourage **cheating** among adolescents, who think education is about getting good marks rather than learning something.
- The results of 'high-stakes' examinations can be **unfair** and depressing to countless young people.

The first three issues really arise from the narrow, rote and outcome-oriented nature of traditional tests. These would

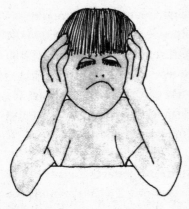

disappear if the tests were more broad-based, qualitative and process-oriented. In simple terms, there needs to be a *better match between what we want to teach, and what is tested, between the way we want to teach it, and the way it is tested.* If a teacher does a long and in-depth project with her students on the Indus Valley Civilization, for example, with open-ended analysis of the evidence, and an emphasis on critical thinking, her students may do rather poorly on a test of 'facts' with match-the-following and true-false items. This does not mean they learned nothing about the Indus Valley or about history. To the contrary, they probably have a greater feel for historical methods and ancient civilizations than the test permits them to show. But if the teacher could test them in such a way that the skills developed during the project were assessed, the match would be good. In such a scenario, 'teaching to the test' and curricular 'backwash' do not arise as problems.

Are there such ways of testing? Some genuine solutions have been developed, such as open-ended questions, demonstrations, exhibits, non-speeded tests, collaborative tests and portfolios. Together these are called **authentic assessment** techniques, and they have been rigorously applied on a small scale, in pockets. Research shows that at many levels authentic assessment is far superior to traditional methods of mass testing. It even addresses emotional and moral issues associated with testing. But there are huge stumbling blocks to authentic assessment being more widely accepted and used. Switching to authentic assessments, given the large numbers of students involved, would simply take more time than our educational system is willing to give. And a second reason why it is difficult to switch over completely is our fear that if we use alternate methods of assessment, we will lose objectivity. This is an important point, and will be addressed in a later section of this chapter. To better appreciate the problems of current testing practices, and to be able to evaluate alternatives, we must first understand some fundamentals of measurement theory.

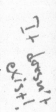

The ABCs of Psychological Testing

An assessment is a measurement of what has been learned, and any such measurement needs to possess two key qualities, namely, **validity** and **reliability**. Validity is the extent to which a test measures what it is supposed to measure; this may sound circular, but you will understand it better by the end of this section. Reliability is the extent to which the test is free of measurement error, which means, for example, that repeated testing should give similar results. Measurement in any field of study needs to possess an acceptable degree of validity and reliability, but you can see that what is acceptable depends on the field. In the field of psychology and education, we cannot expect the same high levels of validity and reliability that one finds in, say, physics. Let us look at how these two properties of measurement work in the context of academic assessment.

Suppose I have taught a student about the mean, median and mode in a statistics class. I teach her how to calculate them, some of their simple properties, and their uses and misuses. Naturally, I would want to know what my student has understood of the lesson. The new learning is encoded in complex ways in her brain, in patterns of interconnections among millions of neurons. If only there were a way to 'scan' her brain to make sure it's all in there. Imagine how different things would be if instead of tests and examinations, students had only to submit to a painless brain

scan at the end of every year. Such measurement would be highly reliable and valid—but it hasn't yet been invented.

To find out what she has learned, I will have to give my student *a context, a task for which she needs to use what she has learned*, and this could be a worksheet, a homework assignment, or an academic test. Her **performance** must allow me to infer something about her **competence** (knowledge, skill level and understanding). Thus, the task becomes an instrument that measures learning, just as a metal ruler or a weighing scale or a blood pressure monitor measures various things. But metal rulers, unlike academic tests, are uncontroversial instruments. You don't find people debating the merits of metal rulers, or getting upset about them one way or the other. The reason why tests are so controversial and require so much of our attention has to do with problems of definition, validity and reliability. We will look at these issues in turn.

The aim of a metal ruler is to measure length. People are agreed on the definition of length (one dictionary says it is the 'extent from end to end'); we don't hear anyone arguing that the length of a line should be the angle it makes with the north-south axis of the earth, for example. Given this **consensus in definition**, the metal ruler does a fairly good job of measuring length. It clearly measures what it is supposed to—the 'extent from end to end'—and thus, it is a **valid** instrument. Also, repeated measures using the metal ruler will give more or less the same value for length, and this makes the instrument **reliable**. Without validity and reliability, the instrument would be virtually useless. Imagine using a crooked metal ruler, or one with wavy edges—an invalid instrument. Or imagine using a calibrated elastic band to measure length—an unreliable instrument.

Now let us look at the case of the academic test, whose aim is to measure the student's knowledge and understanding. Right away, we can see that we do not possess a measuring instrument as valid and reliable as a metal ruler. A person's height is easy to measure, but her level of understanding of a concept is hidden, dynamic, and must be inferred from her behaviour. So first of all, we need agreement on a definition of knowledge and understanding, just as we had for length.

It is interesting to ask yourself as a teacher, how you would define knowledge and understanding. Quite likely, your answer goes something like: my student has *understood* when he can *do* x, y or z. The answer is usually in terms of the measurement process itself; we say that understanding is the ability to answer a particular set of questions correctly. But the problem lies in the choice of questions. Not everybody will

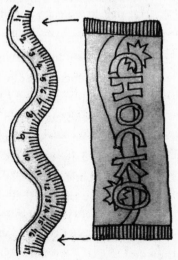

agree on a particular definition of understanding, and not everyone will agree on a particular choice of questions. This fundamental problem with definition is easy to forget, especially in a time when performance on tests has become synonymous with intelligence and understanding. It is an extremely illuminating exercise for a teacher just to step back and ask herself, 'Is this examination or test getting at the essence of what I want my students to learn? What aspects of a subject do I want all my students to master? What are the abilities that will distinguish those who are competent from those who are excellent?'

You can see that it is impossible for a test to be *perfectly valid*, but there are degrees of invalidity. Some tests are so invalid as to be useless; others are valid enough to be useful. There are a few different ways of evaluating the validity of a test, each with its problems, unfortunately!

- One simple way is to see if the test scores *correlate with the teacher's estimates* of the students' understanding. In other words, if the results of a test are completely surprising to you (if students you thought had a good grasp scored very low, and vice versa) you would not consider that test valid. By this yardstick, many tests do fairly well. That is, most teachers feel that tests are valid when their good students do well and weak students do badly. But there is a potential circularity flaw in this reasoning. Our impressions as teachers of who are the 'good' and 'weak' students are shaped by the tasks we structure for our students in class, which in turn are strongly influenced by the tests and examinations offered by the system. Unless teachers' estimates have some independent basis, they will inevitably correlate with test scores.

- Another way to check a test's validity is to see if the scores *correlate well with other tests*. The problem with this kind of validity is that if all the tests are measuring the students' ability to, say, memorize certain facts, they may all correlate well with each other, but it still doesn't mean any of them is really testing understanding.

- Still another way of checking a test's validity is to see how it *correlates with performance in real life*. If we claim that understanding a particular subject should lead to competence 'in the field', so to speak, then that correlation should be high. One problem with this is that real-life situations are dramatically different from academic test situations. Real life involves people working together over a longer period of time on open-ended problems, with information available to them, but testing is typically individual, time-bound, closed-ended and closed-book. So studies have found that performance in school correlates well with performance in college, but beyond college the correlations seem to break down considerably. For example, doing well in the IAS exams requires a whole lot of general knowledge, but being a successful civil servant also requires good interpersonal skills, common sense and integrity.

Both definition and validity are therefore tricky issues when it comes to academic tests. Turning now to reliability, can we say that the test would yield close to the same results on repeated testing? Remember the case of measuring length using an elastic band? We would no doubt find such an instrument useless. In a similar way, if a test would not give us similar results on repeated occasions, of what use can it be?

The question of reliability is actually related to the retrieval of long-term memories given certain cues at the time of recall. Henry Roediger, a psychologist interested in the effects of repeated testing, has discovered that retrieval is quite variable and inconsistent. That is, when a student is given a test on the same material on different occasions, he will not always give the same responses. Often, he will recall things on later tests that he did not recall on earlier tests (and this is without any revision in between, of course). Repeated testing seems to produces *new* memories! These new memories are called 'recovered' memories, and Roediger's studies show that recovered memories are the norm rather than the exception. Often, this improvement in performance was greater than the reduction due to forgetting.

Because of these inconsistencies in the retrieval of things that we know, we cannot set too much store by the results of a single test (*especially* when it is a test of mostly memory). There is *always* some measurement error in a test score. Even though we cannot say exactly what the measurement error is, we can be sure that it is at least several percentage points. Certainly, the error is enough that we are not justified in making distinctions between students based on decimals of a percentage point. For example, if one student scores 88 per cent, his true score may be anywhere between 84 per cent and 92 per cent, and he is, therefore, not clearly superior to another student who scores 85 per cent.

So, I suppose the question is: how can we make a test more like a metal ruler? And the answer is: we can certainly *improve* the quality of a test, but it will never be as valid or reliable as a metal ruler. This means that we really need to change the way we interpret test scores; our current naïve acceptance of what those numbers tell us is simply not justified. The next section briefly discusses the ways test scores are used.

Interpreting Test Scores

If our metal ruler were somewhat (though not totally) erroneous, we would interpret its results with some tentativeness. Similarly, when a teacher assesses his students in the classroom using formative assessment, the results are held more as a working hypothesis than an absolute conclusion. This hypothesis is quickly changed or abandoned when the teacher probes a little, asks further questions, or tests in a different way. Teachers know not to make firm conclusions from the results of the little class tests and assignments they administer. However, the results of summative examinations are not looked upon as hypotheses. We treat those numbers as if they were lengths read off from a perfectly engineered metal ruler! The results of such examinations arrive too late and are too unspecific to be useful as feedback, so instead, they are used to make **decisions** about students (who gets what in terms of further opportunities) and also to **evaluate teachers**, schools and boards of education. These uses make such examinations 'high-stakes'.

In India, test scores are largely used to make crucial decisions about individual children. If an admissions board or a prospective employee relies on a single number to choose whom to accept and whom to reject, mistakes can occur. The figure shows a hypothetical plot of a sample of test scores against some measure of job performance—*were all applicants to be hired*. The correlation between the two is reasonably strong: you can see that most high scorers will go on to perform well on the job, and most low scorers will perform poorly on the job. But, there is also a small group of low scorers whose job performance is satisfactory, and another small group of high scorers whose job performance is not. If only those scoring above the cut-off on the test (drawn as a vertical line on the graph) are hired, the decision will be wrong for both these small groups. And the groups may not be that small, either.

As the relationship between test scores and job performance gets weaker (and this has to do with validity) the false hits and misses become more in number, as you see in the second figure. Of course, there is no such thing as a perfect decision, free from

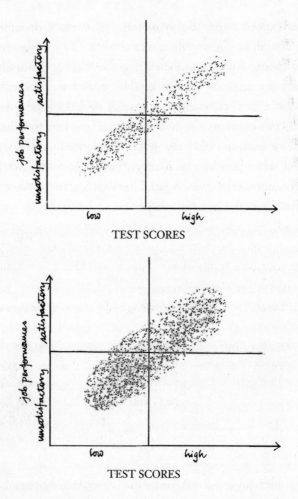

TEST SCORES

TEST SCORES

these two errors. But, even if there is nothing we can do to improve a test's validity, the least we can do is to use multiple criteria for decision making.

Test scores are also used to evaluate teachers and programmes. In some parts of the United States, for example, teachers and schools are actually rewarded and punished on the basis of the scores—teachers can get pay raises or be discharged, and schools with low average scores can be 'taken over' by government-appointed experts. Interestingly, one study in the U.S. documented a group of teachers' strong opposition to the high-stakes testing imposed upon them. Some of their negative feelings naturally had to do with the fact that they themselves were being 'tested', and being held accountable for poor results. But the study showed that teachers were especially bothered about the fact that the tests do not allow for good teaching practices or meaningful learning. The paper, whose authors are Mary A. Barksdale-Ladd and Karen Thompson, includes many long and stirring quotes from teachers, and I have excerpted just a few here:

> 'Just think what you could do if you took all that time spent on testing and preparing for testing, and used it to teach. There's way too much testing';
> 'They don't need real teachers to prepare children for tests, and in fact, I think they could just develop computer programmes to do this';
> 'Learning for the test isn't meaningful...the scores are up, but the kids know less, and they are less as people'; and,
> 'I think they [the tests] were designed because everyone thinks there are so many bad teachers, and this would make the bad teachers improve. But it isn't; in fact, it is giving bad teachers an excuse to continue doing what they've always done—lots of skill and drill. It's a license for bad teaching'.

The problem of using tests to evaluate people and programmes arises largely due to the poor quality of assessment. In this last section, we look at ways to increase the validity and reliability of academic tests.

Improving Assessment

Assessment can benefit from a richer definition of what is to be tested, and this is one of the aims of authentic assessment. While poorer tests might measure only memory, better tests might measure memory, understanding *and* application. Even better tests would assess many more important skills, such as:

- solving open-ended problems,
- framing problems,
- making and specifying assumptions,
- working in a group,
- being open to new ideas,
- dealing with data,
- using multiple perspectives,
- persisting in spite of failure,
- self-assessing and self-correcting,
- presenting information orally,
- ordering chaos.

Basing assessment on such a comprehensive list is good for two reasons. First, these are the skills valued in the real world; assessment that takes these into account will be more valid. Second, the 'backwash' effect of such assessment on teaching and curriculum will only be for the better. Recall that backwash refers to the tendency for teachers and curricula to align themselves to a test's requirements. Thus, improving assessment will lead to improved teaching practice—at least, that is the hope behind many widespread testing reforms.

One well-researched form of authentic assessment is called the **portfolio method**. Psychologist Scott Paris and his colleagues define a portfolio as a selection of students' work reflecting daily classroom curriculum and teaching. Student portfolios have been successfully used as a supplementary and more meaningful assessment in many schools in the United States. Each portfolio contains a representative sample of a student's class work, a variety of evidence of her performance in class. No extra work is required, except for selecting suitable samples, which can be done along with the student. Thus, the student becomes a self-assessor, asking herself, 'Does this work show the effort or skill that I want to share?' Paris suggests that portfolios include three different kinds of evidence: performance (everyday examples of what the student could read/write/calculate), process (evidence of strategies and methods) and perception (written self-reflections or self-evaluations).

Another recent innovation in assessment is **collaborative testing**. Philip Zimbardo, a prominent name in psychology over the past fifty years or so, recently turned his attention to test anxiety and how to reduce it. He decided to try a new idea in his own psychology courses—students were offered the option of doing their exams with or without a partner of their choice from among their own classmates! They were told that the collaborative pair would submit a single paper and receive a single grade—there was to be no individual work at all. An intriguing idea; how do you imagine the students reacted to such an offer? Around 40 per cent of them opted to write the exams with a partner. Most of those who opted to work alone did so because they feared that a partner might end up doing less work. But in fact, only 20 per cent of the 'pairs' reported having 'split the work'; most of them studied the whole portions, or as much as they would have if writing the exams alone. The results showed that those who wrote collaborative tests scored several points higher on average than those who worked alone. Further, they enjoyed the course more, shared their knowledge more, and were less anxious about the exams. They also told Zimbardo that they would like collaborative testing to be used in more of their courses. As Zimbardo says, although collaborative anxiety reduces stress, it is even more valuable for its real-world emphasis on joint work. Students have to negotiate, share, and cooperate, and these are valuable skills in almost any workplace today.

A third example is the use of **rubrics**. Suppose a student has written an essay on the Arab-Israeli conflict, and his teacher is required to grade it out of ten. A single number will reflect several criteria at once: clarity, range of issues, depth of understanding, sophistication of language, and so on. As a first step towards making a rubric for this situation, these criteria need to be listed out. Next, different levels of performance on each criterion can be described in words. For example, for the criterion of clarity, the levels might be:

1. Points not clearly made, overall confused essay.
2. A few points made clearly, rest mostly confused.
3. Many clear points, a few confused areas.
4. All points made clearly, overall very clear essay.

A similar thing would need to be done for all the criteria, and the result would be a matrix or rubric. Rubrics have been tried out in many schools systems with excellent results. The greatest advantage of a rubric is its effect on students when they are shown it *before* they complete their work. It makes them aware of the standards, and encourages them to match the highest levels they can.[1]

Looking at the success and clear advantages of various alternative assessment methods, one wonders why they have not been adopted across the board. What are we afraid of losing if we do so? The answer is probably: objectivity and easy quantitative cut-offs. Authentic assessment may require human judgement on several dimensions of quality. Teachers who grade essays already do this: they judge style, clarity, elaboration and so on. Early research on the reliability of essay marking was quite disappointing, showing that there is very little agreement when two separate people mark the same essay, and even when one person marks the same essay on two different occasions. This has led us to be deeply sceptical of the objectivity of such assessment. The other problem is, of course, that we are used to simple summary numbers with which to decide a student's 'worth'.

Is there a way out of the impasse? We will have to take another look at qualitative assessment, because to dismiss it completely would leave us with no alternatives to the present system and its problems. There are a few properties of qualitative assessment that might worry us.

---

[1] 'Weighing cattle does not make them fatter!' These words were spoken by a well-known educator, Albert Shanker, who was trying to make the point that merely testing children does not make them smarter. However, after acknowledging his point and appreciating his way of putting it, we can continue the analogy in the following way. What if cattle could read weighing scales, wanted to get fat and, further, knew what it took to get fat? This is called 'owning the standards', and it applies to students writing tests and exams. If students can be actively involved in their own learning, if they can be told the standards of good performance, they will 'own' the standards. They will use the results of assessment to improve their own learning. And then, weighing cows *will* make them fatter!

- We know that in some cases, criteria of performance are sharp, in the sense that there are clear rights and wrongs. Examples of these are found in mathematics, physics, chemistry, spelling and grammar, perhaps. But for the many skills listed at the beginning of this section, the criteria are most probably going to be 'fuzzy'. As an example, for an essay, in between 'very clear' and 'completely confused' is a whole range of possible states.

- Qualitative ratings are subjective, and therefore can fall prey to carry-over effects during correction (judging one student's performance as good because the previous student's was poor); halo effects (when personal images of students influence our assessment); personality effects of the person doing the correction (a severe or a lenient nature); and extraneous influences (neatness or handwriting).

- Performance is simultaneously a function of multiple criteria, which means that you cannot compare two students on a single dimension.

These may seem inescapable problems, but it might help to realize that 'subjective' does not necessarily mean arbitrary or biased, and

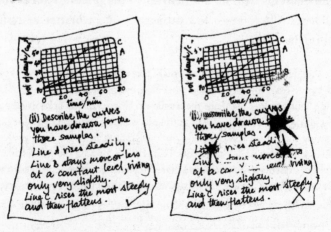

objectivity itself may be an illusion. The steps that go into making even a multiple-choice test—choosing questions, wording and arranging items—are themselves subjective, even though the final step of deciding how many 'right' is perfectly objective. In the case of qualitative assessments, objectivity must be defined as consensus among a group of trained teachers. This can be achieved by i) carefully working out procedures for assessment; ii) training teachers in these procedures; and iii) arranging for consultations between teachers, so that they can build consensus. Even better, the standards can be made public and available to other teachers, parents, colleges, employers and students themselves. Once teachers are trained in the procedures and have some familiarity with them, qualitative assessment need be no more difficult than traditional marking.

A final point is that no single time or testing episode should assume supreme importance. Decision making should be spread over time and tests. In this way, we are minimizing the effects of teacher and student inconsistencies, thus making the final result more reliable. There is, however, a deeper thread here: one that wraps up this chapter rather nicely. **While we mostly measure performance, what we want to measure is competence.** The only way to get better measures of competence is to sample performance of different skills, over time, in different contexts.

In Conclusion

India's National Curriculum Framework of 2005 has a section on assessment and evaluation. Apart from acknowledging many of the issues we have raised here, the document adds some concrete suggestions for reform. Examples are open-book exams, unlimited time exams, offering mathematics and English exams at two or three levels of competency, making a bank of good test questions from teachers and other professionals, and eliminating all board examinations other than at the end of the 10th and 12th standard. These are based on sound psychological principles, as this chapter has shown, and if implemented will really change the face of assessment in India.

One of the biggest reasons for changing assessment and evaluation is the burden of pressure felt by students. In general, school can be a stressful experience for many children. There are challenges of various kinds that young people have to meet, and the next chapter looks at the issue of emotional health in the educational context.

References and Bibliography

1. Barksdale-Ladd, M.A., and K.F. Thomas, 2000. 'What's at Stake in High-Stakes Testing: Teachers and Parents Speak Out'. *Journal of Teacher Education*, Vol. 51, No. 5, 384–97.

2. Bjork, R.A., 1999. 'Assessing Our Own Competence: Heuristics and Illusions'. In D. Gopher and A. Koriat (eds), *Attention and performance XVII. Cognitive regulation of performance: Interaction of theory and application.* Cambridge, MA: MIT Press.

3. Cheng, L., 1997. 'How Does Washback Influence Teaching? Implications for Hong Kong'. *Language and Education*, Vol. 11, No. 1, 38–54.

4. Dietel, R.J., J.L. Herman, and R.A., Knuth, 1991. 'What Does Research Say About Assessment?' North Central Regional Educational Laboratory, http://www.ncrel.org/sdrs/areas/stw_esys/4assess.htm

5. Hopkins, G., 2005. 'How can Teachers Develop Students' Motivation—and Success? An Interview with Carol S. Dweck'. *Education World*, School Issues, 2005.

6. Moon, T.R., C.M. Brighton, C.M. Callahan, and A. Robinson, 2005. 'Development of Authentic Assessments for the Middle School Classroom'. *The Journal of Secondary Gifted Education*, Vol. XVI, No. 2/3, 119–33.

7. Roediger III, H.L., and E.J. Marsh, 2005. 'The Positive and Negative Consequences of Multiple-Choice Testing'. *Journal of Experimental Psychology: Learning, Memory, and Cognition*, Vol. 31, No. 5, 1155–59.
8. Shaughnessy, M.F., 2002. 'An Interview with Henry L. Roediger III'. *Educational Psychology Review*, Vol. 14, No. 4.
9. Stecher, B.M., *Consequences of Large-Scale, High-Stakes Testing on School and Classroom Practice.* 79–100.
10. Zimbardo, P.G., L.D. Butler, and V.A. Wolfe, 2003. 'Cooperative College Examinations: More Gain, Less Pain When Students Share Information and Grades', *Journal of Experimental Education*, Vol. 71, No. 2.

CHAPTER TEN

Emotions, Learning and Emotional Health

Of all the hundreds of languages in the world, the most important one for a teacher to learn is probably 'body language'. A teacher must be able to read things like glazed expressions, mischievous glances and sullen pouts, because these are clues to students' inner feelings. The feelings experienced by students in academic contexts are called *academic emotions*, and they affect a wide range of student outcomes, such as motivation, cognition, achievement, physical health and psychological health. We all know that if a student is unhappy, worried or angry, very little of the lesson will be understood. And we know that when she is attentive, interested and unafraid, she will learn better. But this is only the tip of the iceberg; students experience a great variety of emotions in connection with school work and school performance.

Ideally, we should give as much importance to our students' emotional states as we do to their academic learning. Yet, in a typical school set-up, it is extremely difficult for a teacher to attend to the emotional needs of each student—there are so many students and so little time. Perhaps, because we cannot give the time and energy required to attend to academic emotions, we end up ignoring them altogether. We may even deny their importance in learning, convincing ourselves that emotions are 'irrelevant', to be pushed aside to allow for the important work of study and exam preparation. But this would be a grave mistake.

For one thing, if we do not acknowledge the presence and power of emotions in learning, we risk pouring much of our precious teaching energy down the drain. More fundamentally, emotions are inextricably intertwined with motivation and cognition, and the three phenomena form the basis of all school learning. Although we seem able to separate them in our descriptions, in reality they are inseparable. For example, a student may be withdrawn in class, resistant to learning, or simply aggressive. The sources of these patterns of behaviour lie *jointly* in beliefs or attitudes, as well as in basic negative emotions such as anger, shame and guilt. Similarly, the sources of student engagement and involvement in classroom learning activities lie *jointly* in beliefs about the value or importance of the activities, as well as in emotions such as boredom, interest, love and joy.

In a recent paper, psychologists Antonio Damasio and Mary Helen Immordino-Yang make this point very strongly. Instead of looking at emotion as the toddler who upsets the glassware in a shop, we should be looking at it as the shelf upon which the glassware rests! We tend to think in 'either-or' terms, as when we talk of pure rational thought, or emotion derailing cognition. But, as Yang and

Damasio point out, reasoning and learning involve the perception and use of social feedback, which is an emotional process.

If we accept the importance of paying attention to students' emotions, but are at the same time constrained in our ability to do so, is there any solution? There is another, broader approach to caring for students' emotional health, and that is to create school environments that are affectionate and affirming instead of impersonal and competitive. As I hope to convey through this chapter, the traditional emphasis on performance and comparative evaluation triggers harmful emotional responses in students. I use the rather strong word 'harmful' deliberately—certain emotional states can harm the learning process, relationships among peers, relationships with parents and teachers, and the student's psychological health. This is true, as you will see, even of certain 'positive' emotions such as pride and hope. Given the educational emphasis on performance, there is little we can do for our children other than to help them 'cope' with their harmful emotions, and coping is such an unsatisfactory solution! A supportive educational environment, on the other hand, addresses the issue of academic emotion in a much more holistic way. Of course, a supportive environment for children, in the broadest possible sense, implies societal, educational and familial values quite different from those in place today. While we all need to work at that level too, if each of us can tune in to our students' emotional worlds even in small ways, the returns will be enormous.

The following section will introduce academic emotions, and explore two of them in some depth—enjoyment and anxiety.

Academic Emotions

As an exercise, you might like to write down a list of the academic emotions that you think students typically experience, and compare your list with the one in Box 1. This list was compiled by

---

Box 1

Activity-related emotions

Enjoyment (both excitement and relaxed states)	*When the activity is valued and there is control over learning.*
Frustration	*When the activity is valued and there is low control.*
Boredom	*When the activity is not valued.*

Outcome-related emotions

Prospective emotions

Anticipatory joy	*When success is expected.*
Hopelessness	*When failure is expected.*
Hope	*When the outcome is uncertain, but the focus is on success.*
Anxiety	*When the outcome is uncertain, but the focus is on failure.*

Retrospective emotions

Joy	*When success is achieved.*
Sadness	*When success is not achieved.*
Disappointment	*When success was expected, but did not happen.*
Relief	*When failure was expected, but did not happen.*

Social emotions

Pride	*When success is seen as caused by oneself.*
Shame	*When failure follows high effort.*
Gratitude	*When success is seen as due to another's help, such as a teacher.*
Anger	*When failure is seen as caused by others.*

---

psychologist Reinhard Pekrun and his colleagues, from qualitative data collected from students in schools in Germany.[1] The students were asked to *describe* their emotions during class time, while

[1] This is generally a good approach to begin exploring a new area of research, because qualitative, descriptive, open-ended responses reveal all the complexity and the possible variables involved.

studying at home, and around testing time. From these verbal accounts, the psychologists were able to create a classification with explanations, as shown in Box 1. Anxiety was the most common (fifteen per cent to twenty-five per cent of all emotions reported). However, if we label these emotions as 'positive' and 'negative' in the obvious sense, the findings showed that the overall frequency of positive and negative emotions was similar.

One interesting point that the table shows is the overabundance of achievement-related emotions—those experienced in anticipation of, or as a result of, success and failure. Here is concrete evidence of the fact that school has become a place of performance more than of learning. But the few activity-related emotions listed in the table—enjoyment, frustration and boredom—are extremely important because they are connected with feelings of involvement or engagement in learning. When the conditions are right, students experience a **feeling of 'flow'**, a sense of being engaged in an activity done for its own sake, and at just the right level of challenge. Debra Meyer and Julianne Turner are psychologists

interested in what affects the quality of learning experiences, or what contributes to feelings of 'flow'. The simplest description of this intangible state is quoted in one of their papers, in the words of a young girl describing an activity she enjoyed—she was 'thinking a lot...feeling that I am really understanding it and getting something out of it... really into it'.

There is, naturally, a strong connection between academic

emotions and the quality of learning experiences. Yet, when Meyer and Turner began investigating learning experiences several years ago, they did not initially consider emotions. They examined students' *beliefs and attitudes* in the classroom: goals, risk-taking behaviour, perceptions of ability, and so on. Typically, a study like this is approached by giving students closed-ended questionnaires, with multiple-choice answers or rating scales. Such methods allow psychologists to gather focused, readily analyzable data, but only within the range of what they already expect. Fortunately, Meyer and Turner took a different approach. They also asked open-ended questions to which the students could reply in their own words (a large part of their data was qualitative and descriptive). Thus, they discovered that, rather than dispassionate beliefs and attitudes, the data was filled with reports of how the students *felt* about various aspects of their learning. The quality of the learning experience, it seemed, was determined by feelings of fear, pride, anger, surprise, love, elation and fun within the individual. 'Flow' experiences were closely correlated with the presence of some of these feelings and the absence of others.

Essentially, learning is most enjoyed when there is a balance of one's skill level and the challenge level of the activity, which implies that students at **all ability levels** can enjoy learning. This may sound like a trivially true statement, but it is really very important. Think of the students you've had over the years who you thought were really enjoying their learning—most likely, they were all fairly high in ability level. What we need to explore, as teachers, are imaginative ways to give more students this 'right match' between ability and challenge. In Chapter Eight, I included a series of suggestions on how to make classroom learning optimally challenging for all students, all of which will allow more students to experience 'the feeling of flow' in your classroom.

You may wonder what concrete benefits to learning there are to something like 'enjoyment'. Is there any psychological evidence that a student will learn a lesson better if he has enjoyed it and been happy during learning? This is an important question, especially as schools and teachers these days are making efforts to increase their students' enjoyment of learning. A student may go through twelve years of thoroughly enjoyable learning, but in the final analysis, one does not know whether she has learned more or better than someone who has gone through twelve years of drudgery. In fact, some educators may even argue that in replacing drudgery with joy, we are sacrificing learning. This latter argument can be easily addressed, however. We want children to be happy in school because **emotional well-being is an end in itself**, not because happiness will lead to higher marks in the final examination. Yet, at the same time, enjoyment in the classroom has to come from the learning process itself, not merely from an *entertaining* or *undemanding* lesson or teacher.

To return to the question, there is no directly relevant research on the effects of enjoyment on learning, but there is a lot of related evidence that can be summarized in one nice sentence: happy states promote creative thinking. In a wide variety of studies—some conducted in laboratories, some in real settings, with adults or children, in social or cognitive tasks—it has been demonstrated that even mildly positive states of mind increase cognitive elaboration and flexibility, giving rise to more thoughts, both usual and unusual. This flexibility leads to superior problem-solving ability, especially on tasks that require a creative, unusual response. Two psychologists, among many others, have worked a great deal in this area of **positive affect**, as it is called. They are Alice Isen and Barbara Fredrickson, and both describe the benefits of emotions such as joy, gratitude, enjoyment, interest, curiosity, and so on. Isen's work demonstrates immediate benefits, such as better problem solving or more prosocial behaviour. Frederickson's work is about the long-term benefits of even fleeting periods of positive affect. In her own words, 'not only do positive emotions make people feel good in the present, but also, through their effects on broadened thinking, positive emotions increase the likelihood that people will feel good in the future'. She contrasts this with the 'downward spiral' of depressed moods, which lead to thoughts and behaviours that are narrow and further depress the individual. Fredrickson's **broaden-and-build** theory explains that when we are in a good mood, we have more ideas, are more exploratory and sociable. This expansiveness builds lasting resources (intellectual, physical, social and psychological) which help us in future as well.[2]

A related question is whether enjoyment leads to better memory of a lesson. The evidence here is not so clear. There is a well-documented relationship between emotion and memory, but the emphasis in such research has been mostly on *negative* emotions and *episodic (personal, autobiographical)* memories. We all know, from our own experience, that strongly emotional events are remembered longer and more vividly than other events. This is largely due to the action of the hippocampus and its close neighbour the amygdala, which jointly increase the level of attention paid to emotional stimuli. Both brain parts also seem

---

[2] There is even a fair amount of brain-based research on the effects of happy states. Parts of the brain respond to mild positive affect by releasing greater quantities of a chemical called **dopamine**. Dopamine acts on several other brain sites in ways that help us link ideas together in new and useful ways. For example, one such site is the cingulate cortex, which was described in Chapter One. This small brain area is responsible for 'executive attention', and increased levels of dopamine here probably help the mind select from among competing cognitive perspectives, or switch back and forth between them. Dopamine also acts on the prefrontal cortex, the hippocampus and amygdala, all of which are responsible for various functions of memory.

to influence the process of *memory consolidation*—the 'setting' of relatively fragile early memories into the neocortex (Chapters One and Three have described some of these processes). But as I said, these findings relate mostly to stimuli that arouse fear, disgust or anxiety in us.

This brings us to the effects of negative emotions on learning, and here we can look at academic anxiety, which is rather commonly reported among students all over the world. Research on test anxiety over the decades has consistently shown how destructive this emotion can be, both for test performance as well as for overall well-being. Test anxiety reduces precious resources of working memory, so that performance on complex tasks (that require more of those resources) suffers. Essentially, the problem is that task-irrelevant and unproductive thoughts intrude upon the mind. These thoughts are limited in scope, but can completely derail the process of answering a test paper. A test-anxious student is likely to be preoccupied about his poor performance, wondering how others are performing, and how his performance will be judged by the teacher. With all this cognitive interference, it is no wonder that he cannot perform well on the test.

Early research showed that some students are more susceptible to test anxiety than others, and importantly, that they *perform as well as more relaxed students under non-test conditions.* The psychologist who has probably done the most work in this area is Irwin Sarason, whose research on test anxiety extended from the 1950s to the 1980s. In one of his studies, he tried to reduce test anxiety in students in one of two ways: reassurance ('don't worry; you'll do just fine') and reminders to focus on the task at hand ('concentrate all your attention on the problems; don't let yourself get distracted'). Sarason found the first method was less helpful in improving test performance than the second method—that is, telling students to relax was less effective than helping them refocus. His finding makes sense under the assumption that test anxiety is more of a cognitive-distraction phenomenon than a tension-stress phenomenon.

But tension and stress are, unfortunately, a large part of our students' lives. Students in India face tests and examinations at frequent intervals from a very young age, besides an almost constant pressure to perform to arbitrary standards. Indian psychiatrists have documented this (mostly middle-class) phenomenon, noting that there has been a steep rise in mental health issues, and even suicides, related to the fear of failure at school. But one wonders about the day-to-day experiences of even emotionally healthy students.

A recent study allows us a glimpse into the daily lives and feelings of urban, middle-class, eighth standard students in Chandigarh, using an interesting technique called *experience sampling*. Suman Verma, Deepali Sharma and Reed Larson gave hundred students an alarm watch each, which beeped at random times through the day for a week. At every beeped reminder, the student was to note down several things, including where she (or he) was, what she was doing, whether she wished she was elsewhere, and how she was feeling on a range of scales (e.g., happy-unhappy, cheerful-irritable, and so on). The results were fascinating. Students spent about a third of their time on school work (which included class time, homework and tuitions) a little more than a third on leisure (television, music, talking and sports, in that order!) and a little less than a third on maintenance activities (mainly eating). But there were clear differences in their emotional states during these three times. During school work activities, the students reported feeling less happy, relaxed and excited and more lonely, disappointed and worried. For example, they expressed that they were, 'very bored, I have to study, study and study', 'tired, I had been doing a lot of work at school', 'irritated, I had been woken up early because of a test' and 'worried, I was not prepared for my maths exam'. The students also reported highest levels of attention to their work when they were happy, felt they had chosen the activity themselves, and did not wish themselves elsewhere. The authors conclude that the fear of punishment for not doing homework is a major source of stress among school students, and that 'school education needs to strike a balance between learning and positive emotional experiences'.

Stress!

A young student is walking to school along a path, through tall grass. Suddenly, without warning, a tiger leaps onto the path in front of him and stands there, growling and smacking its lips. The

boy immediately freezes, as unknown even to himself, his body has with lightning speed readied itself to either fight this danger or flee from it. The moment the threat is perceived, a hormone called **adrenalin** is released in large amounts through his bloodstream. This has the effect of making more oxygen-rich blood available to the muscles that will help him survive the menacing tiger; and diverting blood away from non-essential systems such as digestion. In the brain, neural networks of heightened attention and focus are activated.

At the same time, a second and somewhat slower reaction is initiated in the boy's body: a hormone called cortisol enters the bloodstream to release energy from fat and muscle stores. This process is meant to replace what was used up by the first, energy-intensive reaction, and, thus, the second reaction can be seen as helping the body recover from the first reaction after the danger has passed. Meanwhile, in the brain, elevated levels of blood cortisol are picked up by receptors especially sensitive to cortisol— and these receptors happen to be concentrated in our old friend, the hippocampus. This is no accident; the hippocampus, which is responsible for the encoding of memories, is thus encouraged to lay down strong memories of this tiger encounter, so that the young student can avoid this path the next time. Finally, when cortisol levels reach a certain amount in the blood, the brain 'switches off' the production system like a thermostat, and everything returns to normal. The typical human stress response is beautifully engineered!

But of course, few students today are going to encounter a tiger on the way to school. Instead, the boy is probably on his way to an examination. Or, perhaps, because he did not complete his homework the previous evening, he is on his way to a scolding and a punishment. These are non-life-threatening situations, but they will probably bring about stress reactions in the boy. Now, the elevated cortisol in his blood is in *anticipation* of what is to come. In fact, many students' lives today are filled with a series of low-level stressors, which bring about repeated small elevations of cortisol in the blood. The net effect of these is that the brain raises its 'thermostat' setting, allowing higher and higher levels of cortisol to circulate in the blood. And in the long run, chronic elevations of cortisol lead to hypertension, ulcers, heart disease and other medical conditions.

Stress is not good for the body or the brain, and it is not good for academic achievement, either.[3] Some confusion may arise over the point made earlier about the memory benefits of stressful situations. I mentioned that elevated cortisol spurs the hippocampus to lay down stronger memories. And, since memory is so all-important in our schools, could stress actually be 'good' for children? No, a thousand times, no. First, the memory most strongly affected by this process is a certain kind of spatial memory (perhaps because the *location* of danger is so important) and there is no evidence that this would extend to better memory for school subjects such as mathematics or history. Second, there is no evidence that stress *preceding* the stressful event will do any good to memory. Elevated cortisol leads to enhanced memory to help you avoid danger the next time you are in a similar situation, but in situations where *anticipation* causes stress, cortisol doesn't help much. How can you better remember the future?! Third, and most important, research on the developing brain has recently shown that stress and the concomitant high levels of cortisol actually

---

[3] The effects of stress on academic performance must not be confused with a long-known fact about **arousal**; the famous 'inverted U' relationship that all beginner students of psychology learn. It says that a moderate level of arousal can improve performance on well-practised or over-learned tasks, but reduces performance on complex tasks which are at the limits of one's ability. The implications of this are obvious: the arousal of stress will not help students perform better on any but the most trivial tests of their ability or learning.

destroy crucial neurons in the hippocampus, thus impairing memory and learning ability in the long term.

Academic situations are not the only source of stress and anxiety in students. Equally painful is the social stress of being rejected by one's peers, or the stress of witnessing conflict between one's parents, for example. It turns out that there are many risk factors that could derail a happy, healthy childhood, and we can categorize them as follows:

- Psychobiological and cognitive factors, such as hyperactivity, inattention and difficulty reading social interactions, as well as learning difficulties.
- Family difficulties to do with harsh discipline or problematic relationships.
- Ecological factors, such as dangerous neighbourhoods and an antisocial peer group.
- Problematic peer relations, such as bullying and rejection.
- School practices, such as competitive classroom environments, corporal punishment, constant comparative evaluation.

Serious emotional problems in childhood or adolescence are usually the result of more than one of these risk factors simultaneously. As you can imagine, in situations where only a single risk factor is involved, other positive processes can help the student through his difficulties. A supportive family and school can help a student get through the difficulties of being dyslexic, for example. Or, a child with good friends, and who is coping with the academic demands of school, may be able to ride the difficult period of her parents' divorce. But for students with multiple factors at risk, the result can be chronic emotional or behavioural problems. Children can suffer from depression and anxiety disorders, as well as several conduct-related disorders, for which teachers and parents may seek the help of a professional. Understanding the root cause of a child's emotional disturbance allows us to seek the best solutions, besides helping us to anticipate what could go wrong and prevent it.

One group of children that consistently suffer from risk at multiple levels are students from poor families. For instance, lower income children do not receive as much cognitive stimulation at home as do middle or upper income children, and this affects their cognitive and developmental growth. Studies conducted among poor families in Turkey, China, Vietnam, Brazil, Jamaica and South Africa have shown that when mothers are trained to speak and play more effectively with their children, there is a significant improvement in the child's verbal ability, IQ and performance in school. Children in poverty also experience stressful life events and daily problems to a far greater degree than other children, and, therefore, might be expected to have more emotional difficulties as well. An emotionally unhealthy environment for a growing child is one that threatens safety, is violent or abusive, chaotic and unpredictable; and poverty brings many of these risks into the child's life. Even if their lives are

Box 2

CHILDREN OF AFFLUENCE

Here is a curious statement about American adolescents I would like to quote from psychologist Mikhail Csikszentmihalyi: 'The reported happiness of teenagers…shows a very significant inverse relationship to the social class of the community in which teens live…Children of the lowest socio-economic strata generally report the highest happiness, and upper middle-class children generally report the least happiness.' What are we to make of this? While we have often heard it said that money cannot make us happy, we don't expect it to have the reverse effect! Of course, it could be that affluent children avoid presenting themselves as happy. But the work of Suniya Luthar, a psychologist based in the US, points to several sources of emotional stress among these children in particular. Before I summarize these for you, we must remind ourselves that this research was done in the West, and again, its applicability in the Indian context may be limited. Personally, I find her conclusions to be remarkably similar to my own observations of urban Indian middle- and upper-class youth.

Luthar has consistently found higher levels of anxiety, depression and substance abuse in affluent adolescents. Unfortunately, these families do not easily accept the smaller signs of emotional disturbance in their children, although they will avail of excellent mental health services when such disturbance becomes obvious and serious. Perhaps there are privacy issues at work here, or maybe privileged people find it harder to admit that things can go wrong, and try instead, as Luthar puts it, to 'maintain a veneer of well-being'. Two sources of their children's emotional difficulties seem to be achievement pressures, and isolation from adults. Parental expectations of their children are high, and they are often enrolled in several out-of-school activities. This 'overscheduling', as it is called, only adds to the pressure of having to excel in school itself.

It is not at all unusual to find Indian children hopping from tennis class to tabla class…but what is unique to our context is the *fucking Tuition.*

ugly spectre of *Tuition*. Most children in these income brackets spend their evenings in a parallel set of classes, relearning what they were supposed to learn at school in the first place. Their parents, meanwhile, often hold top positions in successful careers, which keep them so busy that they are unable to spend much time with their children either. It is tempting to imagine that a close emotional bond with one's child is not dependent on literal *time spent together*, but there is sufficient indication from the research that such time is absolutely necessary.

Luthar also uncovered an interesting set of peer norms in her upper-class American adolescent samples. Popularity among boys depended on being aggressive and willing to get into substance abuse, while among girls it revolved around being physically attractive. Not surprisingly, these peer norms spelled trouble for their emotional and physical health. These findings may or may not apply to our Indian urban elite (perhaps they are too busy studying) but it would be fascinating to study these matters in the Indian context.

Finally, the problem may also be an overemphasis on **material sources of happiness**. For several years now, there has been a move toward a 'positive psychology', that is, a focus on variables such as happiness and contentment. Studies are showing that although human beings pursue external sources of happiness, these sources simply do not deliver the goods. Luthar says, '...today's economically privileged children...rarely cite life goals such as seeking intellectual challenge or contributing to humankind'. She points out that the mainstream media constantly pushes the value of more power, more money, more physical attractiveness, which ultimately leads to stress in children of affluence. The emotional health of these young people will have far-reaching consequences for society in general, because they are likely to be influential in their spheres of work as adults. Depression and anxiety obviously will reduce their productivity, but more subtly, psychological research shows that unhappy people tend to be more acquisitive than philanthropic.

not severely dysfunctional, research has shown that poor children receive more corporal punishment by the adults in their lives, and their teachers tend to be more authoritarian, and ask them fewer questions that encourage answers.

While you will readily understand that children growing up in poverty must face emotional difficulties, you may be surprised to learn that children from affluent families also suffer their own brand of emotional stress. You will find this research described in Box 2. In the next section, we look at what constitutes emotional health or emotional maturity, and what a teacher could do to foster it in his students.

Developing Emotional Maturity

Two important aspects of emotionality studied by psychologists are **emotion arousal** and the **capacity for regulation**. Arousal can be defined as the intensity of emotional experience, and regulation as the control of this intensity, as well as of the duration of facial, gestural and other behavioural reactions to the emotional state. These two variables are related to a wide range of important outcomes for children, such as social adjustment, academic performance, and even psychopathological outcomes, such as depression or attention deficit hyperactivity disorders. Understandably, both arousal and regulation matter more in the case of negative emotions such as sadness and anger, and regulation is more important for children with tendencies towards high emotional arousal.

How would you measure arousal and regulation, particularly among children? This is an interesting question because it illustrates both the difficulties inherent in psychological measurement, and the ingenuity of psychologists determined to measure the immeasurable! The most common method is to ask children questions, and trust their responses as a fairly good approximation to the real thing. Self-report methods, as these are called, are of different kinds. For instance, the PANAS-C (Positive And Negative Affect Scale for Children) gives ten- to fourteen-year-olds adjectives like *lively, gloomy, daring* and *blue*, and asks them to rate the degree to which they felt these over a few days or weeks. The CSCRS (Child Self-Control Rating Scale) asks them to rate the degree to which, for example, they keep promises, calm down when excited, and think before answering. The HIF (How I Feel) scale asks children to rate statements about the previous three months, such as, *I was happy very often, I was scared most of the time, When I felt sad my sad, feelings were very powerful,* and *When I felt mad, I could control or change how mad I felt.* For moment-to-moment records of emotional states, there is the ESF (Experience Sampling Form) described earlier in the study done by Verma and her colleagues. Of course, the results of self reports must be used with caution, or better still, in conjunction with other measures of children's emotionality. The study described below is a simple example of how this can be accomplished.

Nancy Eisenberg (whose work on moral development you read about in Chapter Six) along with Jeffrey Liew and Sri Untari Pidada studied emotionality in a group of Indonesian children. The psychologists assessed intensity of emotion, capacity for control, and social functioning, by having teachers rate their students, parents rate their children, and students rate each other. Typical items for the parents and teachers were, 'My child responds very emotionally to things around him/her', 'This child can wait before entering into new activities if he/she is asked to,' 'This child gets angry when called in from play before he/she is ready to quit', 'My child acts shy around new people', and 'This child often feels sorry for others who are less fortunate'. Students themselves were asked to list four peers who were most likely to get angry, four whom they liked the most, and four they liked the least. These 'top four' rankings were weighted and averaged across all peers to yield a single score for each student. The psychologists were curious to know whether the emotional patterns of intensity and regulation were related to social status and acceptance by peers in a different culture, since this had been demonstrated several times for students in Western cultures. The answer was 'yes'. In this Indonesian sample too, unregulated children were socially unaccepted. When they expressed a negative emotion such as anger repeatedly and intensely, it led to peer rejection. On the other hand, when they internalized a negative emotion such as sadness or anxiety, it led to shyness and a different form of isolation from peers.

Given the fairly universal importance of emotion arousal and regulation, you will want to know what an adult can do to help young people in these areas. There are four things that psychologists say we can tell our students about the regulation of negative emotions in particular, and these are listed below:

- Deal directly with the emotion (e.g., relaxation techniques or medication).
- Focus on improving your underlying competence in some areas, which will bring in positive emotions.
- Critically examine your explanations for the way you feel.
- Change the situation you are in, if it is making unreasonable demands on your peace of mind.

Options one and two are fairly straightforward, but options three and four are more interesting from an educational point of view. Let us look first at option three, which asks the student to examine the way he explains his own emotions.

One important contributor to emotional stability is the set of beliefs a student has about his personality and abilities. All students are sure to experience failure and setbacks in their school years, in areas such as academic achievement, athletic achievement, personal relationships and social success. In the face of a negative experience, such as doing poorly in a test, being rejected by a peer, or getting punished by a teacher—how do they recover and continue pursuing goals? Perhaps the key lies in the *meaning* given to failures or setbacks. When failure occurs, it is implied that change is required, whether in the form of trying harder next time, or working with a different strategy. If a student believes that such change is possible at all, he will put energy into the change and 'give it another shot'. But, if he believes that his abilities and/or personality are fixed, he will react defensively, trying to cope with the 'knowledge' that failure has provided about his limitations. Thus, a setback may be seen on the one hand as a challenge for change, but on the other hand as disastrous, and therefore energy draining. This determines whether a student will respond passively, defensively, or actively. It determines whether he will spend his time proving himself, or eagerly seeking challenges for learning. And it therefore determines the emotional quality of his school life.

We need to help our students see that **performance is a means to learning, instead of learning being a means to performance**. Obviously as teachers, the way we respond to mistakes or poor performance will make a huge difference. We ourselves may be guilty of viewing performance (whether on homework, tests, assignments or presentations) as an end-point, an indication of a student's worth, rather than as an invaluable guide for improvement. To this extent, we must not be surprised if our students believe the same things we do about performance and failure.

Let us turn now to the fourth suggestion relating to emotion regulation—changing the emotionally stressful situation. It is unreasonable, of course, to suggest to a distressed student to 'change her situation' by herself, but schools and teachers can make changes in the environments that they create for their students. Robert Roeser is a psychologist who has written extensively about healthy educational environments, and he suggests four classroom and school level reforms: *curriculum, competence, community and care.*

- The curriculum must be suited to students from many different backgrounds, and include cooperative learning and graded, reachable goals.
- Teachers must aim for each student to achieve a level of competence, acknowledging mistakes as a part of learning, instead of thinking in terms of success and failure.
- Students must be allowed opportunities for decision making within the school community, so that they value and feel 'bonded' to their school.
- Students must be given opportunities to form close relationships, with each other as well as with the adults, perhaps through the creation of smaller learning groups within the school.

Pekrun, too, has come up with a strikingly similar list of positive ways in which schools and teachers can contribute to emotional stability among students. He elaborates more on areas such as competence and control. We need to give our students demanding tasks that are still within their ability, but not only for cognitive and motivational reasons. There are emotional benefits as well, such as feeling good

about completing a demanding task. In other words, *feeling* competent is as important as *wanting to be* competent and *being* competent. A sense of control comes from being allowed to work in a self-regulated way, whether in groups or individually. In the individual situation, the student can be given the responsibility to plan the way she will work through the material, pace herself and make sure she gets whatever feedback is necessary to master the material. In a group situation, the students as a whole can be made responsible for making decisions about how they will divide the work, assign tasks and make members accountable. The teacher's role is to hover around making sure the learning goals are being met for each student, but the students have to clearly be given collective control. Cooperative group work of this kind, says Pekrun, is also valuable because it serves our social needs to help and to be of help.

This chapter would be incomplete without the mention of another variable that originated in psychological research, but sparked the imagination of the lay public far more than emotion arousal and regulation ever did. Happiness and emotional health have often been associated with a high sense of **self-esteem**, an enticing variable with an interesting history. As has happened so often before, with this variable too, popular psychology presented a picture that was appealing and simplistic, that seemed to lead to easy answers and methods for teachers: make children feel good about themselves, and they will do better. The last section of this chapter tells the story of self-esteem, and the questions that psychologists are raising about it. I should add that I see the concept potentially gaining popularity in urban Indian educational circles, which is why a critical understanding of its meaning and value is so necessary for us.

Self-esteem

Since the early 1970s, over fifteen thousand journal articles have been written about self-esteem, or how a person evaluates herself. Across three decades of furious output in the field, the popular psychology message was that this variable was extremely important because it could result in many positive outcomes, such as optimism about the future, reduced alcohol usage, lower aggression, job success, physical health and longer life. For educators, the claim was that high self-esteem would result in better school performance. Naturally, teachers and parents were immediately advised to avoid criticism in favour of praise, praise and more praise...and tens of thousands of teachers (primarily in the West) followed this advice earnestly.

One of the most important things to understand about self-esteem is that there is **no requirement of accuracy** in the concept—someone with many positive qualities and accomplishments may nevertheless be low on self-esteem, while another who is not particularly competent or talented may nevertheless have high self-esteem. Of course, there are people whose self-esteem *does* match with a more objective evaluation. Thus, self-esteem is a perception, not a reality about oneself. The claim of the movement was that self-esteem, essentially a perception, could have a significant effect on performance, quite separate from the reality of the student's abilities and skills. And if the movement was supported by more than fifteen thousand studies, surely it had to be right?

Wrong! The truth was that all through the years, several studies had failed to show strong relationships between self-esteem and outcomes. These negative results got buried under the enthusiasm of psychologists and lay people alike, who believed passionately that global self-esteem in individuals would bring about beneficial behaviours and thus a better society. One of the leading figures in the self-esteem movement was psychologist Roy Baumeister, who had probably published more papers in the field than anyone else. In 2003, he was commissioned to carry out a rigorous survey of the field, and he and his colleagues set about the task in good faith. To their dismay, the survey showed that the vast majority of the fifteen thousand papers were scientifically flawed. The message from the remaining good papers was that high self-esteem does *not* in fact boost achievement or any of a number of other outcomes. Baumeister, who is said to have called this the biggest disappointment of his career, now conducts research showing how boosting self-esteem can lead to *lower* performance and even failure under some conditions. One reason for the confusion was that most studies were **correlational**, and **causation** cannot be inferred from such data. That is, perhaps good school or job performance resulted in high self-esteem, or perhaps a third variable such as social class was a shared causal factor for both self-esteem and performance. Another source of confusion could have been that much of the research was based on self reports of both self-esteem *and* success. For the former, a self report is by definition necessary. But for the latter, a more objective measure is needed, since otherwise our measure of outcomes will be biased in the same direction as the individual's self-esteem! In other words, people with high self-esteem often have an exaggerated view of their own accomplishments, and this naturally spoils the data.

I cannot resist quoting Baumeister here:

> It is therefore with considerable personal disappointment that I must report that the enthusiastic claims of the self-esteem movement mostly range from fantasy to hogwash. The effects of self-esteem are small, limited, and not all good. Yes, a few people here and there end up worse off because their self-esteem was too low. Then again, other people end up worse off because their

self-esteem was too high. And most of the time self-esteem makes surprisingly little difference...For example, I think the world would be a better place if we could all manage to be a little nicer to each other. But that's hard: We'd all have to discipline ourselves to change. The self-esteem approach, in contrast, is to skip over the hard work of changing our actions and instead just let us all think we're nicer. That won't make the world any better.

You could say that today the self-esteem bubble has burst. Research shows that as the self-esteem movement, and even levels of self-esteem among individuals, have risen in the US, so have rates of depression and anxiety and suicide. No causal links can be drawn here, of course, but the correlation certainly makes you sit up and take notice. There are important emotional issues involved in boosting self-esteem, and we have to tease these out carefully. Greater rigour and attention to the various aspects of self-esteem has helped psychologists to identify several major problems, which are summarized below.

- The self-esteem movement emphasizes making students 'feel good about themselves', with insufficient attention paid to boosting actual skills and competence on which to base that self-esteem.
- High self-esteem *per se* must be distinguished from the **pursuit of self-esteem**. Boosting a student's self-esteem temporarily *reduces* anxiety. But, when the student takes on the work of protecting, maintaining, and enhancing her

own self-esteem, it *increases* anxiety. This is a truism about human beings in general; we all pursue self-esteem at the cost of our own peace of mind!

- While the *successful* pursuit of self-esteem reduces anxiety and other negative emotions, in many classrooms self-esteem can become a scarce resource, gained only at the expense of others. For many students, therefore, the *failed* pursuit of self-esteem leads to increases in sadness, anger and shame.

- Because failure leads to a loss in self-esteem, students whose self-esteem is contingent on academic performance experience great pressure to succeed, and this leads to lower intrinsic motivation to learn.

- If self-esteem becomes a student's goal, she will tend to over-generalize negative events to encompass her entire worth as a person. This can lead to depression.

Of all these damning points, the 'costly pursuit of self-esteem', a term coined by psychologist Jennifer Crocker, is perhaps the most interesting to explore. She and her colleagues have contributed immensely to a deeper and subtler understanding of the whole self-esteem movement, by their focus on the effects of having a self-esteem goal in life. Crocker says that self-esteem or self-worth is *not an essential requirement for personal well-being*, whereas competence, relatedness and autonomy are. Even so, self-esteem often becomes a goal in life for many people, and this can lead to unintended and undesirable outcomes. For instance, it seems likely that such a goal would have an impact on the quality of our interpersonal relationships, and whether they can be mutually supportive. Research shows that people with self-esteem goals tend to blame others following threats to the self. While blaming others protects self-esteem, it is no good for relationships. Another suggestive finding is that people with already high self-esteem often pursue self-esteem through dominance and competence, whereas people low on self-esteem pursue it through wanting to be accepted by others.

All these points may remind you of the section on praise in Chapter Eight. Indeed, these two ideas are strongly linked, and this is where the teacher comes in. When the adult praises a student's personality or ability (implying that these two are fixed) rather than the work she has done, in future she begins to ask herself: am I smart? am I a winner or a loser? Instead, if students can have (in Baumeister's words) 'a sober, accurate recognition of their actual talents and accomplishments', they can ask themselves: what do I want to become? what do I want to learn? what about myself do I want to develop? Again, this is similar to the discussion a few pages ago on the way students respond to failures or setbacks. There, too, we saw that certain beliefs lead the student to view performance as a feedback about fixed ability, rather than as an indication of how to improve the next time around. The connection with self-esteem is obvious.

In Conclusion

The underlying issue throughout this chapter has been the student's emotional health and maturity. We have visited concepts as varied as flow and enjoyment, anxiety and stress, emotion regulation and self-esteem. There is one more 'feeling', if we could call it that, which has only recently come up in the psychological literature, and it is **contentment**. The idea of inner contentment is subtly distinct from happiness in the way we are used to thinking of it. Ancient spiritual and philosophical traditions such as Buddhism say, for instance, that contentment cannot come from strengthening one's concept of self. Perhaps paradoxically, a strong self concept is actually weak, because it is always under threat, constantly in need of protection, and therefore forever at the mercy of external circumstances. A few psychologists, Roeser among them, are successfully bringing these philosophical ideas into mainstream psychological research.

Crocker, Deci and many other psychologists believe that the sources of emotional well-being lie in three key areas: competence, relatedness and autonomy. Interestingly, all three areas are conditional on a strong sense of being a self—a self who is good at such and such, who is related to other selves, and who is in control of her own life. Is this in conflict with the idea of 'true' contentment, as described by several philosophers over the centuries? Crocker suggests that this may be the case, when she says, '...such goals [of having competence, relatedness, or autonomy] do not shift the focus away from the self but instead are still focused on getting something for the self and thus are likely to trigger fears and anxieties rather than motivate people to move forward in spite of their fears and anxieties'.

The emotional fallout of this deep self-interest becomes apparent when we look closely at ourselves and our students. To quote Crocker again, '...people pursue self-esteem by trying to satisfy their beliefs about what they need to be or do to have worth and value; this pursuit has temporary emotional benefits when people succeed but big costs when they fail'. The alternative that she and her colleagues put forth is to have more inclusive goals, which encompass the needs of others as well as one's own. This idea flies in the face of current educational practice which emphasizes the individual's gain over all else.

The late philosopher and educationist J. Krishnamurti wrote in his *Commentaries on Living* (First Series):

You have a certain estimation of yourself, have you not?

We all place ourselves at various levels, and we are constantly falling from these heights. It is the falls we are ashamed of. Self-esteem is the cause of our shame, of our fall. It is this self- esteem that must be understood, and not the fall. If there is no pedestal on which you have put yourself, how can there be any fall?... Why have you put yourself on a pedestal called self- esteem, human dignity, the ideal, and so on? If you can understand this, then there will be no shame of the past; it will have completely gone. You will be what you are without the pedestal. If the pedestal is not there, the height that makes you look down or look up, then you are what you have always avoided. It is this avoidance of what is, of what you are, that brings about confusion and antagonism, shame and resentment. You do not have to tell me or another what you are, but be aware of what you are, whatever it is, pleasant or unpleasant: live with it without justifying or resisting it.

Underlying everything we do is a strong assumption that each of us *is* a separate, permanent and real self. So natural is this assumption that questioning it is seen as the domain of abstract philosophy, certainly not admissible in the classroom, as a part of a conversation between a teacher and his students. Yet in recent years, mainstream psychologists have increasingly come to question the reality of the self. From a brain and biology point of view, there seems to be no particular place where the self resides. Current theories often refer to the self as an illusion created by neuronal processes from instant to instant.

It would be fascinating to learn more about the possible implications of these findings for emotional health, and in the references following this chapter, I have included several sources in the area. Even better, we can think of sharing these tentative ideas in open discussions with our students, especially the older ones. Adolescence is famous for being a time when young people are seeking to establish an 'identity'; this may also be just the time when they can grapple with the intriguing suggestion that true emotional security comes from not having an identity at all! The last chapter of this book deals with adolescents and the many challenges they present, not least of which is that as adults in their lives we must take the exciting opportunity to engage with them on some of the deepest and most fundamental questions of human existence.

References and Bibliography

1. Ashby, F.G., A.M. Isen, and A.U. Turken, 1999. 'A Neuropsychological Theory of Positive Affect and Its Influence on Cognition'. *Psychological Review*, Vol. 106, No. 3, 529–50.

2. Buchanan, T.W., 2007. 'Retrieval of Emotional Memories'. *Psychological Bulletin*, Vol. 133, No. 5, 761–79.

3. Csikszentmihalyi, M. (1999). 'If we are so rich, why aren't we happy?' *American Psychologist*, Vol. 54, No. 10, 821–827.

4. Eisenberg, N., J. Liew, and S.U. Pidada, 2004. 'The Longitudinal Relations of Regulation and Emotionality to Quality of Indonesian Children's Socioemotional Functioning'. *Developmental Psychology*, Vol. 40, No. 5, 790–804.

5. Farmer, T.W., and E.M.Z. Farmer, 2001. 'Developmental Science, Systems of Care and Prevention of Emotional and Behavioural Problems in Youth'. *American Journal of Orthopsychiatry*, Vol. 71, No. 2, 171–81.

6. Immordino-Yang, M.H., and A. Damasio, 2007. 'We Feel, Therefore We Learn: The Relevance of Affective and Social Neuroscience to Education'. *Mind, Brain and Education*, Vol. 1, No. 1, 3–10.

7. Krishnamurti, J., 1956. *Commentaries on Living: First Series*. Krishnamurti Foundation India, Madras.

8. Luthar, S.S., and L.J. Latendresse, 2005. 'Children of the Affluent: Challenges to Well-Being'. *American Psychological Society*, Vol. 14, No. 1, 49–53.

9. Luthar, S.S., 2006. 'Over-Scheduling Versus Other Stressors: Challenges of High Socioeconomic Status Families'. *Social Policy Report*, Vol. XX, No. IV, 16–17.

10. Meyer, D.K., and J.C. Turner, 2002. 'Discovering Emotion in Classroom Motivation Research'. *Educational Psychologist*, 37(2), 107–14.

11. Molden, D.C., and C.S. Dweck, 2006. 'Finding 'Meaning' in Psychology: A Lay Theories Approach to Self-Regulation, Social Perception and Social Development'. *American Psychologist*, Vol. 61, No. 3, 192–203.

12. Nelson, C.A., and L.J. Carver, 1998. 'The Effects of Stress and Trauma on Brain and Memory'. *Development and Psychopathology*, 10, 793–809.

13. Phelps, E.A., 2004. 'Human Emotion and Memory: Interactions of the Amygdala and Hippocampal Complex'. *Current Opinion in Neurobiology*, 14:198–202.

14. Roeser, R.W., J.S. Eccles, and A.J. Sameroff, 1998. 'Academic and Emotional Functioning in Early Adolescence'. *Development and Psychopathology*, 10, 321–52.

15. Roeser, R.W., C. Midgley, and T.C. Urban, 1996. 'Perceptions of the School Psychological Environment and Early Adolescents' Psychological and Behavioral Functioning in School: The Mediating Role of Goals and Belonging'. *Journal of Educational Psychology*, Vol. 88, No. 3, 408–22.

16. Walden, T.A., V.S. Harris, and T.F. Catron, 2003. 'How I Feel: A Self-Report Measure of Emotional Arousal and Regulation for Children'. *Psychological Assessment*, Vol. 15, No. 3, 399–412.

CHAPTER ELEVEN

Adolescence, a Biopsychosocial Shift

In many societies around the world, there is a gap of several years between attaining sexual maturity and becoming an 'adult'. The main reason for this gap seems to be that young people need to master many complex skills before they can be truly independent, and in industrialized societies this is not complete till they are about eighteen years old or more. This period of time is called adolescence, and psychologists are divided about whether it is a social construct, or a true stage of development. Some believe that it is an **artefact of industrialized societies**, but others believe that in *any* society, there is bound to be a period of adjustment between childhood and adulthood. Adjusting to new social roles is compounded by biological changes within the body, and it would be naïve to imagine a young person sailing through these challenges without any stress. From this point of view, adolescence and its various features are a relatively **universal phenomenon**.

Students in India reading psychology textbooks from the West often say that they feel little or no connection with the descriptions of adolescence found there. Yet, this is probably more a result of the way the chapters are written—their audience is primarily Western, and they do not write for the Indian context. There is ample psychological research of a good standard on adolescence that *is* applicable to us. Ideally, of course, we need to conduct our own research on the Indian adolescent, but we have a long way to go before we have a large enough research base from which to develop our own theories of adolescence in India. In this chapter, therefore, I will give you a flavour of the findings from mainstream psychology, drawing from them some useful and interesting lessons for us.

Apart from being biased towards Western conceptions of adolescence, the psychological research is also biased towards *negative* conceptions of this developmental period. Right from the 1950s, psychologists have studied and focused on conflict with adults, criminal tendencies, moodiness, and risk-taking behaviour among adolescent youth. This focus has fed into what is called the *storm-and-stress* model of adolescence. A large part of this can be traced to Sigmund Freud, who had his own colourful explanations for adolescent turbulence. In fact, his daughter Anna Freud apparently believed that 'to be normal during the adolescent period is by itself abnormal'! Since the 1990s or so, several psychologists have begun to re-examine this 'stereotype'. It is interesting that many lay people also carry this rather negative view of adolescence. And because of this, it becomes difficult to be sure that one's research results are valid. How much of the reported difficulty of this age group is a function of 'acting the part'? The methods we have of studying development are far from immune to such problems.

There are only a few ways to get a glimpse into the minds of adolescents. You could simply talk to them and ask them questions, and this is called the self-report method. Unfortunately, one of the hallmarks of adolescence is a strong need for privacy, so this method may not yield an accurate picture. You could talk to the people close to them (parents, friends, teachers) but they may be prejudiced by a storm-and-stress stereotype of adolescence, and so this method may not give accurate results either. Or you could observe adolescents and note the frequencies of various behaviours, and infer what might be going on in the mind. Psychologists have done all this, in addition to some amount of armchair philosophizing based on general impressions about young people. One of the problems with all these methods is that they cannot really track minute-to-minute emotional fluctuations or mood changes, something that rapidly changing hormonal activity would predict. This problem was solved by psychologists Mihaly Csikszentmihalyi and Reed Larson in the following imaginative way. Adolescents were given small beepers timed to go off every two hours or so. When the beeper went off, the young person was to fill in a form asking about his or her current activity, state of

mind, thoughts and feelings. This method revealed the rapidly fluctuating world of immediate sensations and emotions that adolescents inhabit. It also showed that the majority of conflicts they experienced were over seemingly small and trivial matters, even though the intensity of emotion was strong. Perhaps the fact that adults see as 'trivial' the things that adolescents consider important, is itself an important source of conflict.

With an awareness of cultural and popular bias about adolescence, as well as the difficulties of various research methods, we will be better equipped to evaluate the results of studies in this field.

All About Change

Several overlapping topics fall under the rather large umbrella of adolescent psychology. All of these have to do with change, which seems to be the key word for this stage of life. Of course, all of childhood is a period of tremendous growth and change, and we adults would like to feel that we are changing too, not fossilized! Yet the sheer rate and irregularity of changes make adolescence, in particular, a unique developmental stage. Just take a look at this list. Adolescence is characterized by:

- hormonal and other chemical changes in the body;
- changes in physical appearance which are sudden and obvious to others, signalling sexual maturity;
- emotional changes such as increased excitement, anxiety, elation, depression;
- new behaviours (conflict, aggression, taking risks, seeking thrills);
- new psychological issues, such as seeking a sense of identity, rebelling against authority, having romantic interests, increased self-consciousness, greater dependence on peers;
- social changes such as desiring and being given more autonomy and independence;
- cognitive changes, whether quantitative or qualitative, that allow for significantly higher levels of learning and understanding.

Hormonal and physical changes, and the sexual awakening they signal, are a powerful set of forces. These are universal physical markers of adolescence, and, to a great extent, the emotional and behavioural effects they have, might be expected to be similar across cultures. During adolescence, hormones exert their influence via increases in average concentration, as well as via irregularities in cycling pattern. An extremely thorough review of these influences was published in 1992 by Jacqueline Eccles and her colleagues. Eccles is a psychologist who studies many different aspects of adolescence, and without the 'negativity' bias I mentioned earlier. In fact, the summary of the 1992 paper begins with the statement, '...adolescence does not inevitably spell trouble'. And yet, to give you an idea of what is typically studied in adolescence, here are the topic headings in the paper: 'mood swings and mood intensity', 'depression', 'energy level', 'restlessness and concentration', 'irritability', 'impulsiveness', 'anxiety', 'aggression and behaviour problems', 'self-consciousness'! The paper examines the available evidence for hormones being at the root of all these phenomena. In a single sentence: hormones play both direct and indirect roles, and there are several possible paths of influence. The next two paragraphs will summarize the findings.

Changes in a young person's body may allow for certain behaviours, such as increased strength in boys leading them to use aggression to get what they want. Hormone changes (both in levels of testosterone and estrogen) can make the senses more alive and alert, and this can result in feelings of great well-being (almost a 'high'). On the other hand, more sensitivity to painful stimuli could result in irritability and anger. Hormone increases also lead to a more ready and rapid response to stimulation, leading in different situations to snapping back in anger, or laughing easily. Fluctuations in the basal metabolic rate or autonomic reactivity can contribute to energetic feelings at times, lethargy at other times. And finally, hormones can affect adolescents in a really roundabout way: if they and the people around them subscribe to the model that hormones cause significant storm-and-stress, the belief may become a self-fulfilling prophecy. Thus, in many cases even minor mood and behaviour changes may be labelled 'adolescent hormones'.[1]

With all this going on, non-hormonal factors such as school and family environment and temperament play an important role as well. Studies have shown that higher testosterone levels can lead to lower tolerance to frustration, which can mean more aggressive behaviour *when provoked*. In other words, a boy with high testosterone levels who is rarely or never provoked may never exhibit aggression, so the effect of the hormone is mediated by a non-threatening environment. Similarly, hormone changes do influence depression, but the effect is more pronounced for those adolescents who are psychologically vulnerable or in a stressful environment.

The classic adolescent quest is the search for a stable, integrated identity. The roots of this seem to lie in their realization that they behave so differently in different contexts ('Why did I do that, it isn't *like* me', or 'I'm just going to be *myself*', but then 'Which is the *real* me?'). According to the well-known psychologist Erik Erikson, identity formation is the most important task of adolescence. Identity is the sense of the continuity and sameness of one's self, in spite of the feeling of 'multiple selves'. It is also a set of beliefs about the self, including ways in which one is like other people, and ways in which one is unlike other people. Erikson's description of the process of identity formation suggests

---

[1] Hormonal fluctuations may increase vulnerability to an adolescent's psychological predispositions for mental illness, or to environmental stressors such as competitive academic examinations. This can lead to depression, and in extreme cases, suicide.

that it is an impressive and complicated job. It involves four levels of analysis for any adolescent:

- her judgments of others;
- others' judgments of her;
- her judgments of others' judgements, and,
- her knowledge of social and cultural norms by which to make judgements!

To make this clearer, let us look at an example. Suppose a thirteen-year-old sees a classmate getting caught in a lie about homework. Several trains of thoughts are likely to go through her mind, such as, 'She was stupid to lie about her homework', 'She was stupid to get caught', 'Will my friends think I'm a goody-goody girl if I tell the truth?' and 'Will the teacher think I'm bad if he finds out that

I cheated on the last test?' Or if a fourteen-year-old boy is friendly to a new student, he is likely to wonder 'Am I a friendly person? Would I be more 'cool' if I were rude to this new student? If my other friends don't like my being nice to this boy, maybe it's their problem!'

The young person's sense of self is strongly influenced by the values and practices in her environment, and here school plays an important role. Does your school give students a sense of belonging and safety, chances to explore the environment on their own with help available, and opportunities to participate in central activities? Or does it encourage a sense of isolation, pitting student against student and student against teacher, blocking attempts to explore and discouraging participation? No prizes for guessing which kind of school environment helps students to gain a positive representation of self. In the next section, you will find a longer discussion of school environments and their effects.

Another stereotypical struggle of adolescence is the increasing need for autonomy and independence. This is highly likely to lead to conflict with adults. Younger children accept adult authority in a wide range of situations, from personal hygiene and appearance, to how and with whom they spend their time. For adolescents, many of these situations are shifting from moral or conventional domains to the **personal domain** (see Chapter Six for descriptions of these three domain types). After all, eventually an adult sees most of his actions and decisions as nobody's business but his own, except, perhaps, for those actions that break the law. This shift from being answerable to adults on practically every issue, to being mostly answerable only to oneself, has to be gradual, and adolescence is the transition period.

Here, one wishes there was some data on the Indian adolescent, although one might require separate data on India adolescents from different classes, religious groups, and urban-rural settings. In one cross-cultural study that can more easily be applied to the Indian context, Andrew Fuligni asked American adolescents from four different cultural backgrounds (children of immigrants from the Philippines, China, Mexico and Europe) whether it would be 'OK' or 'not OK' for their parents to make rules in a variety of settings. These included sleeping late on weekends, talking on the phone, doing chores, keeping parents informed of activities, how to dress, which friends to socialize with, and cleaning one's room. Fuligni chose these ethnic groups expecting to find that children from cultures that value parental authority and devalue individuality would respond quite differently to European children. Yet he found surprisingly little difference among these groups. He also found a similar developmental pattern for all four groups— with age, many settings were increasingly considered 'personal'. In other words, it was increasingly 'not OK' for parents to have a rule about more and more issues. He summarizes his results in a sentence: 'Even within groups that traditionally emphasize parental authority over individual autonomy, children become more desirous of limiting the purview of parental authority as they progress through the adolescent years'.

Finally, we come to the cognitive changes that define adolescence. Although Piaget's theory of development had proposed a sharp jump in abstraction abilities, the research over several decades has pointed in the direction of gradual improvements in a range of more basic abilities. You may recall from Chapter Four on child development that many psychologists today argue for a more continuous, graded picture of cognitive development. Improvements can be seen in working memory, speed of processing, the amount and organization of long-term knowledge and metacognition, and these continue to get better and better through adolescence. Piaget's famous task involved chemicals in beakers and a tester that turned yellow only with a particular combination of chemicals. The child's job was to discover that combination through a series of trials. Using this task, he found that before the child is twelve years or so, he makes unsystematic and random trials, leaving out some combinations and repeating some, and therefore does not hit upon the exact solution which requires the *presence* of two chemicals and the *absence* of another. However, beyond age twelve or so, children begin to make systematic plans, and test the chemicals in such a way that all 15 combinations are tried in sequence and without repetition. In this way, 'formal-operational' reasoners, as Piaget called them, are able to arrive at the correct answer. Thus, adolescence came to be seen, at least cognitively, as the formal-operational stage.

Large numbers of adolescents all over the world have done this task since then, and the chemicals sloshing around in beakers have taught us two interesting lessons. First, barely twenty per cent of adolescents and adults are true formal-operational reasoners. Psychologists have devised other tasks requiring logical reasoning, such as determining which brand is the better buy and on all such tasks, too, the majority of adolescents and adults fail to reason logically.

And second, with explicit training, not only adolescents but even younger children can be more systematic reasoners. All this points to the power of improved basic abilities and explicit training in improving performance on a wide variety of complex tasks. Adolescents are at a high point in that developmental curve, and we can naturally expect to see changes in their reasoning in many areas.

Developmental and cross-cultural psychologist Michael Cole, whom you encountered in Chapter Four, explains that adolescents are increasingly able to think about hypothetical possibilities, to think about the future, to think about their own and others' thoughts, and to think beyond societal conventions. In fact, this last allows them to see the contradictions in adult life and adult society, leading sometimes to cynicism and a rejection of all tradition. Perhaps this movement feeds into their general need for autonomy, and we should not then be surprised that adolescents turn rebellious or resentful rather than merely *logical* questioners of us adults!

Change is difficult for any of us to adapt to, so we can readily understand the challenges that adolescents face when everything in their lives is changing so rapidly, both within themselves and, in their perception at least, outside themselves as well. We need to look for ways in which a school could support the young student through these changes, to help make the transition smoother. Unfortunately, the research suggests that schools provide more of a mismatch than a match for the adolescent's needs. The nature of this mismatch will be described in the next section, followed by suggestions for schools and teachers that arise from the research.

School and the Adolescent

What are your school's goals and how are they pursued? What messages does the school send about the meaning of success, and how are these translated by the teachers? Are students given opportunities to express themselves and to make important decisions? Do the teachers emphasize understanding and effort, or do they treat the 'smart' students better than everyone else? If the school favours homogeneous ability groups (by 'tracking' or 'streaming' students, for example), institutes prizes for achievement, and publicizes students' ranks, the focus is clearly on competition and social comparison. In such a setting, adolescent students pick up the message that improvement and mastery for individual students is not important to 'success'. This affects their motivation to learn, and can make them frustrated or, at the very least, *self-conscious* about learning. This, at a time when they are particularly prone to self-consciousness anyway. Self-consciousness impairs concentration, and brings in a fear of taking academic risks.

Many aspects of a school environment actually work counter to the special needs of an adolescent. Psychologist Robert Roeser and his colleagues have analysed the connection between school environments and adolescent needs both in the USA and in India. The adolescent needs to be in contact with emotionally supportive adults other than his parents, since in this stage of life he is seeking autonomy and independence from his parents. Romance is in the air, so he is also painfully conscious of how he appears to his peers (not just physically). The slightest social comparison can make him feel publicly humiliated. He is also intellectually and physically ready for more challenging work. But when he enters secondary school, the environment can be very unresponsive to his needs.

In some instances, the school and its demands do in fact change for the worse around the time students hit adolescence. For example, there is less emotional support from their teachers compared to when they were in primary school, more emphasis on comparative evaluation, and a trend toward departmentalized teaching. Large class sizes make close teacher-student relationships difficult, if not impossible, yet supportive relationships with adults other than their parents, are more important now than ever before. In other instances, the adolescent perceives the same type of environment differently, due to his new cognitive, emotional and motivational orientations. Adults are *seen* as more controlling, or less willing to give students opportunities for decision making and autonomy. There is clear evidence for this in a study done by Eccles and her colleagues with late and early maturing girls *in the same class*. The more physically mature girls expressed a greater desire to be involved in classroom decisions than did their less physically mature classmates. They reported a greater 'can't but should' mismatch between their desire for control and the opportunities given to them. For example, they would answer 'no' to the question, 'Do you get to help decide what math you work on during math class?' but 'yes' to the question, 'Should you have a say about this?' Eccles reports that this difference is partly due to changes in an adolescent's perception of the environment during puberty, and partly due to the fact that adults may actually respond to physical maturity with more controlling behaviour.

At a time when adolescents' levels of energy, stamina and strength are increasing, most of them are pushed into increasing amounts of book and desk work, and opportunities for physical activity actually decline. Similarly, a fourteen- to seventeen-year-old's capacities for logical reasoning, efficient information processing (due to better working memory) are increasing. But at around this age, more and more of their time is spent in preparing for tests and examinations. Unless these assessments are challenging in the right ways, this is a great waste of the adolescent's growing capacities for abstraction and comprehension.

The end result of all this mismatch is, in many cases, negative consequences for the student. Common outcomes in the area of academics are falling motivation, reduced interest in school, low achievement and a feeling that one is not competent. So, to return to the question stated in the beginning of this section, what can a school do to make transition smoother for the adolescent? Only you can decide what might work well in your particular setting. This is why I am always reluctant to list 'dos and don'ts', but nevertheless, I do list a few below, based on the research and my own observation.

Give your students more real responsibilities. Make them responsible not only for their own learning but also for things outside themselves. This will not lessen your load, however! More likely, it will require a *greater* investment of time and energy from you (at least initially). Tasks and situations will have to be structured in such a way that students can make decisions and execute them. But the idea is to gradually work towards being less of a controller and more a facilitator of your students' learning.

Allow for the importance of friendships among adolescents. Many of us adults regard such friendships with mild suspicion, and some schools have a policy of deliberately breaking up friendships each year by changing class composition. As teachers, we often have a tendency to 'separate' friends, and we may have sound reasons for this. But we risk alienation if we deny the importance of peer relationships, and further, we are denying the benefits of the peer group to a student's emotional life. And there *are* benefits. Although the term 'peer influence' has a negative connotation, as if it refers only to misbehaviour, there are positive behaviours that are influenced by one's peers. Further, the research indicates that we should not worry too much about our students' ability to resist the pressure of peers. Box 1 briefly explores these ideas.

Don't clamp down on girl-boy friendships. This is possibly the hardest 'don't' to follow, because there are, of course, real dangers in allowing adolescents to 'fully' explore their sexuality. Often, these very real dangers push us into a state of policing, banning and disallowing any sort of contact between girls and boys. This is a mistake, for at least two reasons. First, we are ignoring the fact that most of the adolescent's thoughts and feelings are directed towards physical attraction and romance—a natural, biological movement, if ever there was one. If we don't want them to express these drives in certain ways, we certainly shouldn't want them suppressed either. We *must* think creatively about how to manage this issue; clamping down is too easy, and will not work in the long run. Second, adolescents will explore their sexuality *anyway*, and just take care not to let disapproving adults know about it. Thus, we will have missed the opportunity to communicate with our students about sexuality, and they will learn nothing from us. Not that it will be easy to talk openly on these matters—understandably, adolescents regard these as private and will be reluctant to share their thoughts and feelings with us. Recent research points to the limited effectiveness of talking, however, and this is discussed more fully in the last section of this chapter.

Don't use comparative evaluation. Our whole system of education in India is based on performance and comparison, right from a very young age. Adults even tell toddlers, 'Let's see who eats faster', 'Hurry up or else he will finish first', and 'See how nicely she plays—why can't you play like her?' So when children turn into adolescents, you would think they would be used to it, impervious to the constant emphasis on comparative evaluation in almost every aspect of their lives! But it could also create a strong habit in them of evaluating themselves in comparison with others. Plenty of research shows that this is harmful to their growth and learning (see Chapter Eight on motivation). I don't believe that students are ever comfortable with such evaluation—even those who are relatively successful. In my school days, the most anxious student I knew was the girl who used to be 'first in class'. During adolescence, when students are thinking about and defining themselves, negative feedback will only feed into negative self-images and low self-esteem. So make sure your students know that you respect and value the learning process in each of them, and avoid using comparison as a prod to get better learning out of them.[2]

---

[2] You are almost certain to have a few students who seem to *need* the motivational push of comparison to do anything! However, adolescents are well able to understand and discuss abstract ideas such as motivation and comparison. You can invite them to critically examine these movements in themselves, but be willing to leave the results of such self-understanding to the individual student.

Box 1

THE PEER PHENOMENON

Anyone with even a little contact with adolescents knows that there are many different kinds of peer group values. For example, some peer groups value deep and affectionate friendship, others athletic prowess, and still others academic excellence. Both in psychological research and in the popular media, too much attention has been given to the value that some peer groups place on antisocial behaviours such as shoplifting, property damage and aggression—particularly among boys. Larry Steinberg, a researcher in the field of adolescent psychology, believes that this imbalance can be corrected by looking at neutral peer group values, such as styles of clothing and taste in music, as well as prosocial ones such as volunteering in charities. Decisions to work hard and do well at school are often a function of one's peer group, as are decisions to stay away from alcohol, drugs or sex.

There is also a widely held belief that adolescents have almost no resistance to peer influence. However, using a well-designed questionnaire to measure this interesting variable, Steinberg and his colleagues find that resistance to peer influence increases steadily between the ages of fourteen to eighteen years. The questionnaire requires you to choose one statement from a series of pairs, and rate the extent to which it describes you, such as—'Some people think it's more important to be an individual than to fit in with the crowd', BUT 'Other people think it is more important to fit in with the crowd than to stand out as an individual', and 'Some people go along with their friends just to keep their friends happy', BUT 'Other people refuse to go along with what their friends want to do, even though they know it will make their friends unhappy'.

Steinberg's research, conducted in the US, showed that the gradual increase in resistance to peer influence occurred for both boys and girls, and for students from different ethnic and social classes. Between the ages of ten to fourteen years, resistance to peer influence is quite low. Friends form an emotional safety net for the adolescent who has become emotionally independent of her parents, before she is ready for emotional autonomy. In a way, her dependence on parents is replaced by a dependence on peers. By age eighteen, says Steinberg, the adolescent has developed a sense of identity that allows her to gain more independence from her peers as well. In his words, '...we speculate that the growth of resistance to peer influence is a developmental phenomenon bounded by individuation from parents at its onset and by the development of a sense of identity at its conclusion'. In our context, we can speculate that this developmental phenomenon holds here as well, but that the ages may differ.

Give students challenging academic work. At this age, your students are capable of engaging with conceptually challenging work.

- Expose them to well-written material in the various subjects they are learning in school, and read and analyze it along with them. Sources could be editorials, magazine and journal articles, and excerpts from good books.
- Don't limit their cognitive demands to simply repeating answers or memorizing facts—that would seriously under-use their improved abstraction capacities.
- Particularly in our educational system, students are subject to more and more tests and examinations, and it is not at all clear what cognitive challenges they can create for themselves while endlessly 'studying' on their own. But, when they learn from a passionate and prepared teacher, or work through material that is conceptually excellent, their cognitive abilities are truly stretched and exercised. So look carefully at the proportion of time they spend in various kinds of academic activities, and try to maximize their cognitive challenges.
- By adolescence, students have had exposure to so many phenomena that it would be a pity not to help them connect it with their textbook learning as much as possible. They have built up a good store of knowledge and skills, and this allows for the possibility of learning new knowledge through associations with a wide base of prior knowledge and experience. For example, the topic of pressure can be taught with references to pressure cookers, brakes, pumps and ears popping in at high altitudes. English can be taught using examples from the way language is used in news reports, advertisements, speeches, conversations and letters.

These are all things that adolescents have a fair amount of experience with. So make use of their experience, and as far as possible, don't treat knowledge as if it existed in isolated, watertight compartments.

Make time for adults and adolescents to dialogue with each other. As mentioned above, one of the cognitive advances of this age group is the ability to question existing frameworks and conventions. Paradoxically, they are also in the grip of the influence of their peers, which can sometimes mean that they bravely reject adult conventions only to fall meekly in line with peer conventions. The ability to question 'the way things are' can be widened in scope to include questioning the powerful messages that adolescents receive from television, films and each other. You can have discussions with your students now on advertising, consumerism, the impact of our lifestyles on the environment, social inequity, relationship, morality, and freedom and social order. Hopefully, these are not just interesting armchair discussions, but ones that relate to your and your students' daily lives. Roeser puts it well:

> Education is also about assisting young people in becoming aware of and extricating themselves from habitual (automatic) ways of attending, perceiving, feeling, thinking, and doing by cultivating more mindful approaches to these basic self processes and ways of being in the world...(which) is a precondition for creativity, freedom of thought, and myriad forms of personal and social renewal.

For these dialogues to be meaningful, you must create a space of mutual respect and affection, where students and teachers feel free to communicate openly about their thoughts, feelings and opinions. Some guidelines for such dialogue sessions are listed in Box 2.

Box 2

DIALOGUES WITH YOUNG ADULTS: CREATING THE SPACE

Regular dialogue sessions are ideal for communicating with our students about some of the most important and serious matters in life. Here are a few suggestions for facilitating such sessions with thirteen- to eighteen-year-old students.

- You as the teacher are clearly a facilitator, in that you will give direction to the discussion, but not to the extent that you are constraining it. You might prefer not to give direction at all, and instead allow it to be a free flowing 'chat', but in my experience, everyone feels a sense of coherence and satisfaction when the dialogue has remained focussed. It is useful to have a topic or a question in mind so that you can initiate the dialogue, but make sure there is always an opening for a child to bring up something unexpectedly.

- You must ensure participation from everyone. This will be a real challenge in a large class, but even in smaller classes it is something you need to watch for. Encouraging participation does not mean that you force each child to speak. Silent listening has its value, but you can watch out for 'switching off'. Two simple techniques you can use are to 'go around' for comments, and to keep track of those who are quiet to direct a question to them occasionally.

- Some students need to gather their thoughts and formulate full sentences before they are willing to utter them, while others don't mind 'thinking aloud'. So look for ways to allow both types of student to participate. For example, give enough time for each child to complete his thought. Interruptions are the bane of any dialogue, and beyond a point, one cannot completely remove them. However, everyone can be sensitized to the fact that someone else may wish to speak or to complete their thought, and give that space.

- The language and vocabulary can be simple, and you can allow incomplete sentences and a preponderance (in some circles!) of words such as 'like', 'whatever' and 'something'. Yet, over time, it is good to encourage students to articulate clearly, in complete sentences. Being able to express one's own feelings and emotional states in clear language is a skill worth learning.

• This has to be a **safe space** where everyone feels free to share their feelings, opinions and thoughts freely and without fear of judgement. It takes hard work to create such a space, and one guideline is that the teacher must strictly avoid using it as a 'scolding' session, or to put across a moral lesson, however subtly. When students sense this, or imagine it, they clam up immediately.

Perhaps the most important point of all is that we as teachers must not have grand expectations of these dialogues. On two counts we risk being disappointed: first, because they may hold back from open communication, and second, because their behaviour may not match the maturity of their talk. As the last section of the chapter explains, while adolescents are increasingly capable of sophisticated verbalization, they are often not as 'in control' as they sound.

Perils and Promises of Adolescence

Everyone has heard about the famous risk-taking behaviour of adolescents—in areas such as sexuality, substance abuse and fast driving. One favourite explanation for the phenomenon is that young people cannot judge the consequences of the risky behaviour. For instance, they seem to think that they are immortal, or that they will never get addicted or pregnant. More and more nowadays, schools and other groups are educating adolescents for awareness on these issues. Programmes of raising awareness may have some effect on behaviour, but, for the most part, even those adolescents who 'know' all the facts continue to engage in risky behaviour. Psychologist Larry Steinberg tells us that there is virtually no connection between awareness campaigns and reduced levels of risky behaviour. After all, we do know from research in cognitive development that adolescents are more sophisticated and logical thinkers than younger children, and, furthermore, that they can imagine hypothetical situations, such as the consequences of rash driving. By age fifteen or so, our students are as logically sound in their thinking as we are, so it is unlikely that their behaviour stems from *really believing* that they are immortal, or will never get pregnant, or will not contract AIDS. Yet, it is a definite fact that levels of risky behaviour are higher during adolescence than at any other age. How is this paradox to be explained?

To answer this, we need to get acquainted with two brain networks: one is the **cognitive control network**, located in the outer regions of the brain (prefrontal and parietal cortices) and the other is the **socio-emotional network**, centred in limbic and paralimbic areas, such as the amygdala. Cognitive control includes thinking ahead, impulse control, delay of gratification (working towards a reward in the future) and self-regulation, and the brain regions involved develop gradually and steadily into early adulthood. The onset of puberty seems to have no special effect on the maturation of these regions. The socio-emotional network, on the other hand, governs sensitivity to emotional and social stimuli, sensation seeking and reward orientation (immediate rewards in particular). The brain regions involved become more sensitive and more easily aroused during puberty, and are particularly affected by the hormonal changes of adolescence.

Many decision-making situations bring these two networks into competition with each other during adolescence. When the young person is alone, the socio-emotional network is less strongly activated, and the cognitive control network can guide decision making. However, in emotional situations such as in the presence of peers, the reverse becomes true. The cognitive control system becomes powerless in such situations, *especially* for adolescents in whom the system is not even fully developed. Steinberg hypothesizes that the presence of peers acts like a social reward, thus activating those brain regions that are sensitive to such situations. The resulting impulses to act in a certain way will very likely be carried out because the adolescent is unable to inhibit them. Recent brain scan research confirms this general point in various ways. For example, in one study students with higher and lower resistance to peer influence had different brain activity patterns when shown video clips of angry people. Those who indicated *lower* resistance to peer influence on a questionnaire (see Box 1) had more brain activity in the premotor region (responsible for reading others' actions and preparing for one's own actions) while those who indicated *higher* resistance to peer influence on the questionnaire had more brain activity in the connections between the premotor and prefrontal regions (responsible for reasoned decision making). The greater degree of connectivity between the premotor and prefrontal areas of the brain probably allows for impulsive reactions to be inhibited when necessary. By the way, the differences between high and low resistance students disappeared when they were viewing neutral film clips. It does seem that resistance to peer influence is a matter of being able to balance the emotional and social 'high' (triggered by the presence of peers) with self-regulation and impulse control.

Steinberg reports on another interesting study on the effects of peer presence on risk taking. Adolescents (thirteen to sixteen), college students (eighteen to twenty-two) and adults (twenty-four plus) were given a computer game to play, which involved driving a vehicle as far as possible to gain points. At some points, a traffic light turns yellow and then red; skipping the red light may result in a crash. The psychologists measured the number of times that people tried to sneak past the yellow light—in other words, take a risky decision. Half the participants played this game alone, and the other half played while two friends watched and gave advice. The figure shows the results clearly: adolescents and, to a lesser degree, youths increased their risk-taking behaviour in the presence of peers. While playing alone, all three age groups played very similarly.

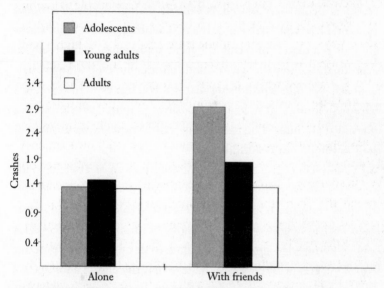

Risk taking of adolescents, young adults and adults during a video driving game, when playing alone and when playing with friends.

The research seems to point to the conclusion that merely talking to our fourteen- to seventeen-year-olds about the risks and consequences of various behaviours will have a limited effect, since in highly emotion-arousing situations they are practically *unable* to exercise control over their decisions. Instead, Steinberg recommends external measures, such as increasing the price of cigarettes, raising the driving age, and increasing access to mental-health and contraceptive services. In his words, he calls for '**limiting opportunities for immature judgment to have harmful consequences**'. This is a lovely piece of advice, but with tremendous potential for misuse! It should not be taken to mean that we have to police and mistrust our students during this difficult phase. A fuller understanding of the research on adolescence can guide us to be more subtle and tentative in our approach than that. At the same time, our adolescent students are both susceptible to irrational behaviour, as well as capable of high levels of rational thought. How you can balance the two to bring out the best in your students is a matter of trying different approaches, being ready to abandon things that don't work, and continually responding to their feedback. No one is promising that this will be easy. However, it is extremely important to keep the positive potential of adolescence in mind at all times. The research described next shows this face of their development beautifully.

In adolescence, we are seeing the culmination of a twenty-odd-year process of tremendous growth and development. Several things are considered to be complete and stable by the end of this stage, such as height, working memory, brain size and IQ score. Of course, knowledge and skills continue to develop throughout our lives. One area where we may believe that the end of adolescence does not spell the end of development is **wisdom**. Most of us believe that you can't be wise unless you are quite old, and we certainly would not describe a twenty-year-old as a 'wise young man' (except in jest!). Psychologist Paul Baltes, who has studied lifespan development for decades, and has studied many aspects of adult psychology, has taken on the formidable task of studying wisdom. With a quality as abstract as this, the first and most difficult challenge is to come up with an operational definition. Baltes and his colleagues define wisdom as 'expert knowledge in the fundamental pragmatics of life that permits insight, judgment, and advice about complex and uncertain matters'. They call this *wisdom-related knowledge and judgement*, and base it on five criteria, shown in the table below.

As with all operational definitions, you may or may not agree with it, but at least it is relatively unambiguous. Baltes and others have studied this interesting variable in adults ranging in age from twenty-five to eighty years, and found surprisingly that **wisdom does not automatically increase with age**; using their definition and methods, older is not wiser. Instead, the factors that make for wisdom-related knowledge and judgement seem to be specific experiences, and personality traits such as openness to experience and the tendency to reflect on things.

Criterion of wisdom	Brief description
1. Rich conceptual knowledge about life	Knowing a wide variety of life's issues in depth, both general and specific.
2. Rich procedural knowledge about life	Knowing how to make decisions, solve problems, reach goals and give advice in a wide variety of situations.
3. Life-span contextualism	Understanding past, present and possible future circumstances.
4. Value relativism	Having both a small set of universal values (for the good of all) as well as the understanding that many values in life are relative.
5. Recognition and management of uncertainty	Knowing that life is inherently uncertain and knowing how to deal with that uncertainty.

Could it be then that wisdom is another characteristic that reaches maturity during adolescence itself? Baltes and his colleagues Monisha Pasupathi and Ursula Staudinger decided to search for the 'seeds of wisdom' in adolescents. A hundred and fifty students in schools in Berlin between the ages of fourteen and nineteen, and sixty young adults, aged twenty to thirty-seven were given hypothetical dilemmas to ponder over, such as:

- 'A teenager learns that he or she has failed a test that is very important for his or her future. What could one or the teenager do and think in such a situation?'
- 'A teenager realizes that he or she is no longer being included in his or her friends' plans. What could one or the teenager do and think in such a situation?'
- 'In thinking over his or her life, a person realizes that he or she has not achieved all he or she once imagined. What could one or the person do in such a situation?'

Students and adults were told to 'think aloud' about the dilemma, and their thoughts were rated for the five different criteria. The results were striking—there was a sharp increase in scores on the five criteria from fourteen- to twenty-three-year-olds. From age twenty-three and above, however, there was no further increase in scores with age (see figure below).

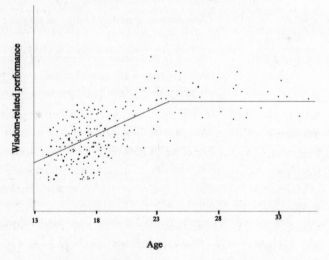

The study clearly indicates that the development of wisdom-related knowledge and judgment between ages fourteen and nineteen is *normative*, that is, determined by factors shared by all adolescents.

Beyond that, however, the further development of wisdom is non-normative, or determined by individual factors. This calls for some shift in our way of thinking about adolescence and early adulthood. Whether you wish to call it wisdom or something else, we will have to credit young people with a quality that we normally reserve only for ourselves, or for people much older. In other words, the seeds of wisdom are truly to be found in adolescence.

In Conclusion

Our students slip into adolescence almost without our realizing it. Suddenly one day, you find yourself looking up to talk to a twelve-year-old girl, or you mistake a fourteen-year-old boy on the phone for his father. While in our eyes they may still be 'children', they so justifiably want to be treated differently now. During these turbulent and exciting years, our greater awareness of what is going on in their minds and lives will help us be more sensitive, understanding and patient in our dealings with them. And maybe then the word 'adolescence' can shed its negativity.

References and Bibliography

1. Arnett, J.J., 1999. 'Adolescent Storm and Stress, Reconsidered'. *American Psychologist*, Vol. 54, No. 5, 317–26.

2. Buchanan, C.M, J.S. Eccles, and J.B. Becker, 1992. 'Are Adolescents the Victims of Raging Hormones: Evidence for Activational Effects of Hormones on Moods and Behavior at Adolescence'. *Psychological Bulletin*, Vol. 111, No. 1, 62–107.

3. Casey, B.J., J.N. Giedd, and K.M. Thomas, 2000. 'Structural and functional brain development and its relation to cognitive development'. *Biological Psychology*, Vol. 54, 241–57.

4. Eccles, J.S., C. Midgley, A. Wigfield, C.M. Buchanan, D. Reuman, C. Flanagan, and D. Mac Iver, 1993. 'Development During Adolescence: The Impact of Stage-Environment Fit on Young Adolescents'

Experiences in Schools and in Families'. *American Psychologist*, Vol. 48, No. 2, 90–101.

5. Fuligni, A.J., 1998. 'Authority, Autonomy, and Parent-Adolescent Conflict and Cohesion: A Study of Adolescents From Mexican, Chinese, Filipino, and European Backgrounds'. *Developmental Psychology*, Vol. 34, No. 4, 782–92.

6. Larson, R.W. and M. Ham, 1993. 'Stress and 'Storm and Stress' in Early Adolescence: The Relationship of Negative Events With Dysphoric Affect'. *Developmental Psychology*, Vol. 29, No. 1, 130–40.

7. Larson, R.W., 2000. 'Toward a Psychology of Positive Youth Development'. *American Psychologist*, Vol. 55, No. 1, 170–83.

8. Pasupathi, M., U.M. Staudinger, and P.B. Baltes, 2001. 'Seeds of Wisdom Adolescents' Knowledge and Judgment About Difficult Life Problems'. *Developmental Psychology*, Vol. 37, No. 3, 351–61.

9. Roeser, R.W., J.S. Eccles, and A.J. Sameroff, 1998. 'Academic and Emotional Functioning in Early Adolescence'. *Development and Psychopathology*, 10, 321–52.

10. Roeser, R.W., and M.G. Galloway, 2002. 'Studying motivation to learn in early adolescence: A holistic perspective'. In T. Urdan and F. Pajares (eds), Academic motivation of adolescents: Adolescence and Education, Volume II (pp. 331–72). Greenwich, CT: Information Age Publishing.

11. Roeser, R.W., C. Midgley, and T.C. Urban, 1996. 'Perceptions of the School Psychological Environment and Early Adolescents' Psychological and Behavioral Functioning in School: The Mediating Role of Goals and Belonging'. *Journal of Educational Psychology*, Vol. 88, No. 3, 408–22.

12. Steinberg, L., 2005. 'Cognitive and Affective Development in Adolescence'. *Trends in Cognitive Science*, 9(2), 69–74.

13. Steinberg, L., 2007. 'Risk Taking in Adolescence: New Perspectives from Brain and Behavioural Science'. *Current Directions in Psychological Science*, 16(2), 55–59.

14. Steinberg, L., and K.C. Monahan, 2007. 'Age Differences in Resistance to Peer Influence'. *Developmental Psychology*, Vol. 43, No. 6, 1531–43.

Index

Mastery orientation, 194, 195, 196, 199, 264
Mayer, Richard, 38
Memorization, 51, 53, 66–68, 88, 168, 209, 271
Memory, Declarative/ Explicit, 53, 54
    Episodic, 54, 229
    Procedural/ Implicit, 53, 54, 59, 60n, 67
    Semantic, 54, 55, 58
    Working, 60–66, 80, 81, 84, 230, 262, 266, 278
Metacognition, 46, 84, 88, 170, 262
Meyer, Debra, 226–27
Misconception, 31, 37, 68
Mnemonics, 67
Morality, Innate elements of, 131, 132
Morals, 119, 125, 126, 127, 129
Motivation, Extrinsic, 176–77, 179, 180, 181, 187
    Intrinsic, 176–85, 192, 194, 248
Mueller, Claudia, 198
Myelination, 73, 75, 89

National Curriculum Framework 2005, 219
Nature vs. Nurture, 72, 73, 94, 97–102, 111, 114, 115, 166
NCERT, 59
Nelson, Charles, 92, 94
Neocortex, 8–9, 12, 13, 17, 60n, 230
Neural plasticity, 18–19
Nucci, Larry, 121, 136

Operantly conditioned, 103–04, 112
Overjustificaion, 123, 182
Overscheduling of activities, 237

Paris, Scott, 169, 214–15
Pasupathi, Monisha, 279
Pekrun, Reinhard, 225, 243, 244
Performance orientation, 194, 196–97, 200, 224, 226, 242, 268
Perkins, David, 43–44, 46, 166, 167

Piaget, Jean, 5, 25, 59, 72, 76–78, 126–27, 128, 129, 262
Pidada, Sri Untari, 240
Pinker, Steven, 24
Positive feedback/ Praise, 122, 184, 185–86, 197, 198, 245, 249
Positive psychology, 238
Positive affect, 228–29
Power assertion, 137–38, 139
Processing, Speed of, 77, 81, 88, 89, 154, 163, 262
Programmes, pre-kindergarten, 86
Psychology, evolutionary, 14, 107, 156n

Radke-Yarrow, Marian, 132–33
Reasoning skills, 22, 23, 24, 43, 47, 82, 167
    Informal, 43, 46, 47
Recall, 10, 43, 51, 54, 56, 62, 67, 79, 80, 84, 88, 109, 168, 209, 210
Recognition, 16, 64, 79, 84, 179
Reev, Johnmarshall, 192
Resilient, 71, 90
Resistance, 112, 113, 199, 223, 276
    To peer influence, 269, 270, 276
Reward and punishment, 42, 122, 123, 176–77, 178, 182–84, 275
Roediger, Henry, 209–10
Roeser, Robert, 243, 250, 265, 272
Rogoff, Barbara, 109
Rousseau, Jean-Jacques, 72, 118
Rubric, 216–17

Salomon, Gavriel, 167
Schooled children, 108, 109, 111
School-like tasks, 108
Self-esteem, 178, 186, 190, 244, 245–51
Sensitive periods, 90, 92, 93
Sharma, Deepali, 231
Shweder, 125, 126
Siegler, Robert, 78–79
Simon, Herbert, 168